# Making More Money on the Internet

# Other Glossbrenner books

*Internet 101: A College Student's Guide—Third Edition, 1996*

*The Little Web Book*, 1996

*The Little Online Book*, 1995

*The Complete Modem Handbook*, 1995

*Online Resources for Business by Alfred Glossbrenner and John Rosenberg*, 1995

*Making Money on the Internet—First Edition*, 1995

*Finding a Job on the Internet*, 1995

*The Information Broker's Handbook—Second Edition*, by Sue Rugge and Alfred Glossbrenner, 1995

*Internet 101: A College Student's Guide—Second Edition*, 1995

*Internet Slick Tricks*, 1994

*DOS 6*, 1993

*Power DOS!*, 1993

*File & Disk Management: From Chaos to Control*, 1993

*DOS 5*, 1992

*Glossbrenner's Guide to Shareware for Small Businesses*, 1992

*Glossbrenner's Master Guide to GEnie*, 1991

*Glossbrenner's Complete Hard Disk Handbook*, 1990

*How to Look It Up Online*, 1987

*How to Get FREE Software*, 1984

*How to Buy Software*, 1984

*The Complete Handbook of Personal Computer Communications*, 1983

*Word Processing for Executives, Managers, and Professionals*, 1983

# Making More Money on the Internet

*Alfred and Emily Glossbrenner*

**McGraw-Hill**
New York San Francisco Washington, D.C. Auckland Bogotá
Caracas Lisbon London Madrid Mexico City Milan
Montreal New Delhi San Juan Singapore
Sydney Tokyo Toronto

*McGraw-Hill*

*A Division of The* ***McGraw-Hill*** *Companies*


Published by The McGraw-Hill Companies, Inc.



pbk 1 2 3 4 5 6 7 8 9 FGR/FGR 9 0 0 9 8 7 6
hc 1 2 3 4 5 6 7 8 9 FGR/FGR 9 0 0 9 8 7 6



ISBN 0-07-024447-2 (pbk)
ISBN 0-07-024300-X (h)

*Making More Money on the Internet* is the second edition of *Making Money on the Internet.*

McGraw-Hill books are available at special quantity discounts to use as premiums and sales promotions, or for use in corporate training programs. For more information, please write to the Director of Special Sales, McGraw-Hill, 11 West 19th Street, New York, NY 10011. Or contact your local bookstore.

Acquisitions editor: Brad Schepp
Editorial team: David M. McCandless, Managing Editor
Lori Flaherty, Executive Editor
Jodi L. Tyler, Indexer
Production team: Katherine G. Brown, Director
Susan E. Hansford, Coding
Wanda S. Ditch, Desktop Operator
Toya B. Warner, Computer Artist
Design team: Jaclyn J. Boone, Designer

WK2

# Contents

**Introduction** *xi*

## *Part 1*
## *Internet essentials: A diagram of the playing field*

**1 How to make (or lose) a fortune online** ***3***
The secret of the ages *6*
A little history *7*
Push-button purchases? Right! *8*
Lessons from the past *9*
*SIMBA Information, Inc.* *12*
Prodigy project: A billion-dollar disaster *15*
"Did I buy the wrong book?" *17*

**2 The seven rules of successful online selling** ***19***
Should my business be online? *20*
Global reach & unique offerings *21*
The right way to view the Internet *22*
The seven rules of successful online selling *25*

**3 Crucial concepts made simple *33***
Understanding & overview *34*
*The bandwidth problem 35*
What about pictures & graphics? *36*
Why is text so fast? *38*
A common-sense approach *41*
Conclusion *43*

**4 Welcome to the Internet! *45***
Behind closed doors *46*
They gotta have a deal *47*
Where did the Internet come from? *49*
Packet switching is the key *51*
Content & features *52*
Five key Internet concepts *54*
The main Internet features *58*
Other features you'll hear about *62*
Conclusion *64*

**5 The World Wide Web *65***
The Web as catalyst *66*
Images & hypertext markup language (HTML) *67*
Where browser programs fit in *69*
Why Bill Gates & Microsoft are worried *71*
*Uniform Resource Locators (URLs) 72*
How Web browsers work *72*
Java, Visual BASIC, & other considerations *74*
The Java language & Netscape plug-ins *76*
A quick-start guide to Web browsing *81*
"Driving" your browser *83*

**6 Other major players *87***
A quick overview *88*
Your secret sales weapon! *91*
Where true wisdom lies *96*
Big Three marketing options *98*
*How to find SIGs on the Big Three 101*
Bulletin Board Systems *101*
Using BBSs as marketing tools *105*

**7 How to get connected** ***107***
A three-step program *108*
What it takes to go online *108*
*Checking your UART 110*
All about communications software *113*
Connecting to the Net *115*
Bringing yourself up to speed *115*
*Free trial offers 116*
Moving to an Internet service provider (ISP) *118*
How to find an Internet service provider *120*
Choosing an ISP *123*
Conclusion *126*
*Leading nationwide Internet Service Providers 127*

***Part 2***
***The tools at hand***

**8 Making the most of e-mail** ***133***
The big payoff *134*
Basic e-mail, all systems *135*
How Internet e-mail programs operate *136*
*E-mail tips & tricks 139*
E-mailing binary files *141*
Addresses on the Net *143*
*International e-mail 144*
The InterNIC & domain name registration *145*
*Choosing a domain name 145*
IP addresses & when to use them *146*
*Encrypt your text for privacy 147*
Sending mail to other networks *148*
*Finding e-mail addresses 148*
E-mail signatures *150*
*Signatures on parade 151*
E-mail marketing & direct mail *152*
Conclusion: A new paradigm *154*

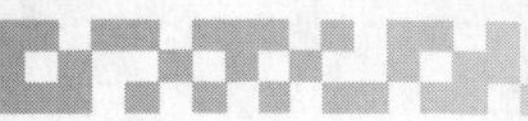

**9 Auto-responders** ***157***

Geared to information distribution 159

*Auto-responders to try 162*

How to pick an auto-responder vendor 163

*Auto-responder companies 164*

*FireCrystal tips on preparing your message 166*

Conclusion: Tell the world 168

**10 Setting up your web site** ***169***

There is no "magic" 170

Options for creating a Web page 171

*Tips for creating your own HTML code 172*

*Home Page Construction Kit & other tools 173*

Hire a Webmaster! 176

*Where to look for award-winning Web sites 181*

Wilson Internet Services—a great example 183

Page design and content 184

Major-league Web page design tips 186

Putting up the page 190

Conclusion: DigiCash, secure transactions, & more 195

## *Part 3*
## *Spreading the word*

**11 Search engines & free directory listings** ***201***

Search engines & how they work 202

*Search tips: How to make the most of a search engine 203*

Free directory listings 207

*What about "malls?" 210*

**12 Making the most of newsgroups & mailing lists** ***213***

Finding out what people are saying 215

*Why are they called newsgroups?* 216

Newsgroup essentials 216

Crucial points 217

*Newsgroup hierarchies 220*

Get your feet wet! 222

Now for the payoff! 222

The *best* way to proceed 223

The best approach of all 225
Hand-crafted selling 227
Net Happenings 229
Mailing lists 229
Thinking about mailing lists 230
Conclusion 232

**13 Announcement services *233***
Step back & think for a moment 234
Free, automated, announcement services 235
Fee-based announcement services 238
Personal attention: Eric Ward's NetPost 240
Finding (& vetting) announcement services 242
Special interest pages 243
Conclusion 246

## *Part 4*
## *Entrepreneurs in action*

**14 Books & music *251***
Amazon.com Books 252
BookBound 254
Windham Hill 256
The Capitol Steps 257

**15 Business & financial services *261***
The Company Corporation 262
Federal Express 264
QuoteCom 266

**16 Computer-related products *269***
Computer Express 270
Dell Computer Corporation 270
Scandinavian Computer Furniture 272
Walnut Creek CDROM 274

**17 Consumer electronics *277***
Shoppers Advantage 278
Cassette House 280
Casio 282

**18 Crafts & collectibles** ***285***
Cards, Comics, & Collectibles *286*
ARJAY Enterprises & the Elvis Inventory *288*
The Doll House *289*
The Knitting Lodge *290*

**19 Food, gifts, & novelties** ***293***
Virtual Vineyards *294*
Hot Hot Hot *295*
Coffee Anyone??? *298*
Foamation World Famous Cheeseheads *299*

**20 Multi-level marketing** ***303***
*Multi-level marketing resources online* *304*
The NuSkin Feelgood Team *305*
Excel Telecommunications *305*
Watkins Products *307*
*Get the MLM FAQ!* *308*

## Appendices

**A FireCrystal Consulting** ***311***
Taken at the flood *311*

**B The Internet Toolkit & Glossbrenner's Choice** ***315***
The Internet Toolkit *316*
Windows/DOS Tools & Utilities *319*
Order Form *322*

**Index** ***325***

**About the Authors** ***331***

# Introduction

## The Naked Emperor Redux

Welcome to the second edition of *Making Money on the Internet*. Over 95 percent of the material in this book is brand new. That's because when it comes to the Internet, you don't *revise* a book, you completely *rewrite* it. The velocity of change is that great.

Of course some things have remained the same. The hype, the breathless cover stories, the articles in major newspapers, the segments on CNN and other networks—in short, the incessant drumbeat for a "point, click, and purchase" future for the selling of goods and services.

And yes, it's still all a crock!

We've served scores of consulting clients in the past year or so, and it's amazing how many have been convinced that if they don't get on the Internet and the World Wide Web today, they'll soon be out of business. Others have the completely inaccurate notion that online space is somehow limited and that they must hurry to stake their claim.

## The problem with the press

The problem, of course, is the press. We have been watching and writing about computers and technology since the 1970s, and, with one or two exceptions, the general-interest press *never* gets it right. This is actually more disturbing than it at first appears. For, if the press can so often be so wrong when reporting on subjects we know a great deal about, how trustworthy is it likely to be when covering subjects about which we know absolutely nothing?

The lesson is: Take everything you read or hear—even this book—with a grain of salt. Then make up your own mind. The difference is that if the press gets it wrong on international politics or on its analysis of why the Federal Reserve board raised or lowered interest rates, it doesn't much matter. Not in the overall scheme of things.

But if the press is wrong in promoting, even unintentionally, the idea of doing business on the Internet, you as a businessperson could be persuaded to invest (and ultimately lose) some serious money. Not to mention a lot of effort, energy, and time.

That's why the single most important truth you can take away from this book is this:

> When it comes to making a fortune on the Internet, the Emperor truly has no clothes! Without the proper guidance, you are far more likely to *lose* a fortune than to make one. That's because most of what you've heard and read in books, articles, and on TV about making money on the Internet is wrong—and demonstrably so.

## It's not what you've been told

There *is* money to be made on the Internet. Time and effort can be saved. There are ways—many ways—for the wonderful technology of the online world to enhance absolutely everything about your business. But the method and means are definitely *not* what you're being told.

That's why we wrote this book. We have been there, and we know what a bill of goods businesspeople are being sold. Whether you're on the Internet, Prodigy, America Online, or CompuServe, you are *not* going to find a pot of gold at the end of the online rainbow. Not without a lot of hard work, imagination, commitment, and some financial investment. The online "market" is just as uncertain and unpredictable as any other. But if you're willing to bring those things to the table, you will succeed.

## Here's what you get

In this book, we'll show you your options, starting with a consideration of whether your business should be online at all, on up through the creation of a home page on the Internet's World Wide Web. And we'll show you how to do it right!

## Part 1, "Internet Essentials"

We've called Part 1 "Internet Essentials: A Diagram of the Playing Field." But before proceeding to the playing field, you've got to understand the game. That's why the first two chapters in this part of the book are aimed at putting online selling and marketing in perspective.

Among other things, you'll learn about the multi-million-dollar mistakes companies have made in the past, and about how important it is to develop a synergy between your online efforts and your current, conventional marketing activities. Should every business have a Web page? Probably. Prices have fallen through the floor since we did the first edition. As you will see in Chapter 2, these days, a Web page and an Internet presence can even make sense for a local TV repair shop or ice cream store.

The remaining chapters in Part 1 will quickly and conversationally bring you up to speed, both as a businessperson and as a consumer and user of online services. These chapters really do lay out the playing field. Forgive the chortling, but we've had readers call with the sole purpose of telling us that the "dummies" books confused them from the first page on, but that they loved our "technical" chapters because they made everything so clear!

## Part 2, "The Tools at Hand"

The chapters in Part 2 are designed to show you how to use electronic mail effectively, how set up and use an auto-responder, and how to create a home page or site on the World Wide Web. We know that not everyone will read the chapters in this book sequentially. So, if you have a basic idea of what e-mail is, feel free to skip ahead to Chapter 9, "Auto-responders: The secret marketing tool." For just $10 a month you can. . . No, go read the chapter. You'll see.

## Part 3, "Spreading the Word"

In Part 3 you'll learn about *search engines*, a powerful class of feature that has revolutionized the way people look for things on the Internet and the World Wide Web. You'll also learn about using newsgroups and mailing lists to market your product or service. And you'll learn about services that, for a fee, will see to it that the major search engines are made aware of the address of your Web site and otherwise help you spread the word electronically.

## Part 4, "Online Entrepreneurs in Action"

Finally, the chapters in Part 4 present dozens of businesses that are doing it right. (And one or two that are doing it wrong!) We'll show you the opening screen for each company's Web site, give you the Web address so you can visit the site yourself, and then suggest what you should look for when you get there.

The key thing to remember about the chapters in Part 4, however, is this: We've organized them by type of business or product. But just because you don't sell books or offer craft items or represent a multi-level marketing company doesn't mean you can't *learn* from what people in these fields are doing.

We think you will want to visit each of the sites in these chapters, and we advise you to do so with this book and a notebook near at hand.

You should also learn to print pages you like with "File, Print" and to capture pages with the "File, Save" option in your Web browser. You can always view them again later with the "File, Open" option. (Don't worry—these technical terms are explained in Part 1.)

We've used the word "entrepreneur" in the full knowledge that it applies not just to people who want to work for themselves. It applies to energetic, creative people everywhere, even in large, Fortune 500 corporations.

# Let the adventure begin!

Finally, we have written this book on the assumption that you are an enthusiastic, curious person who wants to learn more. We do not assume that you are now or ever have been online. You are simply a bright bulb who has been paying attention during the last year or so and who wants to find out whether there's anything to be gained from this online, Internet thing.

Come with us, and we will take good care of you.

If you're a more advanced user, we're glad to have you. But we know your impulse will be to skip over the things you think you know. That's fine. Just remember that each chapter has been written on the assumption that you've read all of the chapters that come before it. So, if you choose to start with, say, Chapter 9 and encounter something you don't fully understand, be sure to go back and read the earlier chapters.

That'll about do it. If we haven't scared you off yet, we'll see you at the start of Chapter 1.

# Part 1

# Internet esentials:

## A diagram of the playing field

# 1

# How to make (or lose) a fortune online

# CHAPTER 1

IN this chapter, you'll learn the secret to making and saving money—or otherwise profiting from putting your business online.

If you have never been online before, don't worry if you're not exactly clear yet on what's meant by terms like *Web site* and *home page*, or phrases like *surfing the Net*. We'll fill you in on those things a little later.

Right now, what you need to know is that anyone with a personal computer, a telephone, and a device called a *modem* can connect with the Internet, the World Wide Web, and the rest of the online world. They can tap a few keys or click a mouse button or two and summon attractive, magazine-style pages to their screens. (See Figs. 1-1 and 1-2 for just one example of a site.) And yes, with apologies to

Figure 1-1

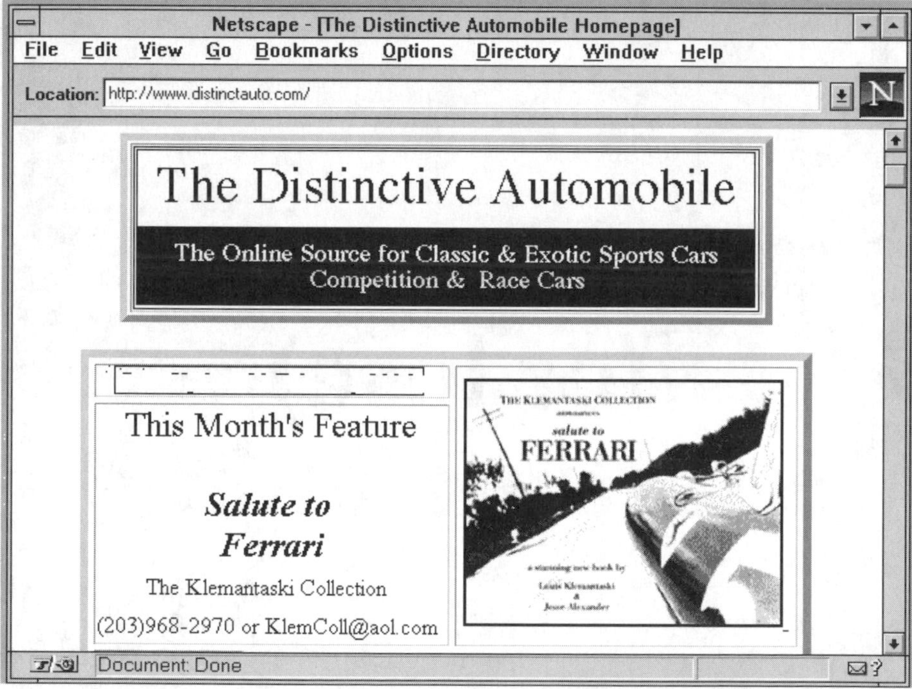


*This is the opening screen for the Distinctive Automobile Web site. Scroll down the page and click on "Classifieds" to reach informative, full-color ads like the one shown in Fig. 1-2.*

Figure 1-2

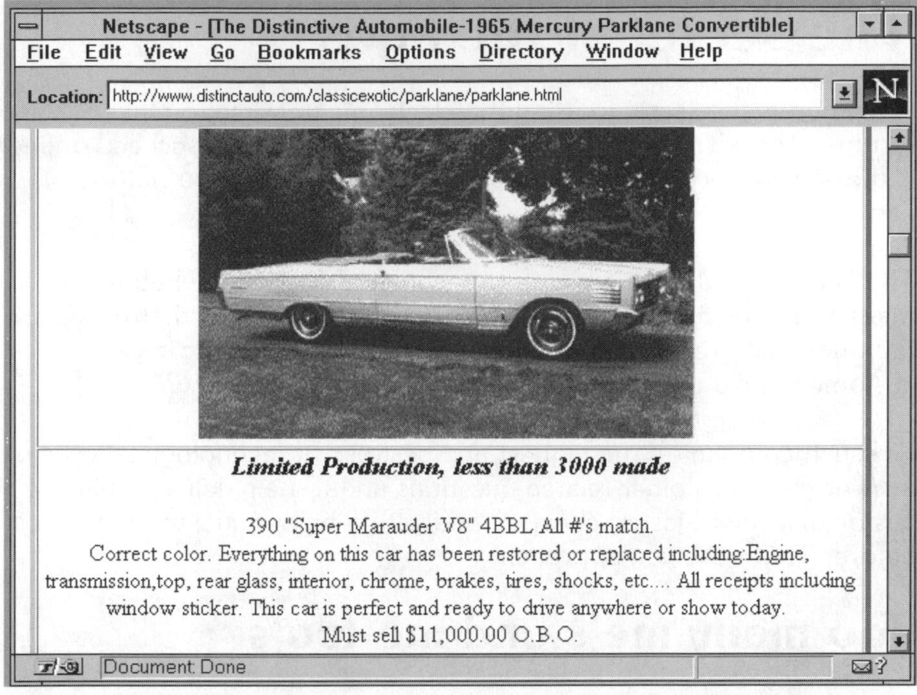


*Here's a sample of the type of information presented in the Distinctive Automobile classifieds section.*

Shakespeare's Hotspur who claimed he could summon demons from the depths, those pages will indeed come when you call them. Usually. Assuming there's no network glitch along the way.

Millions of people do exactly that every day on America Online (AOL), CompuServe, and Prodigy, all of which advertise on television. Millions more log on through independent Internet service providers (ISPs) based in their towns and local calling areas. Internet service providers typically charge $15 to $20 a month for unlimited usage, while America Online and the others charge about $10 a month for five hours and $2.95 for each hour after that.

If you add computer bulletin board systems (BBSs) to the mix, you'll have a pretty good overview of what we have long called the *electronic universe*. A BBS is a miniature online system housed in an individual's personal computer. Some charge a small subscription fee, but most can be used free of charge.

## The secret of the ages

Now, here's the secret to using the electronic universe to make a fortune. There's actually no mystery to it. The way you succeed online is the same way you succeed in any kind of business: You put the customer first!

That's called "taking the you-approach," and it applies whether you make pizza, planes, or concrete pylons. The companies that thrive are the ones that are constantly asking themselves, "What do my customers need today, and what will they need tomorrow?"

For such companies, the highest and best use of technology is to help answer those customer-related questions and to help deliver what the customer wants—faster, cheaper, and with a higher quality than ever before. That's the you-approach.

## Too many me's and me-too's

The problem in the online world is that so many firms have opted for the me-approach. They view technology in general, and the Internet in particular, solely as a means of cutting their costs and boosting their profits.

There's nothing wrong with either of those goals, of course. It's just that when cost-cutting and profit-boosting are your major focus, you tend to see and apply technology differently than if you are driven by anticipating and satisfying customer needs.

A me-approach company looks at the Internet and says, "Hey, terrific! I can get rid of half of my sales force!" A you-approach company says, "Great! The Internet can help me and my employees serve our customers even better, to say nothing of reaching out to gain new customers."

The technology is the same for everyone. But the way you apply it—and the results you obtain—depend on your point of view. That is one of our central themes in this book, and we hope you will keep it in mind as you explore the Internet and the World Wide Web.

As you visit various online locations, for example, always ask yourself whether the site has been prepared by a me-approach company or a you-approach company. Does the site appear to exist primarily to make things easier or cheaper for the company? Or do you sense that whoever set things up was really trying to be of help to you, the prospective customer?

## A little history

It may be that we should not have given you this great success "secret" so soon. Certainly we could have built things up more gradually. But, as defense attorney Johnnie Cochran might say, we wanted you to "get the heart from the start." You're aware that you can reach your customers online, and you know that the you-approach concept is the key to success in the online world, just as it is in the real world.

Now let's pull back for a moment and look at where today's online world came from. The Internet and the World Wide Web may appear to have suddenly burst upon the scene from nowhere. But that isn't at all what happened.

It's very important for every businessperson and entrepreneur to understand that online personal computer communications is nothing new. (Heck, co-author Alfred wrote one of the very first books on the subject—in 1982.) CompuServe, America Online, Prodigy, and several less well-known systems have been around for many years.

CompuServe, for example, began in 1979 as a service called MicroNET. America Online grew out of Quantum Computer Systems, an online service established in the mid-1980s. The first computer bulletin board system went live in 1978. And what we now call the Internet was started in 1969.

Things have been perking along for decades, in other words. And—big surprise—most of the online sales and marketing techniques you read about today have been tried in one form or another *many* times before. Some have worked. Most have not. So there is a golden

opportunity to learn from the mistakes others have made in hopes of avoiding making them yourself.

## Push-button purchases? Right!

In our experience, the biggest mistake of all is to assume that large numbers of people are interested in regularly *shopping* online. Yet that is the siren song sung by promoters of *online* (yes, it has become a noun) and the Internet. It goes something like this:

> All you have to do is put your product catalogue and order form on the World Wide Web and just sit back and wait for the money to roll in. Why pay to write, design, print, and mail a catalogue? Why pay for advertising or marketing? Get yourself a Web site and all you'll have to do is sign on a few times a day to pick up the orders.

This is complete and utter nonsense. But it's a classic me-approach notion, to wit: "Hey, I can cut my costs and boost my profits big-time by getting a World Wide Web home page." And, of course, the company you'll hire to create your home page is encouraging you every dollar of the way. You don't know it, but you're on the fast track toward losing your first fortune!

## Where does it fit in one's daily life?

All right. Maybe you won't lose a *fortune*. These days, you no longer have to spend tens of thousands of dollars setting up a Web page, although some companies do. Now you can get by for a couple thousand dollars, or even several hundred dollars.

And we certainly aren't saying that people won't or don't shop online. We're just saying that you're setting yourself up for a big disappointment if you believe that all it takes to produce a pot of gold is to establish yourself on the Internet. At the very least, you've got to work at giving your customers a good reason to visit your online location. You can prove this to yourself by asking a simple question:

> Where does going online to "surf the Net" or "browse the Web" fit into my typical customer's day?

After all, going online is anything but quick and convenient. A person must turn on the computer and wait for the operating system software (Windows, DOS, Macintosh, or whatever) to load, then click on an icon, wait for the modem to dial, and wait some more for the software to log onto a system. And then, if it's a good day, the system won't be so overloaded that it runs at the pace of molasses in January.

So when do your customers make time to do this?

Sure, kids and college students have plenty of time to log on and surf, but most don't have credit cards or money to spend. Your customers probably spend their days at work, where they may or may not have access to the Internet. (Many managers see the Internet as an even greater threat to productivity than the Solitaire game Microsoft included with Windows 3.1, so they block employee access.)

Again, when does the typical person log on? After work, while dinner is turning in the microwave? Late at night, instead of reading a book or watching *Letterman* or *Leno*?

And, since choosing to do one thing usually means choosing *not* to do something else, what activities are people going to give up in order to spend time online? Activities like reading to their kids or helping them with homework? Or gardening, fixing the faucet, or visiting with friends?

It's crucial to think about these questions before even considering ways to make money on the Internet and the rest of the electronic universe. It's also important to see things in perspective and to try to learn from the mistakes of others.

# Lessons from the past

The year was 1986, and what we now think of as the world of online services like shopping, news, and home banking was called *videotex* (no final *t*). It was the year of the first Big Crash in consumer online services. On March 21, Viewtron, a Miami-based home videotex system created by Knight-Ridder Newspapers, suddenly shut down. It

turned out that during a period of 18 months the company had invested more than $55 million in its system and had succeeded in attracting only about 3,000 subscribers. That's a cost of over $18,300 per subscriber.

The Viewtron shutdown came almost immediately on the heels of the March 7 demise of Gateway, a videotex service created by the Times Mirror Company. That firm invested nearly $30 million and ended up attracting fewer than 1,000 subscribers—a cost of over $30,000 per subscriber. "We found that our subscribers only used the service sporadically," said James H. Holly, president of Times Mirror Videotex Services. "Our goal was to have an average revenue of $20 per month per user. We just didn't see anything close to that. People would sign up for the service, try it out a few times, and then just drift off."

## Oh, but times have changed, haven't they?

One can argue that a lot has happened in the past decade to change the dynamic of this marketplace. The Internet didn't become available to the public at large until 1991, and it didn't really get "hot" until early 1994.

Certainly the fact that Viewtron subscribers had to buy a special $600 AT&T Sceptre terminal and pay subscription fees of $20 to $40 a month had something to do with Knight-Ridder's stunning lack of success. (But wouldn't you have thought that an idea like this would have been crushed in the egg by any executive who had an ounce of common sense? What on earth were they thinking?)

There is also the fact that today's computers and modems are priced like commodities. Nearly everyone can now afford one. And computers can do so many things—word processing, home finance, multimedia, education, and so forth—that it's not a question of buying one merely to go online. Surely that bodes well for the concept of online shopping.

Maybe. But don't hold your breath. Don't believe most predictions. And read every marketing study with your fingers wrapped around a huge shaker of salt.

## All aboard!

For example, in June of 1983, the consulting and research firm Booz Allen & Hamilton proclaimed that a huge home information systems market was only 24 to 36 months away. The prediction, based on a two-year, $2 million study, affirmed that as early as 1985, a $30 billion market would exist, with consumers willingly paying $32 to $35 a month for the convenience such systems would offer (bill paying, information, home security, games, etc.)

The message was clear: "You better get aboard now because this train's leavin' the station!" (Sound familiar?)

That same year, Creative Strategies predicted that sales of videotex services would grow more than 90 percent annually, reaching $7 billion by 1987. Communications consultant Gary Arlen, president of Arlen Communications and a member of the board of the Videotex Industry Association, predicted in *Business Week* (February 27, 1984) that videotex could be a $30 billion industry by the mid-1990s. The U.S. Commerce Department's 1986 Industrial Outlook predicted that videotex could be used in "20 to 50 million homes by 1995."

## Sorry, wrong number

All the pundits and experts were similarly optimistic. And all of them were wrong. Seriously wrong.

As Herbert Brody pointed out in his article "Sorry, Wrong Number" (*High Technology Business*, September 1988), sales in the online market in 1987 totalled a mere $113 million—not even close to the $7 billion predicted by Creative Strategies. And, according to SIMBA Information, publishers of an annual report on trends and forecasts in the online services industry, subscribers to consumer online services

spent less than $1 billion in 1995, a far cry from the $30 billion being predicted a decade ago.

As for the total number of online users, at the end of 1995, there were an estimated 11.4 million subscribers to consumer online services, again, according to SIMBA Information. That's a huge shortfall from the 20 to 50 million the U.S. Commerce Department predicted for 1995.

### SIMBA Information, Inc.

*Billed as "The Information Source of the Information Industry," SIMBA Information is an affiliate of Cowles Business Media based in Wilton, Connecticut. For more information on their reports and other services, visit their Web site at* ***http://www.simbanet.com****, or call 203-834-0033.*

## How many subscribers?

It gets worse. The figure of 11.4 million online subscribers in 1995 is really quite soft since it was derived by simply adding up the subscribership numbers reported by the leading consumer online systems.

That seems like a logical approach, but what most people don't know is that in the online world, there are no standards for calculating and reporting subscribership. For example, at GEnie—the online service started by General Electric—the policy for many years was to count everyone who had ever subscribed to the service. Those who had cancelled their accounts were simply considered "inactive" subscribers.

Prodigy, in contrast, calculates subscribership the way a magazine estimates its readership. Just as the publishers of *Time* or *Newsweek* assume that more than one person in a household reads each issue, Prodigy assumes that each account is used by more than one family member. Thus, when Prodigy claims, say, two million subscribers, that does not mean that there are two million people paying Prodigy's fee of $9.95 per month. According to some analysts, the actual number of accounts may be closer to *half* the number of subscribers that Prodigy reports.

CompuServe's and America Online's numbers are pretty solid, since each account is charged at least $9.95 a month, and no "multiplier formula" is applied. But even the numbers CompuServe and AOL report cannot be accepted without adjustment when calculating the total number of subscribers in the online industry. That's because a significant number of people subscribe to more than one system and are thus counted twice or more.

## And what about the Internet?

The soft-number problem is not limited to the world of consumer online services: it also applies to the Internet. You've probably heard estimates that there are as many as 30 million Internet users. Well, listen to Bob Metcalfe—the inventor of Ethernet, founder of 3Com Corporation, and columnist for *InfoWorld*.

In the August 22, 1994, issue of *InfoWorld*, Mr. Metcalf reacted to a report by Anthony-Michael Rutkowski, executive director of the Internet Society, that stated that there were between 20 and 30 million Internet users:

> A weak link in Rutkowski's chain of estimates is the assumption that there are on average 10 users per Internet host computer. This is a holdover from when the Internet was made up mostly of VAX UNIX hosts, each of which had many users.
>
> Considering that most computers today are personal, the average number of users is closer to one than 10, even accounting for the few really big ones. So, the Internet might have as few as 3.2 million users.

The point: At a time when the press and nearly everyone else had picked up the estimate of 30 million Internet users, the *actual* number may have been only a tenth of that. Not 80 percent or even 50 percent—one tenth! Yet to this day, there are people out there for

whom the common wisdom is that there are at least 30 million Internet users.

No one would want to underestimate the difficulties of calculating the number of people using the Internet. After all, the Net doesn't have a corporate headquarters. But, at the same time, it would be just plain foolish to base *your* projections for making money on the Internet or elsewhere in the online world on any of the published subscribership figures.

## The "real" number

Fortunately, more rigorous efforts have been focused on estimating the actual number of Internet users. In October, 1995, for example, O'Reilly & Associates, a publisher of Internet-related books, and Trish Marketing Systems announced the results of their survey of online and Internet users.

According to the study, some 5.8 million adults in the United States have direct Internet access and use the Net on a regular basis at their work, at home, or at school. So basically, at the beginning of 1996, there were about 6 million adults in the U.S. with Internet access. (For more information, visit the O'Reilly Web site at **http://www.ora.com/survey/**.)

Frankly, that feels about right to us. The actual number at the start of 1996 could have been a few million more, but it is simply impossible to believe that it was *tens* of millions more.

The true number of Internet users isn't really our point, however. Our point is the huge disparity between 30 million Internet users and 6 million. No one is going to admit it, but we all know that some companies swallowed the 30-million figure hook, line, and sinker, and invested in their Internet sites accordingly.

The subhead of the Herb Brody "wrong number" article cited earlier was, "Market-research firms routinely mispredict the course of technology businesses. Why do executives still listen?" Why indeed? Particularly when, like your local TV weather personality, the same pundits and industry experts are once again predicting sunny skies—without acknowledging for a moment that the last time they said it would be fair, it rained cats and dogs.

So, please, please be skeptical of any statistics or figures you read about this field. Invest your time in getting to know what's what on the Net and on the Web before you invest your money.

## Prodigy project: A billion-dollar disaster

We've told you about the Knight-Ridder and Times-Mirror disasters of 1986—ancient history in computer terms. Now you're ready for a current event. The fact is that one reason why people still listen to rosy predictions about the money to be made selling products online is that the me-approach dream of a pot of gold simply will not die. Everyone wants to become the online "point, click, and purchase" equivalent of the television-based QVC home shopping network, at least before that company's numbers began to fall.

The vision is so captivating that companies simply will not listen when *Business Week* (November 14, 1994) reports that, "So far, online shopping has not been a winner for network operators such as Prodigy and America Online. Forrester Research figures that online shopping will generate only about $200 million in revenues this year—not even a drop in the $1.5 trillion bucket U.S. consumers spend in stores and mail-order channels."

They say, "That was 1994. This year will be different." Really? What do you say to going back ten years to 1984 and look at how a system that has been dedicated to online shopping from its start has fared? We're speaking, of course, of Prodigy Services, Inc.

## In the beginning . . .

It all began in 1984. That was the year that a number of formidable corporate combines were announced. RCA, J.C. Penney, Bank of

America, and others formed various alliances that appeared to offer a wonderful synergy. The goal was to bring shopping, financial, and other services into the home.

One such combine was called Trintex, a three-company joint venture that originally included IBM, Sears, and CBS. The notion was that IBM would supply the technical expertise and computers. Sears would supply the merchandise that would be sold to subscribers. And CBS would provide the news and entertainment content that would attract subscribers in the first place.

In 1986, CBS dropped out after spending nearly $20 million on the project and facing a reported possible additional investment of $80 million. Shortly thereafter, Trintex became Prodigy.

The people at Prodigy have done their best, and as a former IBMer herself, co-author Emily well knows the kind of corporate direction they have labored under. But the fact remains that IBM and Sears have spent more than $1 billion on Prodigy since 1984, and after ten years, it still had not had a profitable year. (Our source is the CNN *Moneyline* program aired November 17, 1994, that featured Prodigy's then-president as its guest.)

## But the Internet is different, right?

What you need to know at this point is that every screen users see while logged onto Prodigy carries an advertisement of some sort. That's because Prodigy was from the beginning designed primarily to sell products. It's been trying to do so for over a decade with on-your-screen, in-your-face ads, and it has failed miserably. In fact, as you read this, IBM and Sears may well have sold Prodigy to someone else.

Now ask yourself: Is there any reason why on-your-screen, in-your-face ads will work any better on the Internet?

We don't think so. Millions of people have tried Prodigy over the years. Most would qualify as "upscale." But they haven't made enough online purchases for Prodigy to be profitable.

That should be a lesson to us all: Online shopping—at least in the sense of "see a product, click, and purchase—doesn't work. Nor do the advertising approaches used by magazines, newspapers, radio, and television work in the online world.

If forcing users to view ads in order to get the information or entertainment they want has not been effective on Prodigy, where such ads are impossible to avoid, why would similar ads be any more effective on the Internet, where a user can get the same content and information from many different sources?

To put it another way, if the latest sports scores are available from a dozen different Web sites, why would a given user opt for a site that carries ads over one that is advertising-free? On a closed, controlled system like Prodigy, a user has no choice. But on the Internet, your customers have dozens, even hundreds, of choices. They can go where they want to go and do what they want to do.

## "Did I buy the wrong book?"

With apologies to *Magnum, P.I.*, "We know what you're thinking." You're thinking, "Gee, so far this book has been little more than an attack on online selling and a catalogue of failures by companies that have tried it. Maybe this really isn't the book for me."

And maybe you're right. But we don't think so. We have gone after the conventional idea of online, push-button (or mouse-click) selling with both barrels. And we have told you things you probably did not want to hear, true as they may be, for a very specific reason. Our goal has been to do the verbal equivalent of shaking you by the shoulders and saying, "Wake up! There are opportunities galore out there, but they are not at all what you assume or have been told!"

Think about this: Television, radio, newspapers, and magazines are all a form of communication, and all such media carry advertising and marketing information. Indeed they are all supported by advertising and marketing dollars. But each is a distinctly different medium. So a

TV ad obviously won't work on radio, and a newspaper ad won't fly in a magazine.

The Internet is yet another medium. So why would anybody assume that what works on TV, radio, or in print would also work on the Net? Yet you will find many a Web page that is clearly nothing more than a magazine print ad, with huge graphics files that take forever to transmit and offer nothing of value other than a pretty picture, and very few words explaining the benefits of the product.

No, you didn't buy the wrong book. You can indeed make money on the Internet, regardless of the product or service you have to sell, and we will introduce you to businesspeople who have done just that. But you've got to go about it the right way.

The worst mistake you can make is to assume that the Internet and the World Wide Web are like every other communications medium you have used to carry your advertisements over the years. The next worst mistake is to assume that lots of people will "point, click, and purchase" your product online just because you are indeed online. As Paul Reiser might say on *Mad About You*, "Never happen, my friend."

Probably the third worst mistake you can make is to skip the next chapter. :) (That innocent looking colon and right-parens combination is called a *smilie* in the online world. It is the typographical equivalent of a grin, a fact that becomes clear when you tilt your head to the left and realize that it is two eyes and a smile.) Continue with us to Chapter 2, where you'll learn "The seven rules for successful online selling."

# The seven rules of successful online selling

ANYONE with a product or service to market can do so online. The electronic universe is closed to no one. You can use CompuServe, America Online, Prodigy, the Internet and the World Wide Web, BBSs, and lots of other small commercial systems to provide prospective customers with the information they need to decide to buy from you.

And the cost can be as little as $30 a month for a basic *home page* (or site) on the World Wide Web. In short, it has never been easier or cheaper for a small businessperson or entrepreneur to establish a presence in the online world. Whether it makes sense for you to do so or not is another matter.

## Should my business be online?

You might think that everything depends on your particular product or service. You might assume that you've got to offer some high-tech gadget, or something of interest to people all across the country or around the globe. But that really isn't the case.

Certainly the product or service matters a great deal if you're expecting people to "point, click, and purchase" online. However, as you know from Chapter 1, that probably isn't going to happen. If, on the other hand, you plan to use your online presence primarily as a *marketing* tool—as a way to communicate with your customers—then your product, service, or geographical location really don't matter at all.

The only thing that matters is whether your customers have access to the Internet.

## A TV repair shop on the Web?

For example, suppose you operate a TV repair shop. At first blush, you might think that it wouldn't make sense for you to be on the World Wide Web. A fair percentage of your customers may have computers and go online regularly. But what good is "global reach" when most of your business comes from people who live within a 15-

mile radius of your shop? And besides, no one is likely to ship you a broken TV set from Kuala Lumpur.

The fact is, though, that the Internet and the World Wide Web offer an ideal way for you to communicate with your *local* customers.

##  Leverage your current advertising!

For example, our local TV repair shop has dozens of used and reconditioned VCRs, TVs, and boomboxes for sale. The owner advertises regularly in our local papers, but he couldn't possibly afford to buy enough space to list each of these used items.

But what if he were to set up a Web site that lists each item and its price? He could then include a simple line like the following in his newspaper ad: "Great Buys on Used Equipment! For details: http://www.teevees.com."

If he wanted to take things a step or two further, he could present visitors to the Web site with a menu that included "clickable links" to items like these: "New Equipment," "Great Buys on Used Stuff," "How to Get the Most From Your VCR," "Our Ironclad Guarantee," "Today's Special," and "Mort-the-TV-Answerman." And, to get an idea of whether his Web site was helping sales, he could insert a line like this: "For a free gift, just bring a printout of this page into the shop!"

##  Global reach & unique offerings

Of course the conventional wisdom applies to online selling as well. Which is to say, you really can expand your market by reaching people all over the world with your message.

The London Connection is one good example. The company specializes in vacation rentals of London flats, Cotswold cottages, and similar properties. We found them in the *New Yorker*, where they had

taken a plain, one-and-a-half-inch ad listing their phone and fax numbers in Europe and the U.S., along with their Internet address: **http://www.ditell.com/~london/**.

When you visit this site, you will find that you can click on the name of a London tube stop and be taken to a description of that part of the city. You'll also find detailed descriptions of the flats currently available at those locations.

There are a few rough edges. For example, the rental fees are not given. And the "let-in" fee you pay when you arrive at the flat is specified in pounds, while the damage deposit is in dollars. But the overall approach works splendidly. This is worth thinking about. The product is unique. The appeal is international, since London is surely one of the most visited cities. And the Web site lets you, the customer, point and click your way through London in a manner that is far more convenient than thumbing through a printed catalogue.

Oh, and speaking of catalogues, think about this: the London Connection Web site can add and remove listings at a moment's notice, so it's always current. That's good for the company, the flat owner, and you, the customer. And because there are no printing or postage expenses to be concerned about, customers can get longer, more detailed descriptions of the properties than would be affordable in a traditional catalogue.

## The right way to view the Internet

Does your business belong on the Internet? Probably it does. Certainly at today's prices, you have little to lose but your time.

Note, however, that if you expect customers to point, click, and purchase at your site, your products will have to be either quite unique or deeply discounted. That's because the only reason to actually *buy* anything online is if you can't get it anywhere else, or if you can't get it as cheaply anywhere else.

As we'll see later, Wisconsin-based Foamation, Inc., maker of the world famous "Cheesehead" line of foam headgear, perfectly fits the bill when it comes to offering a unique product. You can visit them at **http://www.arcfile.com/cheesehead.html**.

On the money-saving side, Cassette House (**http://www.tape.com/ch**), a supplier of just about any kind of magnetic tape you can imagine, offers its products at discounts of 40 percent or more off the already discounted prices you'll find at Wal-Mart and similar stores. Of course, cassette boxes and paper "J-cards" are extra, but they're available in bulk at a deep discount as well.

Yet, as we've said, you will probably be better off if you don't expect people to actually complete a sales transaction while they're online at your site. Instead, view the online world the way they do at The Big Dipper Old-Fashioned Ice Cream Parlor (Fig. 2-1)—as an absolutely

Figure 2-1

*Visitors to the Big Dipper Web site are treated to a complete list of the company's gourmet ice cream flavors—some 75 in all—and a colorful description of what makes their products special.*

incredible marketing tool, a mechanism that offers you the chance to promote goodwill and engender good feelings about you and your products and to tell your story while building a relationship with your customers.

## Where to find you and why bother to visit

Even if none of these "warm and fuzzy" notions appeals to you, there's still a no-brainer of a reason to be on the Web. And that is simply the amazing leverage that an online presence brings to all of your current advertising and marketing efforts.

Your co-authors would be the last to promote setting up a Web site for its own sake or merely because it's fashionable to do so. But at $30 or so a month, how can you lose? Set up a site, include its address in all your print materials (letterhead, business cards, brochures, local newspaper ads, Yellow Pages listing, etc.), and see what happens.

Naturally, there's more to it than that. As we'll see later, establishing a World Wide Web site is only one of many options when it comes to marketing online. So there's more to it in the sense of additional tools you can use. But that's not what we mean here.

What we mean is that setting up a Web page is only the first step. Whether your potential customers are online, on foot, or on the road, they must somehow learn about your place of business on the Web. Then they must be persuaded to exert the effort and expend the energy needed to get there.

It's not enough to simply open a store or set up a Web page. You've got to advertise! You've got to promote! You've got to tell people that you're there and where to find you.

You've also got to give your prospective customers some reason for making the trip. You will understand this much better once you've made the trip yourself. It may be that when Time-Warner and other cable companies begin offering Internet access, getting into the Web will be as easy as changing channels on the TV. In the meantime, as we said in Chapter 1, getting online is something of an ordeal. It's usually worth the effort, but it is not always easy.

# The seven rules of successful online selling

We've given you a lot to think about here. And we will explore additional options and alternatives later in this book. But you will find the experience most profitable if you keep the following seven "rules" in mind. Don't worry if you're not familiar with all of the terms or concepts. Read "The Seven Rules" and absorb whatever comes easily. Then read the rest of the book and come back here after you've had a little more experience.

## Rule 1: Make it worth the trip

The first rule of successful online selling is that you've got to make it worth the trip for a person to seek out and visit your site. You've got to give online users an incentive to pay you a visit.

It doesn't take that much. If your company can save $10 by taking an order online instead of via your toll-free phone number, split the difference with your online customers and offer the merchandise for $5 *less* than the customer would pay ordering by phone. You'll be surprised at how many people will eagerly make the trip to save a mere $5.

Consider putting online merchandise on sale or running special promotions. Is there some item you can make available *exclusively* via your online store? What about a service or convenience that's not available any other way?

For example, imagine giving customers the power to specify the features they want in a TV or VCR, and having a computer scan your inventory for just those units that match that profile. That's service! In

many instances, that's reason enough for a user to make the effort. You won't have to offer any financial incentive at all.

The biggest mistake you can make is to assume that online marketing is just like selling through mail-order catalogues. The *next* biggest mistake is to think that online selling will ever free you entirely of the expense of printing and mailing a catalogue or whatever other advertising and promotion you may be doing right now. You may be able to reduce those expenses by making the information available online. But as long as any competitor is offering merchandise comparable to yours via print ads, color catalogues, and toll-free phone numbers, you will have to do likewise.

And don't forget, with a catalogue, you can go to your customer. The catalogue arrives, unbidden, in the customer's mailbox. When you're online, your customer must be persuaded to come to you. Your customer must say, "Yes, I am going to key in the address that will take me to this site," and then do so. All of which further reinforces the need to "make it worth the trip."

## Rule 2: Integrate your online efforts with everything else

It's amazing, but true: Even today, you can page through *Internet World*, *Wired*, *Boardwatch*, and many other high-tech, online-oriented magazines and discover that many of the ads do not include an e-mail or Web address.

At the very least, every print ad should include your e-mail address, as well as your land address, voice phone, and fax phone numbers. And, once you've got things set up, you should make a real effort to use your print and conventional efforts synergistically with your online presence.

Use the leverage! There are all kinds of ways to do this, but here's a quick example:

> If you want to get prospects to come to your online site, consider running a trivia contest in your most successful print publications.

Put the questions in the ad and tell readers that in order to play, they must go online and visit your electronic location. Perhaps every correct entry will be placed in a random drawing for some prize. Naturally, once they are at your location, there will be items for them to buy and other things to do.

## Rule 3: Keep it fresh

So many companies in the past have assumed that if they offered some information or created an online feature, that there was no need to keep an eye on it. Internally, the online area is assigned the lowest priority. Some staffer is supposed to take care of it, but only if time permits. Which it rarely does.

This is a huge mistake. Neglect of this sort not only hurts sales, it creates an extremely negative impression in the minds of prime prospects—those 20 percent of customers who account for 80 percent of your business.

For example, assume you're in the model-airplane-kit business. You create an online presence that lets users instantly get informative descriptions of your product line. They can easily place orders when they see something they want. And they can get transcripts of interviews with masters of the field and download pictures of prize-winning models.

This is not a difficult thing to create. So, assume you do so and then just walk away. Or, more accurately, assume you fail to assign someone to maintain this feature and make it a top priority.

Here's what will happen: Once the word gets out about your site and what you offer, you'll get a good initial boost as model-airplane enthusiasts gravitate to your feature. They love it! Fantastic! Great job!

But when these same people check in two weeks later, they will expect changes, updates, and new information. If no one has updated the product descriptions and price list . . . if no new interviews or images have been added . . . if, in short, it's the same-old, same-old, you're in trouble!

Okay, two weeks is a very short time. Maybe they'll cut you a break. Particularly if you are the only model airplane kit company online at the time. They'll wait another two weeks—making a month between the time they first checked you out and now. Surely, your company will have uploaded a new interview or two or a batch of new images.

No? It's been four weeks, and nothing has changed? So long, guys. We're outta here!

Possibly never to return.

Through plain, stupid neglect, you have just alienated your prime, platinum-plated online customers. To persuade these folks to give you another look, you'll have to do something spectacular. And you'd better hope that no competitors have come online in the meantime.

## Rule 4: Start small and keep it simple

Everyone loves a visually pleasing magazine page, rich in color and detail. The trouble is that what works for magazines does not work online. A big, beautiful photograph can take several minutes to transmit, and few online users will sit still for that. To see what we mean, try visiting the DealerNet Web site shown in Fig. 2-2 (**http://www.dealernet.com**) using a typical 28.8 kbps (kilobits per second) modem.

Don't worry about the technical details right now. The fact is that people who use the Internet from locations at large companies, government agencies, and college and university computing centers usually will see a full-color, full-screen image like the one in Fig. 2-2 in just over one second, thanks to their high-speed connections to the Net.

But those connections are at least 50 times faster than a 28.8 kbps modem can deliver over regular phone lines. And 28.8 kbps is very close to the maximum speed the common phone line can deliver. Not until the phone system is totally fiber-optic, or until cable companies begin offering access via coaxial cable, will Internet images appear any faster in the typical American home.

Figure 2-2

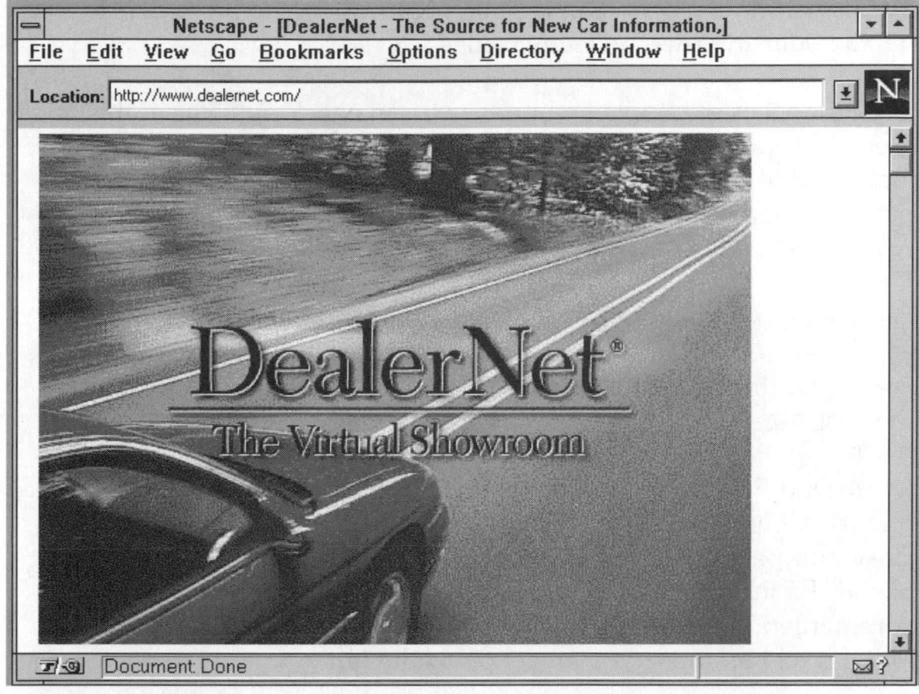


*Graphic images like this one at the DealerNet Web site look great, but with a typical modem connection, they take forever to appear on the screen.*

That's why we strongly suggest that you think small and simple. After all, as pretty as they may be, most big color images do not carry much in the way of information about the product they feature.

Fortunately, as we will see later, there are ways to create a visually pleasing page that appears quickly and does not force users to wait for some huge graphic file to be pumped over the Net and into their machines.

##  Rule 5: Hire an expert

There are many, many things you can do yourself on the Net. Or, if you personally can't do them, they can be done by someone you assign. But—just as a desire to be freed from worrying about ad copy, design, layout, and media schedules may have prompted you to hire

an advertising agency—you may be better off hiring an expert to handle your Internet/online activities.

You'll find lists of people and firms you can check out later in this book. (You might even give us a call!) You will also learn how to plug in and look at what other firms in your line of work are doing. If you like a particular service, you may want to hire the people who created it.

You may be the smartest, cleverest person in the world. But like everyone else, you only get 24 hours to spend each day. So, even if you know you have (or could easily acquire) the necessary knowledge and skills, think about concentrating on what you do best and hiring the rest.

Our friend Robin Raskin, editor of *PC Magazine*, once recounted the remark an eminent scientist made to her at dinner: "If I was ever in close competition with another scientist, and I wanted to get a year ahead, I'd just go out and buy him a computer." As Ms. Raskin commented, "True words, but if I really wanted to put someone on idle, I'd add an Internet connection to the gift!"

## Rule 6: Test it personally—always!

One of the most amazing things about the current collection of advertising and marketing efforts on the Net is how bad so many of them are. Many of them just don't work. You can follow the instructions and click on something and nothing will happen.

There are lots of very rough edges to many online efforts. And some are so rough that it is impossible to believe that anyone from the company sponsoring the ad or the online presence has ever actually tried it out.

Don't make that mistake. Make sure that you and everyone in your group signs on and pretends to be a prospect. Keep notes on what is confusing and what should be improved. Think of it as a debugging process of the sort every software product must go through. Hire the experts, if appropriate, but don't let them "publish" your material until you and your group have thoroughly, and personally, checked it out.

##  Rule 7: Make the commitment!

Finally, the absolute worst thing you can do is to attempt to market your goods or services on the Internet or via some other online system without first making the commitment to doing so. Indeed, commitment is the essential element in all of "The Seven Rules."

You can't do this kind of thing off-the-cuff and have a hope of being successful. You and your company have got to take the time to make a thorough study of online options and alternatives.

You'll have to assign the online marketing and sales project to some specific person—even if that person is yourself. And you will have to make it clear that this is a primary task, not just one more thing on the to-do list. You will have to monitor progress and results and fine-tune things as necessary. In brief, making the commitment means treating the online effort not as a poor stepchild but as a full-fledged member of the family.

If you are not willing to do this, you should close this book and put it back on the shelf for someone else to find, for neither the book nor online marketing will do you any good.

On the other hand, if what we have said here is of interest and you are indeed willing to make the commitment, then we will really enjoy working with you, sharing our knowledge and insights, and generally showing you how to make the most of the online medium in general and the Internet in particular.

We firmly believe that the informed, intelligent, and committed use of the Internet and the online medium can boost sales and improve the image of any business or profession or anyone else with something to offer. The trick is in offering it the right way!

# Crucial concepts made simple

## How the online world works

# CHAPTER 3

DO you read magazines? Well, if you do, you know that there's no need for you to understand how ad pages are produced and inserted into your particular copy of your favorite magazine. Nor do you need to be aware of postage rates, ZIP code sorts, or anything else that is part of the mechanics of producing and delivering the magazine and its advertising.

The same thing would be true about the mechanics of the online world if you were a typical user interested in the features offered by America Online, CompuServe, the Internet, and the rest.

But you're *not* a typical user. You're seriously considering adopting these tools to market and advertise your product or service.

If you want to be able to do so with confidence, you've got to know how the online world works. You've got to know about text and graphics files and communications speeds. And you've got to have a broad overview of the landscape your customers will be traversing.

## Understanding & overview

We'll give you a quick tour of the online world in the next chapter, and after taking it, you will have a much better idea of where everything fits. In this chapter we'll concentrate on the mechanics. And—we promise—we won't force you to master a lot of mindless technical details. We start with the fact that computers can exchange information over the telephone. At this point, that is surely obvious. But you need to know a little more about the process.

## How do computers communicate?

All computers communicate using on/off signals or pulses that we humans usually refer to as 1's and 0's. Physically, those pulses can consist of literally anything. They can be two different voltage levels or two different conditions, like the presence of a hole or the absence of same in a punched card or strip of Mylar tape. They can be regions of a disk that are either magnetized or not magnetized, or the pits and plateaus of a laser-read CD-ROM.

All that matters is that there be two, and only two, distinct signals and that the computer has some way of receiving them.

When it comes to sending two distinct signals over the phone line, a piece of equipment called a *modem* is needed. The modem translates the voltage pulses used inside the computer into sounds that are suitable for the phone line. It also reverses the process when receiving data, translating sounds into voltage pulses.

## The bandwidth problem

*Modems come in all shapes and sizes. Some are designed to be inserted into the computer as a circuit board. Others are free-standing boxes that are connected to the computer and phone jack by cables.*

*The most important characteristic of any modem, however, is its speed. Modem speeds are often loosely referred to as their* baud rate, *though* baud *technically applies only to 300 baud units. Fortunately,* bps *(bits per second) is gradually replacing* baud *as a modem's speed designation.*

*Available modem speeds range from 300 bits per second to a high of 28,800 bits per second, which is usually expressed as 28.8* kilobits *(thousand bits) per second or 28.8* kbps. *Often it is pronounced "twenty-eight eight," just as 14.4 kbps, the next speed down, is pronounced "fourteen four." Modems are classified by their top speed, but, with very few exceptions, all modems can handle every possible slower speed. They are* downward compatible, *in other words.*

*Not too long ago, the standard top modem speed was 9600 bps. Then it became 14.4. Today, as modem prices continue to fall, we can confidently say that 28.8 is becoming the standard. That doesn't mean that the majority of your customers already have 28.8 units yet, but they will in the future.*

*The 28.8 standard is officially called V.34, a designation that is pronounced "vee-dot-thirty-four." It was established in June 1994 by the international body responsible for such things, and it is widely considered to be the maximum speed that ordinary copper telephone lines can handle.*

*Some modem makers use data compression techniques to boost the effective transfer speed. But to get that kind of throughput, you may have to use modems from the same manufacturer on both ends of a connection. In any case, the* bandwidth *(the diameter of the pipe) is still limited by the physical characteristics of copper wire.*

*Not until the nation has been completely rewired with fiber-optic cable will there be enough bandwidth to pump graphic images, sound, and video clips into the home at an acceptably fast speed.*

*The actual lines that are used might belong to the phone company or to a cable TV company. That's not our concern here. What you need to know is that the "data pipes" leading into American homes aren't nearly "wide" enough to speedily deliver all the images and information you may have heard about or seen on CNN.*

*The pipes will be widened eventually. But huge investments will be required, regulatory issues will have to be sorted out, and some time will be required. Unfortunately, we are not likely to become a fully "wired" nation anytime soon.*

# What about pictures & graphics?

Computers have two modes: text mode and graphics mode. As we will see in a moment, sending and receiving text is easy for a computer, even for one with a 9600 bps modem, or slower. Graphic images are another story. Graphic images take much longer to transmit than plain text. Much, much longer.

You will understand why this is so if you think of your computer screen as consisting of hundreds of thousands of tiny picture elements or *pixels*. Each pixel consists of three dots (red, green, and blue), and each of those dots can be controlled individually. The *intensity* of each pixel can also be controlled. In short, four computer bits—one for each color and one for intensity—are required for each pixel when you're in graphics mode.

That sounds reasonable. After all, it means that the typical 16-color, 640 × 480 pixel VGA screen can produce very pleasing images. For photographic quality, you've got to go to 256 colors, but let that go for now.

Here's the key point: The total number of pixels on a standard 640 × 480 screen is 307,200. Each pixel requires four bits of data. That means that filling an entire screen with a graphic image requires over one million bits. (The exact number is 1,228,800 bits, which you get by multiplying 307,200 by four. Call it 1.2 million bits.)

## Unacceptable, even at the fastest speed

We already know that the fastest data speed possible for the vast majority of your customers is 28.8 kbps. In the best of all possible worlds, then, nearly 43 seconds will be required to transmit the 1.2 million bits needed for one full-screen graphic image. (At 14.4 kbps, 86 seconds would be required.)

The majority of users will find 43 seconds far too long to wait, and that's the *best* possible speed. (Remember the DealerNet example, **http://www.dealernet.com**, we told you about in Chapter 2?) So you give them half a screen—call it 20 seconds to transmit. That doesn't sound too bad. And it wouldn't be, if, in the real world, things didn't conspire to slow transmissions down.

For one thing, the software procedures and protocols needed to transport an image from Point A to Point 2 add a considerable amount of overhead in the form of additional bits of data. Then there are the delays introduced by noise on the phone lines and the need to retransmit faulty data.

And let's not forget the fact that the "server" computer sending the image to your customer may be handling several other people at the same time. It may have to divide its attention on a round-robin basis, doling out portions of bits to each person in turn. Or it may be connected to the Internet via a relatively slow line.

There are other complications as well.

All of which leads to the fact that, in the *real* world, even with a connection operating at 28.8 kbps, your customers could easily find themselves drumming their fingers for two minutes or more, waiting for a half-screen image to appear.

Of course, you can further reduce the time required to paint a page by further reducing the size of your graphic images. Or you can set things up so that people entering your page see small "thumbnail" images and are given the option of clicking on them to request a full-size representation.

# Why is text so fast?

One of the really neat things you can do on the Internet is download the full text of most of the great works of literature. (Check out Project Gutenberg at **http://jg.cso.uiuc.edu/pg/** and the Online Book Initiative at **gopher://world.std.com**.) We recently picked up a copy of *Moby Dick*.

In book form, this great work is 730 pages long. As computer bits, however, it occupies the same space as about eight full-screen graphic images and requires less than seven minutes to transmit.

How is it that so much information can be crammed into such a small space and be sent so quickly? After all, each character of text requires a certain pattern of pixels to be lit up on the screen .

The answer is that every computer has a chip called a *character generator*. That chip contains the instructions needed for drawing on the screen every character in the alphabet, as well as many special symbols. Each of these pixel patterns has a number. So there is no need to transmit all the bits that form the graphic image of a character. All you've got to do is send the *number* of the pattern. (America Online and Prodigy use a similar technique for their standard graphic images. Once a copy of the image is on your hard disk, the main system can simply send your software the *name* of the image and it will be displayed.)

## ASCII and the binary numbering system

Everyone agrees on which numbers are assigned to which character patterns. If they didn't, no one would be able to communicate with anyone else's machine. The standard is called ASCII (pronounced "ask-ey"), short for American Standard Code for Information Interchange.

The ASCII code assigns a number to every upper- and lowercase letter of the alphabet. It assigns a number to most major punctuation marks (period, comma, colon, etc.). And it assigns a number to some 26 *control codes* ranging from Ctrl-A through Ctrl-Z.

Thus, thanks to the ASCII code, if you are a Macintosh user and you enter a capital *D* at your keyboard while chatting online with a DOS/Windows-using friend, you can rest assured that your Mac will send your friend an ASCII 68, and that your friend's machine will know that it should respond by displaying a capital *D* on the screen.

Similarly, if you as a businessperson want to offer your product catalogue as a text file on the Internet, you can key in the information and store it as a plain ASCII text file in full confidence that everyone will be able to read it, regardless of the computer or word processing program they use.

## Caveats, of course

There are caveats, of course. First, we are assuming that your text file will be in English. Reaching non-English-reading users requires a special effort that is beyond the scope of this book. (See your DOS/Windows manual for information on *code pages*.)

Second, we're assuming that you've limited yourself to just plain text characters. For technical reasons, computers communicate using eight-bit packages called *bytes*. In the binary numbering system, eight bits—a series of eight 1's and 0's—can express any number from 0 through 255.

But the universally accepted ASCII code set runs from 0 through 127, exactly half of the total possible numbers that can be communicated using eight bits. As it happens, the 128 numbers of the standard ASCII code offer more than enough slots for all the letters, numbers, punctuation marks, and control codes most users will require.

## Non-standard "high" codes

Thus—and here's the key point—no universally accepted standard applies to the ASCII code numbers ranging from 128 through 255.

Computer makers have been free to do what they will with these 128 "high" ASCII codes. In the world of IBM-compatible machines, for example, the ASCII codes from 128 through 168 are devoted to foreign characters, including the sign for the British pound and the one for the Japanese yen. After that come a lot of shading and box-drawing characters, followed by codes for mathematical symbols.

The Macintosh is different. If you're a DOS/Windows user and you send your Mac-using friend an ASCII 227, which shows up on your screen as the Greek letter *pi*, there's no telling what will appear on your friend's screen. (You can generate any ASCII code on a DOS/Windows machine by holding down the Alt key and tapping its number on the numeric keypad.)

You may not be aware of the fact, but the vast majority of word processing programs do not limit themselves to the standard "low"ASCII codes. As an example, consider the matter of soft and hard hyphens.

A *soft hyphen* is one that the program is free to add or remove when it reformats a paragraph. A *hard hyphen* is one that you have entered from the keyboard and that the program will never remove. Both look the same on the screen. Indeed, only your word processing software knows the difference. And the way it knows is by tagging the characters with a high ASCII code.

You never see these non-standard ASCII codes yourself nor will anyone else using the same word processing program. But the codes are stored in the file, and if you send that file to someone who uses a different program, the result may be garbage on his or her screen.

The lesson is this: If you want your words to be easily readable by the largest number of people, make sure that what you offer consists of nothing but plain, pure, ASCII text. (Check your word processing software manual for instructions on how to save a file in plain ASCII text mode.)

## A common-sense approach

We've talked about text and graphics modes and about how computers communicate. Now let's take just a moment to look at some of the ways this information applies to your online sales and marketing efforts.

You already know the importance of saving anything you want everyone to be able to read as standard ASCII text. This also applies to any electronic mail messages you plan to send over the Internet. Most Internet e-mail sites are not able to deal with anything but standard ASCII.

And you know that the fastest way to get a significant amount of information into someone's hands is to send it as text. You'll see how this works later in the book when we discuss *auto-responders*. (If you want to try it right now, send a brief message to **books@mailback.com**. Within minutes, a catalogue of books written by your co-authors will appear as an e-mail message in your mailbox.)

Yet the appeal of graphics, multiple fonts, and all the other elements that make a page on the World Wide Web visually appealing cannot be denied. Indeed, these days, it is *expected*.

What's happening with the Web is the same thing that happened to DOS users with the advent of Windows. There is absolutely no reason for most people to use either Windows 95 or Windows 3.x. A simple DOS-based menu program would serve most people just as well and wouldn't require anywhere near the memory and disk space needed by

Figure 3-1

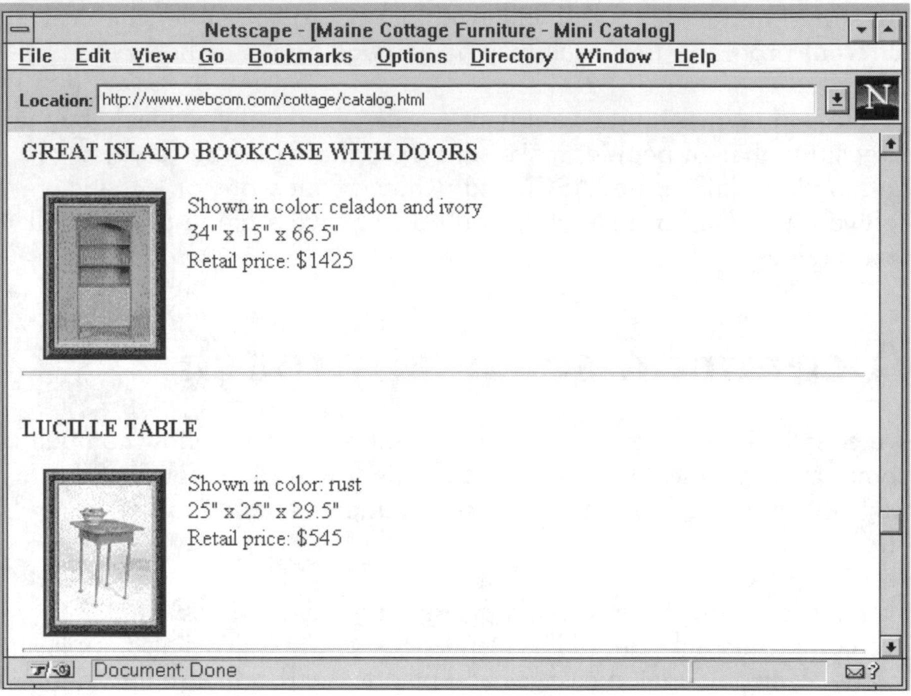


*Maine Cottage Furniture presents thumbnail images—rather than large, slow-loading graphics in their catalogue on the World Wide Web.*

Windows and its applications. But Windows looks pretty, and Microsoft was able to persuade people that it was easy to use.

Similarly, not too long ago, plain, type-written memos in pica or elite used to be the norm. Today, you're nowhere if your memos aren't laser-printed with three different fonts and laced with color-graphic illustrations and charts. The information in today's memos may be the same as before, but as we all now know, presentation is everything.

## Coining a word: infoferrous

While it makes no logical sense, your co-authors have to admit that we were initially disappointed when we tapped into the London Connection, the site discussed in Chapter 2. We expected to see

Figure 3-2

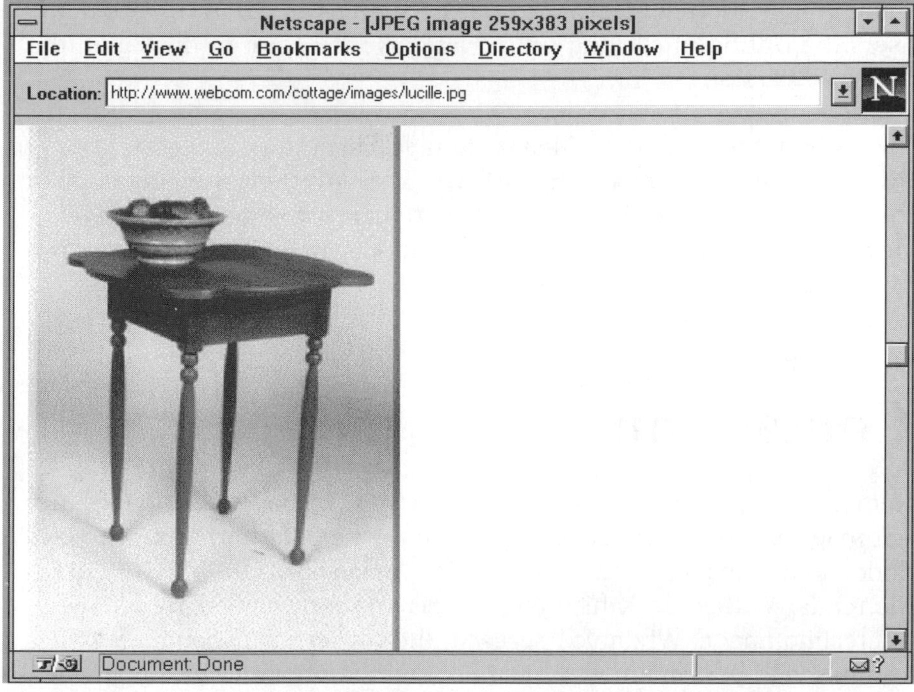


*All it takes is a single mouse-click to turn the small thumbnail image shown in Fig. 3-1 into the full-sized version.*

photos of the flats and cottages being offered and were somewhat taken aback when no images appeared.

This expectation is irrational. Apartments, flats, cottages, and houses are rented all the time via the print media with nary a photo in sight. And, as we have said, big, gorgeous pictures take far too long to transmit. Furthermore, many of the pictures and graphic images on the Web add very little real information. They are not, to use a word we've coined, *infoferrous*—which is to say, they don't carry much information.

The key to graphics on the Web is to use them to make your site visually pleasing and to help your customers find the information they need. If graphics are truly important for your particular product, by all means use them. But don't force your customers to sit still while lots of large, four-color images are sent to them unbidden. Opt instead for

small images—often referred to on the Web as *thumbnails*—and give users the option of clicking on the images they want to display in the full-sized version.

That's how the owners of Maine Cottage Furniture (**http://www.webcom.com/cottage**) present their mini-catalogue on the World Wide Web. Visitors to the site can scroll down the page, viewing thumbnail images and brief descriptions of a dozen or more offerings like the ones shown in Fig. 3-1. A full-sized image (Fig. 3-2) is just a mouse-click away.

# Conclusion

Remember, for all their resemblance to a printed page, Web pages are not magazine pages. They are something quite different, and, when well-done, something significantly better. In a magazine, you've got to grab the reader's attention, which you typically do with a headline or interesting image. When you succeed, the reader may spend a few seconds with you and may or may not dial the phone to give you a call.

On the Web, once you get someone to visit your site, you can get them to spend several minutes or even the better part of an hour with you. And you can get them to come back voluntarily. As for requesting more information or even placing an order, it's only a mouse-click away, which takes even less effort than dialing the phone.

These are things to think about as we plunge into the Internet in the next chapter.

# Welcome to the Internet!

CHAPTER 4

NOW we're ready to discuss the Internet and the World Wide Web in more detail. That's what we'll do in the next two chapters.

We'll focus first on the Internet itself—the collection of wires, cables, computers, protocols, and software that makes it possible to send information from location to location. The Internet is rather like the telephone system in this respect—a mere transport mechanism.

The World Wide Web is just one of many features you can access via the Internet. We'll introduce you to all the major Internet features in this chapter. But the Web is such an important part of the Internet that it's covered in a chapter of its own, Chapter 5.

# Behind closed doors

Thinking about the Internet—where it came from and what it is today—often brings to mind the *hothouse* metaphor. This notion is important for all kinds of reasons, as you will soon see. But basically, for more than a decade, consumer online systems like CompuServe and America Online, plus the nation's BBSs, developed in the *national* marketplace.

Unbeknownst to most of their subscribers, however, another system, funded by the U.S. government, was developing and growing behind closed doors. If you happened to be a defense contractor, a military officer, or a computer-wise university student or professor, you were well aware of this network. But if you did not fall into one of those categories, you probably never heard of it. And even if you did know about it, you couldn't get access unless you belonged to one of those groups.

## The year everything changed

Then, in 1991, everything changed. The U.S. government effectively broke down the wall that separated this system from the rest of the world and more or less let everybody in. Those of us who had heard about the system were amazed at what we saw.

The system we're talking about, of course, is what we now call the Internet. Discovering it was like discovering some long-lost civilization that had been growing and developing on its own on the moon or in some series of isolated underground caverns.

## Perfect timing!

The Internet seemed to come out of nowhere, and its advent instantly re-drew the boundaries of the electronic universe. In retrospect, public access became available at just the right time. If the same thing had happened two years earlier, it is doubtful that it would have made such a splash.

As it was, by 1991, the prices of the modems and computers needed to get onto the Net had fallen dramatically (as they continue to fall). There was an audience of tens of millions who had been developing their computer skills over the last decade or so. Prodigy, CompuServe, and AOL were advertising on television, raising the general awareness of the online world.

Most powerful of all, perhaps, was that the "Information Superhighway" concept introduced by Vice President Al Gore caught the nation's fancy. Although no one really knows what this Information Superhighway will consist of, the globe-girdling Internet is clearly the closest thing to it now in existence.

## They gotta have a deal

Actually, we may be overestimating the influence of the Information Superhighway metaphor here. Our recollection is that what motivated most new Net users was that it was *free*. Indeed, we should warn you that, despite their terrific demographics, in our experience, many online users are extraordinarily cheap.

Like someone who races from one supermarket to another clutching coupons clipped from the Wednesday food section, many online users are only happy if they think they're getting a deal. Just as the coupon

clipper doesn't count the time, effort, and gasoline required to pick up all those "bargains," many online users fail to factor in frustration, inconvenience, and time when calculating their savings.

There's no better example of this than the headlong rush of many of them to the "free" Internet. Men and women who only a few months ago would groan and moan about how difficult it was to use CompuServe or Delphi now demand instant access to the Internet. Never mind that the Internet is a kingdom built on the most obscure, bytehead, complex and confusing, UNIX-based commands you have ever seen!

## Case-sensitivity

People who only yesterday could not be bothered to learn a few simple CompuServe commands—like keying in M for "take me back to the previous menu"—are eagerly diving into Internet features for which the commands are not only obscure, but they've got to be entered in the right *case*!

On the Internet, for example, keying in the command menu is not the same as keying in MENU or Menu. Most of the time, case counts. For example, the Web address **http://www.tv.com/TV.html** is not the same as **http://www.tv.com/tv.html**. If you fail to key in the address correctly, you will not be connected.

This is very much the situation as it exists today. The Internet is not some freestanding entity. It is part of the whole matrix of the online field that happens to have developed its own culture and ways of doing things.

## An earthquake in the online world

At the same time, the advent of public access to the Internet has radically changed the market that AOL, Prodigy, and CompuServe—the "Big Three" consumer online systems—have spent so much time and treasure building. Subscribers have demanded that the Big Three provide Internet access, and many individuals, faced with monthly

connect-time charges of well over $100 on a Big Three system, have defected to local Internet service providers who charge a mere $20 a month for unlimited hours.

Advertisers and information providers have also re-examined their relationships with the Big Three. After all, why would any company pay CompuServe tens of thousands of dollars a year to host a feature designed to sell the firm's products, when that same company can set up a Web site for a fraction of the cost? And such a site will be accessible by *anyone* with a modem, not just CompuServe subscribers.

In our opinion, consumer online systems are far, far from dead. Right now, millions of people want "the online experience." They don't much care what information they retrieve online. The *process* is everything. Later, these same people will get bored—in the "been there, done that, got the tee-shirt" sense—and stop going online.

Or they will become frustrated at how difficult and time-consuming it can be to extract any really good information from the Internet or the Web. That's when they will realize that the filtering and packaging services offered by the likes of CompuServe and America Online are well worth paying for.

In short, while the Big Three and the conventional model of a consumer online system may be down right now, we predict a huge backwash composed of sadder but wiser Internet and Web users. Which means that as a potential online marketer, you neglect the Big Three and similar systems at your peril.

## Where did the Internet come from?

And speaking of "peril," though it may seem surprising, the system we know today as the Internet is a direct by-product of the Cold War and the "peril of communism."

In the early 1960s, some bright bulb in the United States Department of Defense realized that in the event of a thermonuclear holocaust, a

single bomb or two could eliminate any form of "command and control" communication between the Pentagon and military installations around the world.

As it often did in those days, the government called in the Rand Corporation. It hired experts from Rand to think about the problem and present one or more solutions. In 1964, the results of their thinking became known. The experts proposed a new concept in system structure. Instead of a hub-and-spoke arrangement in which, if the hub—the Pentagon—is destroyed the nodes at the tip of each spoke are cut off, they suggested a network *without* a hub or "boss." Instead, it would be composed of peer-to-peer interconnections that put no single system in charge.

If the old arrangement was a *wheel* in which all communication from one spoke to another flowed through the central hub, the new system was a *sphere* in which the node on the end of every spoke was connected to every other node, plus the Pentagon center, through *multiple* links.

## The invention of "networking"

You can destroy a wheel by bombing its hub. But how many bombs is it likely to take to sever every connection in a ball of fishnet? Practically speaking, it cannot be done.

If Site A wants to relay a message to Site Z, and it finds that a dozen sites in between have been destroyed, it just keeps trying until it finds a site that is still active. The message is transmitted to, say, Site T, which keeps trying to find a path to the site that is nearest to Site Z, the ultimate destination.

This is pretty neat, but when you look a bit deeper, it is neater still. The reality is that the computer at Site A does not send the entire message to Site T. The first page of the message might go there, but the second page might go to Site D, which would be equally vigorous in finding the next step on the path toward Site Z.

The two pages might arrive at Site Z in reverse order, but the computer at Site Z will know how to reassemble them correctly.

##  Packet switching is the key

All of this sounds like a lot of work, and it is. But since everything takes place at computer speeds, the actual time required can be minimal. The concept that makes it all possible is *packet switching*.

Packet-switching technology was designed and developed in 1969 by Bolt, Beranek, and Newman (BBN), working under contract for the Defense Department's Advanced Research Projects Agency (ARPA). The network that was created was called the ARPANET. In 1973, the name became DARPANET, the initial *D* standing for *Defense*.

Packet switching is the same technology used by SprintNet, Tymnet, the CompuServe Network, and many other companies that offer access to online services—including privately owned bulletin board systems. Indeed, many of these public packet-switching networks were created by former BBN employees.

##  Packet number and address

There's no need to get technical about it. But you should know that the concept involves chopping any file or message into uniformly-sized packets of bytes, stamping each with an address and packet number, and firing them out into the network.

Once these packets are in the network, the route they take to reach their destination differs with network conditions that change each fraction of a second. If the source is Columbus, Ohio, and the destination is Los Angeles, Packet 1 might go down to St. Louis, up to Portland, Oregon, and then down to Los Angeles. Packet 2 might go to Miami, and then to Las Vegas, and then to L.A. All of the computer nodes on the network have been programmed to seek the best route for each packet at any given moment.

##  Consumer benefits

This is great from a national defense perspective because it makes it all but impossible to take out the entire network. If you doubt this, all you need do is recall how hard it was for the Allies to disable Iraq's command-and-control system during the Gulf War. (That's right, Iraq was using an Internet-style packet-switched network.)

Yet there are consumer benefits as well. When you call someone on the phone, an actual *circuit* is set up between you. The circuit remains in existence for the duration of your call. But think of how many pauses there are in normal human conversation. During those pauses, no data is exchanged—yet the wires and equipment used to create that circuit are not available for anything else.

Packet switching, in contrast, sets up a *virtual circuit* that makes very efficient use of the phone lines. Theoretically, all the wires and all the equipment that make up the network are in use all the time. Sitting in front of your computer in L.A., you cannot tell that no direct, physical connection exists between you and CompuServe's computers in Columbus, Ohio. The results and performance are the same as if you had indeed placed a long-distance voice call to CompuServe directly.

Thanks to packet switching, with the exception of most BBSs, users of most online systems can connect with a distant computer by making a *local* phone call to their nearest SprintNet, Tymnet, or other packet-switching network node.

##  Content & features

In the commercial world, the *protocol* (the set of rules and procedures) adopted to make packet switching possible is called X.25 ("X-dot-twenty-five"). This is a universal standard, promulgated by an arm of the United Nations which, for reasons we need not worry with, labels all standards either "X-" or "V-dot-something."

The protocol used by the Internet is called TCP/IP, short for Transmission Control Protocol/Internet Protocol. TCP defines the way in which packets are to be handled, while the IP portion does the same for the addressing of those packets. Anyone who plugs directly into the Internet today—as opposed to going through one of the Big Three systems or an Internet service provider, must use software that supports TCP/IP. (In fact, even the Big Three have announced plans to establish separate, subscription-based TCP/IP networks separate from their main systems.)

##  The end of the Cold War

We well remember having lunch with a communications consultant friend many years ago and hearing him say that a directive had gone out to all scientists using the ARPANET not to store their notes on the system. Apparently it was not at all uncommon for Soviet scientists to somehow gain access to the network and download copies of those notes.

Or maybe someone at the Pentagon was merely speculating that this *could* happen. We didn't pay all that much attention. While we knew about the ARPANET, we also knew that ordinary people couldn't gain access to it and, thus, this was but a fascinating footnote.

With the Cold War over and the Internet now open to the public, it does indeed seem possible that really good computer experts in other countries could find a way to tap private files stored on the Net. Perhaps someday someone will write a book about the Net during the Cold War—one that will be the equivalent of the books about the Ultra machine that gave the Allies access to all of the Third Reich's secret codes during World War II.

The Internet thus began as a high-speed rail line linking key sites at the Pentagon, defense contractors, and colleges and universities. But other networks were developing independently at the time. It wasn't too long before these other networks began seeking permission to connect themselves to the high-speed lines or *backbone network* of the ARPANET.

There's no need to rehearse every step of how the Internet grew. You should know, however, that the ARPANET was taken down in June 1990, but hardly anyone noticed because, by that time, most of its functions had been taken over by the National Science Foundation (NSF) and its network, NSFNet.

The key point is that, before it became available to ordinary citizens in 1991, the Internet had become a "network of networks" that spanned the globe. Colleges, universities, companies, and government agencies worldwide hooked up to the Net. The Internet had thus ceased to be a network dedicated to a particular purpose (defense).

# Five key Internet concepts

It had become, instead, the electronic equivalent of the U.S. interstate highway system. The Internet isn't an "end," it is merely a means to an end. Physically, it is just the *transport* mechanism that links tens of thousands of locations (computer sites or networks). That's Concept Number 1.

Concept Number 2 is the essential oneness of every location on the Net. This sounds quite mystical and Zen-like, and, in a sense, it is.

Thanks to the speed of computer communications, the distance from any single point on the Net to any other single point is essentially the same, which is to say, zero. Time and geographical space don't count. That's why, from your computer on a farm in Idaho, you can pull in information from a computer located in Hong Kong one second and then click your mouse and instantly connect with a computer located in Paris—and you will never notice the difference!

It will all seem as if you are using one, single, gigantic online system. Which, of course, you are. It seems amazing, and it is. But it is only slightly more amazing than the fact that you can pick up a telephone handset, punch in a few numbers, and establish voice contact with any one of billions of people around the world.

Concept Number 3 is that no one controls the Net. It is true that the U.S. government used to provide the bulk of the funding for the backbone links. But the Net has taken on a life of its own. If the U.S. government were to instantly withdraw its support tomorrow, the Net would survive. As it happens, the government is indeed gradually withdrawing support as the Net makes the transition to corporate, private, and user-based funding.

## Community standards

While the Internet may be the modern equivalent of the Wild West, even in Tombstone Territory unwritten community standards controlled the way most folks behaved. People who violated those standards were shunned. The modern day equivalent on the Internet is for violators to be *flamed*—which is to say, subjected to strong verbal criticism via e-mail and in public forums.

That's Concept Number 4, and it is the most important concept of all for would-be electronic marketers. There are innumerable doctoral theses waiting to be written on the phenomenon of the development of the Internet electronic community.

## The evolution of the community

For example, someone comes up with an idea, with a way to push the envelope of the network structure. The next thing you know, *newsgroups* have been created. Newsgroups, as we will see, are essentially "piano rolls" of messages, one tacked on to the next, in which discussions can take place over time. Net users like the idea, so the number of newsgroups mushrooms. Of necessity, the community independently establishes a procedure for creating and approving newsgroups. And in typical Net fashion, the process is very democratic.

No government committee in Washington, D.C., sat down and deliberated over whether newsgroups should be created and how they should be implemented. The Net decided, debated, created, and implemented. And no one could stop them.

People from all over the world could register their opinions, make their arguments, and participate in the process. It didn't make any difference who you were.

## When you're on the Internet, no one knows . . .

You may recall the now famous Steiner cartoon in the *New Yorker*. The one that showed a mutt sitting in front of a computer screen and, paws on the keyboard, saying to another dog nearby, "On the Internet, nobody knows you're a dog." Well, on the Internet, nobody knows your name, age, gender, or nationality. All they know is what you say, and if what you say makes sense, people will listen to you.

The ingrained prejudices and other baggage all of us bring to any human encounter no longer exist. The Internet, e-mail, and other forms of electronic speech are the closest thing this side of heaven we are likely to come to absolutely pure, soul-to-soul communication.

This process has taken place again and again on the Internet, and over time, as with any group of serious, hard-working human beings, standards of behavior have evolved. Unwritten agreements have developed on what is acceptable and what is not.

## Respect the culture

It's completely irrelevant whether or not you personally agree with those standards. Violate them and you're dead. The Internet is a community of users that has been developing for over two decades. Certainly, most members of this community have benefited from free, taxpayer-subsidized access. So as a taxpayer you may feel that it's your network too. That may be technically true. But again, it's irrelevant.

The best way to approach the Net as a businessperson is with the same regard for culture that would inform your approach in a non-American country.

In Japan, for example, it can be important to know that white, not black, is the color of mourning. If you're invited to dinner at a male business associate's home in Germany, it is a faux pas to bring flowers to his wife since this is considered a sign of romantic interest. The thumbs-up gesture Americans use to signal that everything is "A-Okay" is considered obscene in some middle eastern countries.

The list of tiny, but significant, differences goes on and on. Culminating, perhaps, in the colossal blunder made by a major American electronics firm that invested millions in Christmas promotions in a certain European country, all of which were designed to debut on December 25.

Trouble was, no one bothered to investigate the local customs. If they had, they would have discovered that in this particular culture, St. Nicholas's feast day, December 6, is the day on which children receive their Christmas presents. Needless to say, millions of dollars were lost as a result of this stupid mistake. And it all could have been a success had the marketers taken the time to investigate the local culture.

## A place for everything, and everything in its place

We want to help you avoid similar blunders on the Internet. As you'll discover, the Internet is open to anything. But everything must generally be in its appropriate place. That's Concept Number 5.

What upsets veteran Internet users is not that you have placed an ad or solicited customers or announced a new service on the Net. There are places for all of these things. What bugs them is that you've placed your ad for business stationery, your accounting services, or your "E-Z" business incorporation kit on a newsgroup designed to let small-business owners exchange tips and tricks. Your logic is, "Hey, this group is read by precisely the people I want to reach! I'll just upload a few ads."

Their reaction is, "Get the heck out of here! Put your ad in any of the many business/advertising groups on the Net. But not here. We, the

users of this newsgroup, do not want to discover that every fourth message in the queue is some kind of advertisement. So get thee gone!" (There are several widely circulated "Blacklists of Internet Advertisers" available on the Net. For specific, detailed examples of the kinds of marketing activities that have angered some members of the Internet community, visit the Web site at **http://math-www.uni-paderborn.de/~axel/BL/blacklist.html**.)

## The new Internet culture

We could have relegated this cautionary advice to the back of the book and simply plunged ahead to present the Internet's main features. We did not do so because we believe that learning to use a system's features is not nearly as important as becoming aware of its culture.

It's true that the Internet culture of old is changing. As literally millions of people from America Online, CompuServe, Prodigy, BBSs, and local Internet service providers charge into the Net, the old hands are being driven out. They simply don't have the numbers to dominate things any more.

But why would you or anyone else assume that the newcomers wouldn't eventually establish their *own* culture? The norms, the requirements, the do's and don't's may be different, but you can bet that a culture will emerge. And you can count on the fact that if you violate it, you will be flamed.

## The main Internet features

Now, with all of that out of the way, let's look at the main Internet features and how you might use them to market your goods or services.

Obviously, the World Wide Web is the standout. It shines so brightly in public consciousness that it can be hard to see the many other Internet features at your disposal. In fact, we once did a radio interview during which someone called in and asked "What were you saying about 'newsgroups?' I didn't realize that there was anything else but the Web on the Internet."

You yourself may feel the same way. That's why, before we hit the Web in the next chapter, we'll introduce you to a set of other Internet features any prospective online marketer needs to know about. We've said it before: The Web is the newest and most talked about of all the Internet features, but there are millions of people who use the Internet everyday without ever visiting a Web page. These are people you'll miss if you focus exclusively on the Web.

##  Making the most of the Net

We are about to discuss a dozen Internet features, placing the major emphasis on the four or five that you can most effectively use for marketing. But you must first grasp an essential point: No particular person or group "creates features" on the Internet.

Executives at America Online, CompuServe, and Prodigy may "take a meeting" or "do lunch" over some proposal for a new feature they might offer to their subscribers. But on the Internet, no one runs a return-on-investment or creates a spreadsheet to predict whether a particular feature is worth having.

On the Net, basically, someone has an idea for a feature; he or she writes the necessary program and puts it up; and if the community likes it, the feature is widely adopted. If there is no interest, the feature dies or is relegated to the electronic backwaters.

In the past 20 years, the Internet has had tens of millions of users, and you can bet that many of them have created features, some of which have attracted something of a cult following. For a businessperson, however, there are really only five generally accepted Internet features that matter. The first is the World Wide Web, of course. The other four are:

- Electronic mail
- Newsgroups

- Mailing lists
- File transfers via FTP

## Internet e-mail

Everyone with an account on any system connected to the Internet automatically has an Internet e-mail address. Subscribers to every consumer system (CompuServe, America Online, Prodigy, Delphi, eWorld, and so on) can exchange mail with friends on different systems or on Internet-connected systems. All you need to know is the correct Internet address of your correspondent.

Unfortunately, Internet e-mail messages can generally be no longer than 64K (64 kilobytes or 64,000 bytes or about 16 single-spaced pages) and must consist of nothing but standard seven-bit ASCII text. With seven 1 and 0 bits you can symbolize any number from 0 through 127. These are the "low" ASCII codes everyone agrees on.

No "extended characters" or "eight-bit" or "high" ASCII codes may be used. (With eight bits, you can symbolize not only 0 through 127, but 128 through 255, sending you into the non-standard half of the ASCII code.) That means that you can't use Internet e-mail to send anything other than plain, pure, standard ASCII text.

Then again, anything can be converted into standard ASCII characters for transmission and then reconverted after it is received. That's right: You can take a binary graphic image file and convert it to plain old ASCII text for transmission over the Net. Your correspondent can record this plain text on disk and, once he or she is offline, convert it back into a binary graphic image file, a native Word for Windows file, or whatever it was before.

The software needed to perform these various conversions is free, but you've got to know where to find it, how to get it, and how to use it. (For more on this, see The Internet Toolkit at the back of this book.) That's why, from a marketing standpoint, we recommend that you confine all of your Internet e-mail to plain, pure, ASCII text. Doing so makes everything so much simpler for all concerned.

## Newsgroups

*Newsgroups* are essentially ongoing conferences devoted to a specific topic. They began as a way of discussing and conveying the latest news about the Internet and the UNIX programming language. Hence, the name. But they have grown far beyond that narrow focus.

Today, there are over 15,000 newsgroups devoted to every topic you can imagine—and many that you would not want to imagine. There are no membership requirements for any group. Anyone who can read a newsgroup's messages is free to add comments to a given *message thread*—the list of messages and replies that constitute the discussion.

The main drawback is that at any given time, a newsgroup will be able to show you only a limited number of messages. Previous messages will have "scrolled off" the board, unless some user has taken the time to collect them all into an archive file somewhere.

Fortunately, someone has. The DejaNews service has announced its intention to maintain a searchable database containing one year's worth of postings in leading newsgroups. You'll find DejaNews at the Web address **http://www.dejanews.com**. If you're an America Online subscriber, look for the DejaNews icon on AOL's Internet screen.

## Mailing lists

Mailing lists are similar to newsgroups, but they are far less interactive. The items uploaded to a list are more likely to be articles and longer pieces rather than the short comments that typify newsgroups. Also, while one must key in a command or two to read the latest newsgroup messages, the material sent to mailing list members automatically arrives in their electronic mailboxes.

In most cases, getting your name added to or removed from a mailing list is as simple as sending an e-mail message to a given address.

## Files via FTP

The uploading, downloading, and transfer of files is probably close to the heart of any online system. The files in question could be anything from a piece of music to a graphical image to the full text of a Supreme Court decision. The main Internet technique for locating and downloading files is called FTP, short for File Transfer Protocol.

Basically, you go to some FTP location, take a look around, select the file you want, and tell the system to send it to you. It used to be that you had to key in obscure DOS-like commands to get files via FTP, but now it's all point-and-click. In fact, it's often possible to FTP files directly from a World Wide Web page.

## Other features you'll hear about

As you traverse the Net and the Web, you will undoubtedly hear references to features like Archie, Telnet, IRC, Gopher, Veronica, Jughead, and WAIS. These are vestiges of the old Internet, which is to say, the Internet as it existed for most of its 20-odd years.

Here's a quick rundown to enable you to pass yourself off as an old Internet hand:

- *Archie* is based on the word *archive* and refers to a file-finding system based on the name of the file you're looking for. Imagine a database made up of nothing but the filenames that appear when you key in dir at the DOS command line or bring up File Manager in Windows. Then imagine searching that list of files for one specific file and you'll have a good idea of what Archie is all about. It's a very crude tool, but for many years it was the best that was available.
- *Telnet* is the Net function that is most like signing onto CompuServe or some other commercial system. You "Telnet" to a site and sign on. After that, everything you see on your screen, everything you can do, is controlled by a program running on the host system you have dialed.

Systems accessible via Telnet include libraries, universities, government agencies, and private systems. In libraries you can call up the card files. In universities you can look into campus directories and library files, access databases, and see what's new on campus.

- *Internet Relay Chat (IRC)* is the Internet version of the real-time chat features long offered by the big consumer systems. As on those systems, "chat" resembles text-based CB-radio conversations.

- *Gopher* is a program designed to let educators, administrators, and others present information collections as a series of nested menus. This means that every Gopher you encounter is a unique creation. It also means that nothing appears on a Gopher menu unless some human being decided to put it there. This human filter is absolutely invaluable, a fact you'll appreciate all the more once you've done a few searches of the Web with an Internet *search engine* like Yahoo! or Infoseek.

  You should also know that a Gopher menu item can point to just about any kind of Internet feature, whether it's FTPing a file, Telnetting to a location, or going to a Web page. In this respect, a Gopher is like a site on the World Wide Web without the graphics.

- *Veronica* and *Jughead* are searchable databases of Gopher menu items. Dedicated people at sites with Gopher menus all over the Net regularly send their menus to other sites that have agreed to run the Veronica software. The menus that get sent include *everything*—both the visible text and the hidden commands lying behind each menu item.

  When someone logs onto a Veronica site and does a Veronica search, what gets searched is the database of Gopher menus. This database is what Net users call *Gopherspace*.

  Using this database, Veronica then assembles a customized Gopher menu for you. If you have told Veronica to search on, say, "Supreme Court," *every* item on this customized menu will contain that search phrase. Jughead, in contrast, is used to search the line items on a *single* Gopher menu system.

- *WAIS* (pronounced "ways") is an acronym for Wide Area Information Servers. WAIS lets you search the actual text of a document or group of documents. But it does so in a manner that eliminates the complex AND/OR/NOT Boolean logic and nested expressions used by people who search databases for a living.

  The trick is in the creation of an index containing every word in a given file. Unfortunately, this means that WAIS searches can be conducted only on files for which such an index has been previously prepared. To give WAIS a try, visit the Web site at **http://sunsite.unc.edu/cgi-bin/fwais.pl**.

  For more information on WAIS, call 415-617-0444 or send an e-mail message to **info@wais.com**. At this writing, responses are still being handled by a human being, not an auto-responder.

  As a matter of interest, a product called ZyIndex is generally considered much more powerful and easier to use than WAIS, though the Internet version lists for around $5,000. Still, if you want to offer visitors to your Web site the ability to search, you might consider ZyIndex. Call 800-544-6339 or visit the company's Web site at **http://www.zylab.com**.

# Conclusion

Later in this book we'll show you how to use e-mail, newsgroups, mailing lists, and FTP as powerful marketing tools. Indeed, each can be an effective standalone technique. By making them all work together, however, you can create a marketing effort of amazing synergy.

The element that pulls all of these tools together, of course, is your home page on the World Wide Web. You may say, "But I don't need a graphical Web page to tell my story." To which we would respond, "That may be absolutely true, but you've got to have a Web page anyway because people *expect* it!" So turn to the next chapter and let's get busy as we explain the World Wide Web and how it works.

# The World Wide Web

# CHAPTER 5

THE World Wide Web is simply unavoidable, and we don't mean just when you're talking about the Internet. The Web is everywhere! The *New York Times* and the *Wall Street Journal* routinely carry stories about the Web and advertisements urging readers to "visit our Web site." Our local Bucks County paper even has a regular column about what's happening on the Web and in the online universe.

The computer trade magazines we read are stuffed with stories about the World Wide Web, but you'd expect that. What you don't expect is to take a break from work, switch on CNN, and find—as part of the regular entertainment feature—a whole segment about the wonders of the Walt Disney home page (**http://www.disney.com**).

Or after work, you're doing a little NordicTracking in front of the TV set, and your program is interrupted by commercials for CompuServe and America Online urging you to sign up so you can "surf the Web." Later, during your shower, you're listening to National Public Radio, and *they're* doing a story about the Web or urging you to "check the Web" for their weekly program guide or some other offering.

This is precisely the kind of popularity and interest in the online world that we predicted nearly 15 years ago. Trouble is, we were off by a dozen years or so, and neither we nor anyone else at the time envisioned anything like the World Wide Web.

## The Web as catalyst

The Internet was growing in popularity from the moment the public at large was permitted access. But it wasn't until the graphical version of the Web (and the software to "browse" it) was introduced that things really went through the roof.

The Web is clearly the catalyst that has created the online explosion. It has seized the popular imagination like nothing else since the introduction of the original IBM personal computer.

You've seen a few screen shots and images and heard us talk about it. Now you're ready to learn what the World Wide Web is all about. And you know what? The fundamental simplicity of it all will surprise you.

# Images & hypertext markup language (HTML)

Key concept: World Wide Web *home pages* are physically nothing but plain, pure, 7-bit ASCII text files. What makes them different from ordinary text files is that they contain instructions on how the information they hold should be displayed. Those instructions control things like which font and type-size is used and where the words appear on your screen.

The instructions also contain pointers to graphic image files—the equivalent of "Slug in that picture of the space shuttle right here." And the instructions contain pointers to other locations. These are the equivalent of "If the user clicks on this button, show him this page, or connect her to this site." (See Figs. 5-1 and 5-2 for examples of an HTML file and how that file looks on the World Wide Web.)

The name used for this set of instructions is *hypertext mark-up language* (HTML). The *hypertext* concept is based on the idea that users should be able to click on an on-screen button, image, or line of text and be taken automatically to a different, relevant, page or location. Naturally, though, HTML includes many commands that go far beyond this *hotlink* idea.

# It started as plain text

In the beginning, the World Wide Web was *text-based*. It had no graphics or desktop-publishing-style fonts at all. That beginning was in March 1989, when Tim Berners-Lee of the European Particle Physics Laboratory (known as CERN) proposed a way of using the Internet to make research information more easily available to the scientific community.

Figure 5-1

```
<html>
<head><title>Windham Hill Home Page</title></head>
<body background="/images/bghome.gif">
<p>
<br>
<center>
<p>
<br>
<img border=0 ALT="Windham Hill" SRC="/images/home.gif" width=460>
<p>
<a href="/quicktour/"><img src="/images/quicktour.gif" border=0></a>
<a href="/ourmusic/"><img src="/images/ourmusic.gif" border=0></a>
<a href="/interact/"><img src="/images/interact.gif" border=0></a><br>
<p>
<a href="/ontour/" border=0><img src="/images/ontour.gif" border=0></a>
<a href="/justin/"><img src="/images/justin.gif" border=0></a>
</center>
<br>
</body>
</html>
```

*An example of HTML text. Take a look at Fig. 5-2 to see how it looks on the World Wide Web.*

Mr. Berners-Lee was operating within long-established Internet norms. Which is to say, he proposed a feature, made the coding available, and sat back to gauge the reaction of the Internet community.

What Berners-Lee suggested was that scientists look at the Internet as a huge, round-the-clock library when preparing their scholarly papers. As every college student knows, such papers are filled with cross-references and footnotes. If you want to follow up on these sources, you must hunt them down yourself, using conventional library resources.

The Berners-Lee "Web" approach made all those cross-references *clickable*. Click on a cross-referenced book, article, or paper, and the cross-referenced information itself instantly appears on your screen, thanks to the Internet and the concept of hypertext.

That's how the World Wide Web began. Only it wasn't really clickable in the beginning. The *hypertext* or *hotlinks* that would deliver a copy of a footnoted article to your terminal screen were all text, so you had to enter items from a menu.

Figure 5-2

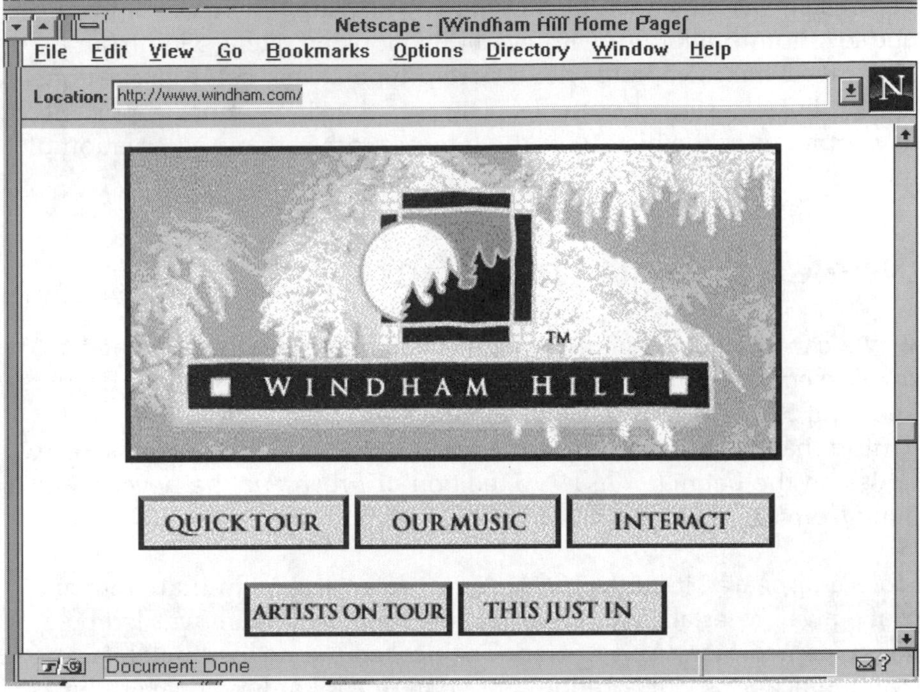


*This is what the HTML text in Fig. 5-1 looks like when displayed on the World Wide Web.*

# Where browser programs fit in

It was the so-called *browser programs* that made everything graphical.

The Berners-Lee concept of the World Wide Web began to take hold as an accepted Internet feature. But it didn't really take off until the National Center for Supercomputing Applications (NCSA) began a project to create a *graphical* user interface for it. That happened during 1993 and 1994, and the program was called *Mosaic*.

Mosaic not only made it possible to click your way through the Web with your mouse, it also allowed documents with images to be pumped to your screen. And it allowed video clips and sound files to be transferred to you as well. In essence, Tim Berners-Lee established the idea of hypertext hotlinks, and Mosaic added a graphical, Windows/Macintosh-style interface.

The result was a means of using the World Wide Web to click from one location to another, with everything looking like a page from a slick magazine, complete with different type styles, color illustrations, and hotlinks to still other pages. This was the single most important development in the history of the Internet, other than the creation of the Net itself.

## Netscape and the others

As we can see once again, the World Wide Web was not planned by some executive committee. It was started in one form by Tim Berners-Lee, and the Mosaic people came along and improved it. (Unfortunately, as Mr. Berners-Lee told National Public Radio's Terry Gross on the February 7, 1996, edition of *Fresh Air*, he never made a dime from his invention.)

Mosaic appeared in early 1994. A year later, the team that created it broke away to establish a separate company. The team was led by a fellow named Marc Andreessen. They called the new entity Netscape Communications Corporation, got venture capital funding, hired a computer industry heavy-weight or two to manage things, and settled down to create an improved Web browser program called *Netscape Navigator*.

In the interim, Mosaic was licensed to other companies, each of whom produced its own version. Other browsers, like Netcom's NetCruiser, appeared. But it was Netscape that raced ahead to gobble up over 85 percent of the market. A year after leaving to form Netscape Communications Corporation, Mr. Andreessen, at age 24, was worth over $131 million, thanks to the company's stock offering, and had appeared on the cover of *Time* magazine. (You can read this cover story yourself by going to **http://pathfinder.com** and selecting the Time magazine icon. Look for the issue dated February 19, 1996.)

## Why Bill Gates & Microsoft are worried

Today, everyone refers to Netscape Navigator as simply *Netscape*. The company was able to move quickly into such a dominant position by making its *client* software (the browser program) available for free and making its money selling the necessary *server* programs to firms wishing to establish a site on the Net.

Shrink-wrapped versions of Netscape can be purchased at software stores, but the latest version is available online free of charge. (Go to **http://home.netscape.com** to get your copy.)

Still, it is doubtful that Netscape would have succeeded if it wasn't such a terrific program. And that's what's driving Bill Gates and Microsoft crazy.

Why? Because the key to Microsoft's success has never been the creation of truly superb software. Rather, it has been the ability to set and control industry *standards*. So here is Netscape with a lock on 85 percent of the Web browser market, and it's just tearing up the track with innovations.

You will even encounter sites on the Web that display a special message reading, "This site looks best with Netscape." And, it's true!

Netscape is in a position to say, "Okay, boys and girls, this is how sound, video, and image files will be transmitted on the Web. Which is to say, this is *our* approach, and we hope you will agree to follow it." The words were different, but Microsoft used to say the same kind of thing a decade ago.

In our opinion, this is a battle that Microsoft is going to lose. As we said, the real reason Netscape is so far ahead is that it is so superior to its competitors. And it keeps getting better and better. Whether Microsoft's impending loss here matters very much, however, remains to be seen.

## Uniform Resource Locators (URLs)

*The official name for what is commonly called a "Web page address" is* Uniform Resource Locator *or URL (pronounced "you-are-ell"). In technical terms, a URL is a means of specifying a location (or* object) *on the Internet. This doesn't make a lot of sense until you understand that you can use Netscape and other browsers to tap not only Web pages but also Gopher menus, Telnet locations, and numerous other tools.*

*Here are six of the URLs you should be able to use with your browser. We qualify that statement because, while Netscape can use them all, other browser programs may not yet be able to handle e-mail. Notice, too, that the newsgroup and mail URLs do not include a pair of forward slashes:*

| Location | URL prefix |
|---|---|
| *World Wide Web site* | *http://* |
| *Gopher menu system* | *gopher://* |
| *Telnet remote access* | *telnet://* |
| *File transfers* | *ftp://* |
| *Newsgroups* | *news:* |
| *Electronic mail* | *mailto:* |

*Don't forget that you will be best off if you pay close attention to the case of the letters in any URL you key in by hand. Also, check your browser's toolbar for options like "Bookmark," "HotList," "Favorite Places," or the like. When you are at a particular location on the Net, you can use such "bookmarking" tools to record the location's URL on a list. Returning to that location in the future can then be as easy as displaying your list of bookmarks and clicking on the relevant entry. No need to type anything in by hand, in other words.*

# How Web browsers work

Now let's summarize what happens when you use Netscape, Mosaic, or any other browser program. People use a browser to get into the Internet and go to a specific location. Once they are at that location, the computer hosting that site transmits an HTML text file to them.

The key point is that the browser program knows how to respond to the HTML commands in that text file. It knows, for example, to tell Windows that it wants a particular font and type-size to be used to display certain words, and a different font and type-size to be used for other words. The browser program also has the built-in ability to display the graphic images that the host system sends.

Basically, a Web browser is a lot like a desktop publishing program like Ventura/Corel or any sophisticated word processor. It accepts files containing nothing but plain-text instructions and produces beautiful screens.

##  Standards, multimedia, and beyond

Please hold that notion in your head. Everyone who is interested in setting up a Web site uses the same programming language—HTML—to prepare the site. And everyone who is interested in visiting a Web site uses a browser that understands HTML programming. Everything, in short, is compatible with everything else, and sweetness and light reign in the online kingdom.

Cool. But what if you want to go beyond pleasant text and pretty pictures? What if you want to offer sound and full-motion video clips? What if you want to offer 3-D images? And, hey, how about this—what if you want to offer your images not in the generally accepted JPG, GIF, or PCX formats but in the GONZO format?

This is a murky area that will undoubtedly be clarified over time. But here's what you should remember: The ultimate goal is to create what might be described as "an interactive, push-button, high-definition television system with CD-quality sound that is linked to the Web and the Internet."

The standards to make this possible will evolve. In the meantime, we're stuck with scores of different formats for graphics, sound, and video files.

# Java, Visual BASIC, & other considerations

We need to talk in a bit more detail about graphics, sound, and video files. We'll be as brief and non-technical as possible. But you're going to hear about *Java* and *Visual BASIC* and other technical stuff when you go to set up your own Web page or Internet presence, so you need to understand something about them.

Remember, displaying text is not a problem for browser programs. They simply use the text-displaying capabilities and fonts offered by Windows or the Macintosh. Displaying graphic images isn't a problem either, thanks to the fact that the Web world has standardized on the Graphics Interchange Format (GIF) originated by CompuServe for most small images, and the Joint Photographic Experts Group (JPEG) format for larger images. The ability to display such text and such images is built into all Web browsers.

The incompatibilities, at this writing, occur with sound, video, compressed file archives, and non-GIF/JPEG images. If you're new to online and personal computing, it is impossible to fully appreciate the number of different ways these things can be—and are being—done.

For example, not only will you encounter GIF and JPEG graphic image files, you will also encounter PCX (PC Paintbrush) and BMP (Microsoft Windows) image files. Plus Targa, RLE, PCT, WPG, DCX, and Kodak Photo CD files. And then there are TIF or TIFF (tagged image format files), which must come in nearly a dozen different "flavors."

# A Tower of Babel

To one degree or another, the same bewildering variety of file formats exists in every application area. Everyone thinks they've got a better way of doing things, so they introduce some new way of handling compression, video, sound, or what-have-you that is incompatible with everything else. And this has been going on for decades.

There was no huge problem as long as everyone more or less stayed within his or her own computing community. In the DOS/Windows world, for example, you can "zip up" a collection of files into a single, compressed ZIP file and send it to any other DOS/Windows user with reasonable certainty that they will be able to unpack and uncompress it.

That's because, while there are half a dozen other programs that can do the same thing, there is a general agreement that archives created by Phil Katz's PKZIP program are the standard. In the Macintosh world, a similar agreement exists regarding the StuffIt program.

The problem today is that the Internet has brought together not only the DOS/Windows community and the Macintosh community, but also the many worlds of UNIX and every other computing community you can imagine. Thus, online file libraries that were created for and by Macintosh users can now be accessed by DOS/Windows users, and vice versa. Sounds great in theory, but the devil is in the details.

## A quick external "helper program" example

For example, suppose you fire up your PC, hit the Web, and click on an icon that promises to display a video clip. A moment later, your browser software asks you what program you want to use to deal with the file the site is sending.

Excuse me? Can't the browser just play the clip on my screen?

Nope. It turns out that the video-clip file is in Apple's QuickTime format, and you haven't "configured your browser" to call the needed QuickTime viewer *helper program*. Heck, you don't even *have* the necessary program on your disk.

And even if you did, Netscape could load the program and the clip would play, but it would not be seamlessly integrated into your online experience. Because it is an external program, you would have to shut it down by hand before you could return to your browser.

# The Java language & Netscape plug-ins

That's where we are today. We know the goal—the interactive-TV concept and all—but we don't know how we're going to get there. At this writing, most of the attention is on Java and Netscape *plug-ins*.

You may have heard of the Java language introduced by Sun Microsystems, Inc. Certainly it has received its share of hype. The main purpose of Java is to make it possible to *include with the file itself* the program needed to view a video clip or graphic image, or to listen to a sound file.

It's as if you went to a hardware store and bought a shrink-wrapped package that contained everything you needed to put up a shelf: wood, knee braces, drill bits, screws, paint, a screwdriver, and an electric drill. No need to supply any tools of your own, in other words.

As long as your browser knows how to "interpret" the Java language, which resembles C++, the format of the video clip or other file you encounter on a Web site doesn't matter. When you click on the icon, you will be sent not only the file but also the viewer/player program, written in the Java language, needed to present it.

Microsoft has scrambled to enter the fray by offering its Visual BASIC 5.x as an alternative to Java. At this writing, however, Netscape Communications Corporation has implemented support for Sun's Java, but not for Visual BASIC. As President Bush used to say, "Stay tuned." Perhaps Microsoft can take consolation in the fact that only users with 32-bit operating systems like Windows NT and Windows 95 can run the version of Netscape that supports Java.

# Why it won't work

Sending both a data file and the program needed to process it via the Net is a clever idea, to be sure. But in our opinion, it will never be widely adopted. There are lots of very obvious reasons for this.

First, people who today find themselves drumming their fingers as they wait for the Web to send them a single image file will not be willing to wait for transmission of *both* an image file and the program needed to view it. As noted earlier, even when you are using a 28.8 kbps modem, the "diameter of the pipe" is still pretty narrow.

Second, *interpreted* programs like the ones written in the Java language always run slower than *compiled* programs. That's because, one way or another, every computer program must eventually be translated into the machine language of 1s and 0s that is the only thing that microprocessor chips understand.

It's possible to write a program using nothing but the 1s and 0s of machine code, but it is quite difficult. So years ago, so-called *high-level languages* like BASIC were created that let you program in English-like text. That makes it easy for human beings to write and debug programs. But every time such a program is run, each line must be translated into machine language. So performance suffers.

The way to improve a program's performance while preserving the benefits of a high-level language is to compile it. All this means is that once you've written and perfected a program with an interpreted language, you make a final, one-time translation into machine language and save the results on disk. From then on, you use the compiled version of the program, which will run faster because the translation to 1s and 0s has already been done.

## Will Netscape replace Microsoft Windows?

On the other hand, since they consist of plain text, interpreted programs can be transmitted virtually anywhere via the Internet. And theoretically, as long as your Web browser program contains a Java interpreter, it doesn't matter whether your computer is a Mac, a PC, a Sun workstation, or something else.

Software producers love this idea because it means they can write a single program for all computer "platforms." That represents a huge

savings, and if they can distribute their products over the Net (no disks, no manuals, no middlemen) they further cut their costs and boost profits.

This has led some analysts to seriously suggest that Netscape Navigator may replace Microsoft Windows as the world's leading computer operating system. The notion is that you will be connected to the Net virtually all the time, and whenever you need to write a memo or do a spreadsheet, you will click with your mouse to download the necessary Java program. You'll pay a small fee for the one-time use of this *applet*, which will disappear once you've finished.

## A case of Microsoft envy

This is sheer nonsense. The fact is that people resent the way Microsoft so completely dominates the personal computer industry and, of course, the company has made numerous enemies over the years. There is thus an extraordinary amount of interest when someone suggests that Microsoft's days may be numbered.

Leave aside the bandwidth (size of the pipeline) problem and assume that everyone's got a high-speed connection to the Net. Leave aside the reality of Microsoft's power. Just ask yourself two questions.

First, why would any company ignore all the money and time that it has invested in training people to use word processing, spreadsheet, database, and other shrink-wrapped programs? Second, why would any company want to switch from the fixed costs of such programs to an open-ended approach under which it is charged each time a program is downloaded and used?

The concept of online, on-demand, pay-per-use software just doesn't make sense. It has all the markings of yet another one of those "we're doing it because it can be done" ideas that litter computer history. The press and the analysts hop onboard (after all, they've got to write about something), and no one thinks to ask, "Yes, but *should* it be done?"

## The Netscape "plug-in" approach

Another possible solution to dealing with graphics, video, and sound files is what Netscape calls *inline plug-ins*. The quick handle on this concept is that a plug-in is a helper program that runs seamlessly within Netscape. Unlike the helper programs of the past, a plug-in is not an external program. It's an add-on that gives Netscape additional powers. It therefore offers a truly seamless approach.

Version 2.0 of Netscape Navigator, which was officially introduced February 5, 1996, contains what you might think of as "sockets" designed to accept such third-party plug-in programs. The company claims that as of that date, there were some 88 companies developing plug-ins for Netscape.

It would appear that many of those firms plan to give their viewer or player or other end-user software away free of charge and make money selling the software needed to create animation or video or whatever to Web page creators. Of course, we users will still have to take the trouble to download the stuff and install in into Netscape. So we're really back to the helper-program problem again.

For example, suppose there are five different sound-file formats, each being promoted by a different plug-in maker. Are you going to offer a given sound clip in all five formats on your Web page? And how pleased do you think the average Web surfer is likely to be at the prospect of having to download and install five separate sound-playing plug-in programs?

Now multiply that situation ten times to account for animation, 3-D graphics, video, and all the other "Live Objects," as Netscape refers to such multimedia elements on a Web page. Then ask yourself, "Does this make sense?"

## What does make sense

What makes sense to us is a third possible approach—for the online world to settle on the file formats that will be used for sound, video,

file compression, and so on. Once that has been done, every browser can include the programming needed to seamlessly display or play or unpack such files, and the problem will disappear.

After all, the GIF and JPEG standards have been established for Web page images. How difficult would it be to settle on a single format for each of the other types of files?

Probably more difficult than we all imagine. For one senses that there's money and market share involved. Among the early plug-in developers are such respected names as Adobe, Software Publishing Corporation, Macromedia, and Apple Computer. And, naturally, everyone's looking for the next software megahit.

So there will be battles. Some time will be required. But in the end, standards for all "Live Objects" will evolve and be widely adopted. Then Microsoft will probably buy the winning plug-in makers and change the software so that it will no longer work with Netscape but only with its own Microsoft Explorer Web browser. (Just kidding . . . we hope.)

## How you will be affected

Now, here's how all of this impacts on you. When it comes to actually setting up your Web site, a topic covered in Chapter 10, it is quite likely that some of the people you might hire will suggest including Java or Visual BASIC applets. You may wish to do so, or you may wish to wait. Our advice is to wait. Keep an eye on things, but don't be rushed into adding Java applets simply because the programmer you hire says they're "cool."

In the first place, any kind of custom programming, whether it's in Java or any other language, costs money. It is not unreasonable to suggest that adding one or more Java applets to your page could increase your costs by several thousands of dollars.

In the second place, many of your users may not be equipped to run the Java applets on your Web page and will not be so equipped for some time to come. The fact is, at this writing, any DOS/Windows user who wants to be able to use the Java-enabled version of Netscape must be running Windows 95. Unfortunately, to be able to run Windows 95, the vast majority of people must replace or spend hundreds of dollars to dramatically upgrade their computers. (And Microsoft wonders why sales of Windows 95 have fallen so far short of expectations.)

## A quick-start guide to Web browsing

We won't attempt to provide a hands-on tutorial for using Netscape and other browsers. There simply isn't space in this book to do so. We can, however, give you some of our best tips and tricks for using browser software. For more information, please consult *The Little Web Book*, written by us and published by Peachpit Press.

We're going to assume that you have access to the Internet. (If that's not the case, you might want to come back to this section after you've read Chapter 7, How to get connected.) We're also going to assume that you're using Netscape and that you have gotten that program successfully installed.

## WINSOCK.DLL and dialer programs

To use Netscape or any other browser, you need two other files, both of which will probably be supplied with your browser. One file is called WINSOCK.DLL. The other is a *dialer program*—a program designed to dial the phone and log you onto your Internet service provider (ISP).

If you have installed only one Web browser program, you aren't likely to have any problems. If you have more than one, as might be the case if you are using both America Online and a local Internet service provider to access the Net, then conflicts can occur.

What you need to know is that the WINSOCK.DLL file supplied with a particular Web browser is *unique* to that browser. So make sure that

whatever WINSOCK.DLL file came with a given browser is located in the same disk directory as that browser. Then make sure that no file called WINSOCK.DLL is located in any directory in your "path." (We know that all this computerese may be foreign to you. If that's the case, find a computer guru friend and ask for help. Be sure that person understands that a given WINSOCK.DLL program and a given phone-dialer program usually go hand-in-hand.)

# Setting your cache size

The single most important thing you can do to improve the performance of your Web browser is to boost the size of its *disk cache*. A cache, as you may know, is a storage area, an easily accessible place where a computer or a program can put things that it is likely to use again.

In Netscape, click on "Options" and then "Network Preferences" and then "Cache." If you have enough available disk space, you should probably change the cache size to at least 10,000 kilobytes (10 megabytes).

Browser programs store the text and images of the Web pages you have visited in their caches. So, the *second* time you visit a site, the graphics and text will be displayed faster, since they are being pulled out of the cache instead of being downloaded from a remote site. In general, the bigger the disk cache, the better. Particularly if you frequently return to the same group of sites.

## How to view your cache

*Netscape stores the components (text and in-line images) of its cached Web pages in the path* **\netscape\cache**. *It uses filenames with the extension .MOZ for the HTML text files and .GIF or whatever for the in-line images.*

*To look at a given MOZ file with Netscape, follow these steps:*

*First, copy the file to a different directory and rename it anything you like, as long as you use .HTM as your filename extension. Then load Netscape, click on "File" and then "File Open," and tell Netscape where to get the HTM file. The text of the page will appear on your screen looking just as it did when you visited the site. The in-line images, however, will show up as question marks.*

*If you want to see both text and images, you'll need to get a Netscape* cache-management program *like UnMozify. Such programs create an index of your cached pages and fix things so that you can see everything as if you were actually online. To download a copy of UnMozify from its producer, Info Evolution, go to* **http://www.evolve.co.uk/unmozify**.

# "Driving" your browser

Driving a Web browser isn't difficult. But you'll need a starting location and some basic commands. Quite understandably, companies like America Online, Netscape, and CompuServe have set their browsers to start you off at their own home pages. But you can alter this default using one of the Preference-style setup menus.

In Netscape, for example, clicking on "Options," then "General Preferences," and then "Appearance" takes you to a screen that lets you specify your starting home-page location. Just key in the desired URL address and click on OK to save the setting.

Probably the most important "driving" command of all is learning to hit the Escape key or clicking on the Stop icon in the toolbar. Both actions have the same effect: They tell the Web site to *stop* sending you graphics and text. Once you've stopped the loading of a Web page, your browser will be able to give you its full attention, allowing you to tell it to go someplace else or do something else.

# Hypertext links and getting back

Regardless of your particular "home" location, once you're there, the steps are the same. You can click on the icons, buttons, or colorfully-highlighted words of text you see on your screen. Those are the hypertext links we spoke of earlier. Each click will take you someplace else.

Alternatively, you can click on the box labelled "Netsite" or "Location" or something similar that you'll find near the top of the screen. Then type in the URL of the place you want to visit.

You'll always end up someplace. The question is: How do you get back to where you started from? And how do you return to some page you encountered along the way? The answer is: You click on "Go" on the main menu bar, and then on "Back" on the drop-down menu that will then appear. That will take you back to the page you just left. From there you can do another Go/Back to return to the page before that.

Fortunately, browser programs keep track of where you've been. So you do not have to "back out" of a location sequentially. If you've visited ten pages in your current session, and if you then click on "Go," you'll see that each location has been given a number. Click on the entry you want, and you will be whisked to it as if you had booked a direct flight. Don't forget what we said earlier about "bookmarking" any location you visit to make it easy to return later at the click of a mouse.

## Saving a Web page

The last basic skill any browser user needs is being able to save to disk what appears on the screen. Start by practicing what we've told you so far. Go to a site, then go someplace else by clicking on a hotlink, then go back to the first site. Add one or more sites to your Bookmarks or Favorite Places list. Then use those features to return to those sites.

Convince yourself, in other words, that you know how to drive in forward and reverse and how to easily return to places that you like. You now know how to surf the Web. You can get where you want to go.

To *save* what you find, remember that the typical Web page physically consists of several different files. There is the master HTML text file that contains all of the words you see and codes that say what size type should be used when displaying each word. And there are the in-line graphics files, each containing a separate image. The master HTML file includes instructions telling your browser which graphic file to display and where.

Thus, while what you see on your screen may appear to be a single, smoothly scrolling file, in reality, its components are no more unified than the various text and image files you pulled together with your word processor when preparing, say, your company's latest sales bid.

First, be sure to wait for the entire "screen" to arrive at your PC before saving or printing it. Wait until you see a phrase like "Document Done" in the lower left portion of your browser screen before taking action. Then, either print it or click on File and then Save As to tell your browser to write the page to disk using the name you specify.

That will get you the HTML or plain text file, but there will be no graphic images. (You can later view this HTML file in Netscape by clicking on "Open" and then "Open File," just as we suggested doing with the MOZ files stored in the cache.)

To save the graphics to disk, move your mouse to each graphic image and click the *right* mouse button. If you're using Netscape, you will then be prompted for the name you want to use when saving the image to disk. (Not all browsers offer this right-mouse-button feature.)

You can save the graphics files under whatever names you want. Then, once you're offline, you can go back and make your filenames square with the filenames called for by the HTML file, either by editing the HTML file or by changing the filenames of the graphic images.

As you may recall, all of the HTML and graphic file components of the page you want to save are probably in your cache. But they are a hassle to find. Saving Web pages and images the way we've suggested will save you a lot of time in the long run.

One final tip: If you're running Netscape and you want to go to the Netscape Communications Corporation home page, perhaps to download the latest version of the program, you can simply click on the Netscape "N" icon that appears in the upper right corner of your screen.

# Other major players

## America Online, CompuServe, Prodigy, & BBSs

# CHAPTER 6

As you know, the electronic universe does not consist of the Internet alone. In this chapter we're going to look at those *other* online components, especially the ones likely to be of interest to anyone who wants to market goods or services online. We're speaking, of course, about the Big Three consumer systems—America Online (AOL), CompuServe (CIS), and Prodigy—and computer bulletin board systems (BBSs).

There are a number of very good reasons for taking this little sidetrip. For one thing, among them, the Big Three have over 10.7 million subscribers, each of whom pays at least $9.95 a month. (Our source is SIMBA Information, Inc., as contributed to the *New York Times*, February 21, 1996.) And these folks don't spend all of their time on the Internet. There are ways to reach them on their chosen system that will not cost you any money.

There's also the fact that you might want to establish a presence on one or more of these systems, in addition to your Internet activities. And, as for BBSs, they are the cheapest of all forms of online presence. They may not be the most convenient, but many companies have been successfully using their own BBSs for years to service customers. They are clearly something you should know about.

## A quick overview

The two fundamental features of the online world are *information* and *communication*. But like the simple components of an atom of helium, these two features can be combined and presented in an apparently infinite number of ways. In general, there are five main categories of online systems used by consumers, businesspeople, and professionals:

- Information-only systems
- Communications-only systems
- The Big Three consumer online systems
- Bulletin board systems (BBSs)
- The Internet

We've already got a pretty good handle on the Internet. And as you know, this chapter zeros in on the Big Three and BBSs. But you should at least be aware of the existence of information-only and communications-only systems

## Information-only systems

People have been using online systems to search for and retrieve information for decades. The information can be anything from the full text of the *Wall Street Journal* to population figures from the Census Bureau.

At this writing, for example, there are over 5,511 databases available on 860 online systems, not including what's available on the Internet. Our source is the authoritative *Gale Directory of Databases*, published by Gale Research, Inc., in Detroit, Michigan. (Ask your local reference librarian if there's a copy on the shelf; you'll find it an eye-opener.)

These databases and systems include such familiar names as Dialog, Lexis/Nexis, and Dow Jones News/Retrieval, as well as many other far more obscure entities. Like HORSE, a system from Bloodstock Research Information Services in Lexington, Kentucky, that can supply you with the pedigree and racing record of every thoroughbred in North America since 1922.

The information on such systems almost always exists in a structured database consisting of many separate *fields*. If the name, address, and phone number of everyone in your town were to be entered into such a database, for example, there would be a separate field for first name, last name, street address, city, state, ZIP code, telephone area code, and telephone number.

That means that someone who knew how to search the database could instantly produce a list of everyone named "Smith" in your ZIP code. Or a list of everyone who lives on your particular street. Or everyone with the first name of John or Mary and their phone numbers.

At this writing, the search capabilities available to people via the Internet are quite crude by comparison. But this kind of information-retrieval power comes at a price. After all, someone has to be paid to collect and then key in all that information. Thus, searching the patent databases on Dialog costs upwards of $120 an hour. Standard & Poor's costs $60 an hour, and Books in Print is $30 an hour.

Users are also charged anywhere from 40 cents to $4 for each complete record they display on their screens. That's why many people hire *information brokers*, professionals who know how and where to find the information you need at the lowest possible price. (If this is of interest, you'll want to see *The Information Broker's Handbook* by Sue Rugge and Alfred Glossbrenner, published by McGraw-Hill.)

## Communications-only systems

On the communications side of things, there are systems that specialize in transferring messages. The leader here is MCI Mail, which can take a message you transmit and send it to your recipient as an e-mail message, a fax, a telex/TWX message, a cablegram, or a laser-printed paper letter delivered by the post office or an overnight delivery service. If you like, you can even have the paper letter printed with your letterhead and finished off with a facsimile of your handwritten signature.

Communications-only systems are becoming rare. MCI, for example, has long offered a gateway connection to Dow Jones News/Retrieval, and it is a major behind-the-scenes player in building Internet "backbones."

## The Big Three consumer online systems

The third general category of online system is a hybrid. It is a system that offers both communication and information features. This is the category generally referred to as *consumer online systems*, and under it you will find America Online, CompuServe, and Prodigy.

There are other online systems in this category, including the Microsoft Network (MSN), Delphi, GEnie, and Apple Computer's eWorld. But none of them has over a million subscribers.

## Bulletin board systems (BBSs)

A BBS consists of one or more phone lines and modems connected to a computer that is running BBS software. Any kind of computer will do. The neat thing is that current BBS software is so sophisticated that callers can easily be fooled into thinking that they are actually logged onto a Web site or a system like America Online.

The vast majority of the country's 60,000 or more boards are free, run as they are as hobbies by their *sysops* (system operators, pronounced "sis-ops"). Still, any number of entrepreneurs have been attracted to the field. And many of them are doing quite well, charging quarterly or yearly subscription fees and offering Internet access, newsgroup "feeds," chat rooms, and much more.

# Your secret sales weapon!

Of the non-Internet components of the electronic universe, the Big Three and BBSs are the most relevant to anyone's effort to make money on the Internet. As you know from our "Seven Rules of Online Selling Success," you can't simply put an advertisement on TV or in a magazine or someplace else your prospects are likely to see it. You've got to reach out and give your customers a good reason to enter your tent and listen to your message. The Big Three offer you yet another opportunity to do just that.

That's why you've got to know about them. All of your competitors will be focusing exclusively on the Internet and the Web. Most won't even know about how to use the Big Three to work synergistically with their Web sites. But you will.

## The state of play back then

At this writing, the online world is in the midst of an enormous upheaval caused by the wild popularity of the Net and the Web. To

appreciate this, you've got to know what the old model was. The best name for that model is *information utility*.

That term was coined by a system called The Source. Established in the late 1970s, its goal was to turn Radio Shack TRS-80s, Apple IIs, and NorthStar CP/M personal computers into "information appliances" serving up news, weather, and sports, airline schedules, job listings, stock quotes, and articles from magazines. There were online games, e-mail, and chat rooms. And there was Comp-u-Card, or CUC as it is now known, which let you search a database of over 250,000 products for the best price.

There was an initial sign-up fee of $100, and a minimum monthly cost of $10. Connect time was billed at $20.75 an hour for 300 baud during the day, and $7.75 an hour during evenings and weekends. Service at 1200 bps was also available, but at higher rates.

The Source was owned by Readers Digest Corporation for most of its life, and it tried to do what America Online does today. (Indeed, one of the founders of The Source founded the company that later became America Online.) The idea was to collect, edit, package, and deliver information electronically, much as phone service, water, or electricity are delivered to the home. It also offered most of the same kind of entertainment features now found on the Big Three.

The trouble was that The Source was 20 years ahead of its time. CompuServe, its arch rival, eventually purchased The Source and quickly shut it down. CompuServe had survived during the same period because it was owned by H&R Block and did not have to carry its own weight. Nor did CompuServe spend much money on features in the early years, so expenses were low.

## CompuServe triumphant

For several years, CompuServe ruled the roost. Prodigy was out there, of course, but its business model of making money from selling ads and from purchases by online users wasn't working. With its roots in the 1970s, CompuServe was, like The Source, text-based.

Having come along a bit later, Prodigy, a joint venture of Sears and IBM, used what was then a relatively new technology called NAPLPS (pronounced "nap-lips")—North American Presentation-Level Protocol Syntax—to transmit and display its text and CGA (color graphics adapter) graphic images. Prodigy had to do this because a portion of every screen it sent users was devoted to advertising, and advertisers demanded something more than plain ASCII text.

Unfortunately, both CompuServe and Prodigy missed the move from text-based DOS to graphical Windows. As inveterate DOS users, we don't blame them a bit, but you can't argue with what the customer wants. So along came America Online, a system that was graphical in the Windows sense from the very beginning (see Fig. 6-1), and its popularity just exploded.

Figure 6-1

*The America Online greeting screen.*

Without a doubt, AOL was the right system at the right time, and it was and is run by creative, flexible people who really know what they're doing. Plus they were willing to spend $40 in advertising and free disks to acquire each subscriber.

Now the Internet and World Wide Web boom hits! Subscribers to the Big Three are clamoring for access. And the Big Three deliberately drag their feet. After all, none of them wants to become a mere pass-through or gateway to the Net. What would happen to all their "value-added" and the fees they could charge?

## Face-lifts all around

AOL broke ranks first. It decided to fully embrace the Web and the Net and to weave them into the AOL system. Now, when you access an AOL news page, you may be given six options, three or four of which may take you to proprietary America Online features, and the rest may take you out onto the Internet.

Prodigy quickly embraced the Net as well, but only in terms of giving users access to it. It did not initially weave the Net and the Web into its system. Prodigy also began a major re-vamp of its appearance, getting rid of NAPLPS graphics and making itself look more like the World Wide Web. (See Fig. 6-2.)

CompuServe (Fig. 6-3) was the slowest to allow its users full access to the Internet. For over a year, it would enable a feature here and a feature there, but there was no coherent strategy to bring subscribers full access to the Internet. To this day, CompuServe is still a text-based system. Its CompuServe Information Manager program and similar packages can give you clickable icons to get to a feature and once you arrive you may find additional custom images and artwork, but the heart of every feature is still good old ASCII text.

## The big sell-off

That's more or less where things stand among the Big Three at this writing. America Online leads with 5 million subscribers, CompuServe

Figure 6-2

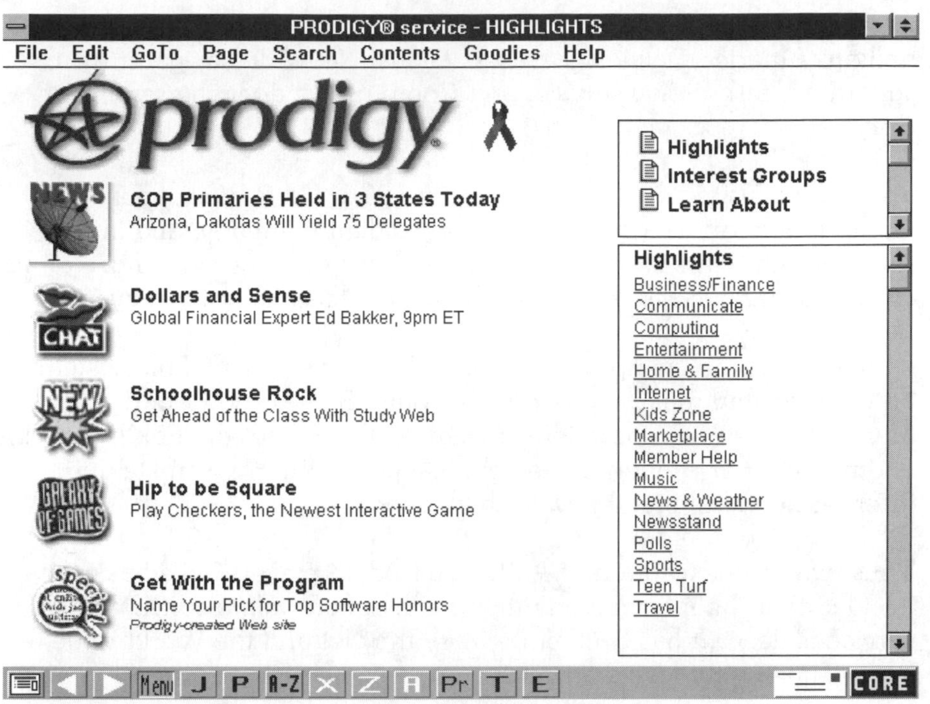


*Prodigy now looks like the World Wide Web.*

Figure 6-3

*CompuServe via CompuServe Information Manager software.*

is second with 4.3 million, and Prodigy is a distant third with 1.4 million. America Online now offers Global Network Navigator as a separate Internet-only service, and CompuServe does the same with SpryNet.

You should also know that in February 1996, H&R Block spun CompuServe off as a completely independent company, and in that same month Sears announced that it wanted to focus even more on its core retailing business and was thus selling its stake in Prodigy.

During the same time period, General Electric sold its GEnie system, an online entity that once vied with CompuServe, and Rupert Murdoch's News Corporation—owner of *TV Guide*, the Fox Network, and many other properties—essentially pulled the plug on Delphi Internet Services' brand new Web presence.

Thus, with the exception of AOL, the leading players have basically decided that the information-utility model of an online consumer service is dead. It has been done in by the Net and the World Wide Web. Time to cut losses and move on to something else.

## Where true wisdom lies

In our opinion, this is a colossal mistake. And we needed to give you this encapsulated history so that you are not misled by such developments.

Everyone is clamoring to get onto the Net and to surf the Web. It's cool! It's hot! It's . . . well, it's chaos. The huge advantage that the Big Three offer to online users is *order*. Each enforces standards for editing, organizing, presenting, and searching for information. On the Internet, in contrast, anyone who puts up a Web site is free to do things his or her own way. That's a wonderful boost for creative programming, but it ultimately hurts the end user.

Pick a topic or a question about any field you can imagine, and there's a good chance that the information you want exists somewhere on the Internet. But this information is useless to you because there is no way to find it within a reasonable amount of time.

There are *search engine* features like Infoseek, WebCrawler, Yahoo!, and many others, to be sure. And they do a good job. But in the end, a search engine can't be any better than the material it is searching. So you conduct a search on a topic like "mortgage refinancing" and you end up with literally hundreds of Web-page hits. Who has time to check out 300 Web pages?

## Discipline, editing, organization, and performance

The Big Three, in contrast, have the ability to bring discipline, editing, and organization to information collections. They have to charge for this service, of course, since a great deal of human time, effort, and judgement are involved.

It may well be that the current Big Three rate of $10 a month for five hours and $2.95 per hour thereafter is too high. But somewhere there is an hourly rate that users will gladly pay to be able to find what they're looking for online with a minimum of fuss and bother. Ultimately, in other words, online users will be willing to pay a small premium to gain access to a well-organized, easy-to-use service that brings them the "best of the Internet" as well as many other outstanding features.

There is also the fact that, according to some, the Internet as we know it today is sagging under the weight of the millions of new users who have signed up and signed on in recent years. True or not, your co-authors have certainly noticed that performance of the Net has suffered in the past few years. There are times when it is simply impossible to connect with a given site.

## "Internet Premium Plus" services

Not that the Big Three haven't had their problems as well. For example, there were many times during AOL's rapid growth spurts in 1994 and 1995 when the system was simply impossible to use. Similar problems have affected CompuServe and Prodigy over the years during peak hours. But eventually, capacity always caught up with demand.

That's because the demand came from paying subscribers. If the Big Three had failed to upgrade their capacities, they would have quickly lost those subscriber dollars. On the Internet, in contrast, virtually anyone anywhere in the world can "demand" access to a given Web page or Net feature, and the Internet's computers will do their best to make the connection.These users are not paying $2 to $3 an hour. They are paying $20 a month for an unlimited number of hours. If you assume that the person spends just three hours a day online during the month, the cost would be a mere 22 cents an hour.

In effect, these users have done the equivalent of purchasing a monthly pass on a city's bus, train, or subway network. Time used and distance travelled do not matter—but at these prices, don't complain about the quality of the service. If you want something more than the basics, you'll have to pay someone to provide it.

The most logical companies to offer such "taxicab" or "limousine" services in the online world are the Big Three. There will always be people willing to pay for faster access, better service, and easier information retrieval. And that is where the futures of America Online, CompuServe, and Prodigy lie. The Big Three have the potential to recast themselves as "Internet Premium Plus" services.

The bottom line is this: In the not too distant future, the novelty of the Internet and the Web will have worn off for large numbers of users. Many of these recent initiates to the online world will actively seek something better than plain old Internet access, and they'll be willing to pay for such a service. Their natural instincts will be to flood back to the Big Three. Or to some similar systems.

# Big Three marketing options

There is thus all the more reason to take the Big Three systems seriously. Anything can happen, but with a few breaks and some enlightened management, the best days of the Big Three are yet to be. So if you're serious about online marketing, it makes good sense to explore the options these systems present.

The first and most obvious option is to go to AOL, CIS, or Prodigy and ask about establishing a feature or other presence on their systems. Lots of leading software and hardware companies provide customer service and technical support via special CompuServe *forums*, for example. Prodigy will happily accept your ad. And executives at America Online, if you can ever get them on the phone, will willingly discuss establishing a "relationship."

Trouble is that even the least-expensive "relationship" with one of the Big Three will cost you many thousands of dollars a year. The programmers at your chosen system or systems will be in complete control—do things their way and don't ask for too many updates, or else—and in any case, only subscribers to *that* particular system will be able to access your feature.

You will be much better off setting up your own Web page for a few hundred dollars and a small monthly maintenance fee and devoting any spare time and cash to telling the world—including, but not limited to AOL, CIS, and Prodigy subscribers—how to reach your site.

## Wait for it, people!

Yes. Yes. That makes sense. But not all of the dots have been connected.

You're right! So here goes. The best way to bring the Big Three into play as you market your product or service is to first set up a Web site and/or an auto-responder. (Both are covered in more detail in later chapters of this book.) Then get a subscription to America Online, CompuServe, and Prodigy and plant messages in their *special interest groups* (SIGs).

Yes, we have just sprung a new term on you. But don't scratch your head too hard. Instead, think back to our description of Internet newsgroups in Chapter 4. As you may recall, newsgroups consist of nothing but "player piano rolls" of messages devoted to a particular topic.

Well, each Big Three system has an equivalent. They may be called clubs, forums, groups, or something else, but the traditional term for this feature has always been SIG. And there are hundreds—if not thousands—of them devoted to every topic you can imagine on each of the Big Three. There are SIGs devoted to topics like organic gardening, wine tasting, or Microsoft's Windows 95 software.

## The essence of the SIGs

There's no charge for joining such SIGs. And, regardless of the Big Three system you choose, you'll find that the SIGs offer many more powerful and sophisticated features than Internet newsgroups. You can't truly appreciate this until you've actually experienced an Internet newsgroup, but Big Three SIGs are far better organized, because they're run by a sysop and his or her assistants.

SIGs offer *message boards* where members can discuss topics of interest; *conference rooms* where many users can gather to chat or listen to a guest speaker; and *file libraries* from which members can download text, graphic, and program files related to the SIG's focus. (Each Big Three system handles the file library function a little differently.)

So here's the key. Once you've got your Internet Web page, auto-responder, and the like set up, your main task will be to spread the word. You'll find lots of specific recommendations for doing so in later chapters, but here it is appropriate to say that you should not neglect the SIGs on the Big Three.

For example, if you market a line of sterile, organically prepared potting soil, you might create a list of ten do's and don'ts for organic gardening and put it on your Web site. Then you can enter the organic gardening SIGs on the Big Three and post a you-approach note saying that your ten tips are available at such-and-such a Web address. You should also identify yourself as a maker of organic potting soil, but you can do so discreetly.

The notion is one we will return to again and again—you've got to give people something of real value to get them to come to your site.

You've got to have the right attitude and approach. The old "hard sell" simply will not work online.

Remember, every subscriber to a Big Three system now has the ability to tap your Web site, send mail to your auto-responder, or enjoy any other feature of the Internet. So it just makes good sense to—properly—use the SIGs the Big Three offer.

## How to find SIGs on the Big Three

*You will find a much more detailed treatment in our* Complete Modem Handbook *(MIS:Press) or* The Little Online Book *(Peachpit Press). But if you want to locate the SIGs of greatest interest on the Big Three systems, here's how to start:*

***America Online (AOL)***
*800-827-6364*

*To locate special interest groups on AOL, do a Ctrl-K to pop up the keyword box. Then search on the keyword "club."*

***CompuServe Information System (CIS)***
*800-848-8990 or 614-457-8650*

*To find SIGs on CompuServe, click on the "Go" (green light) icon and key in* go ind *to access the Index feature. Then search on the keyword "forum."*

***Prodigy***
*800-776-3449*

*On Prodigy, click on the "A-Z index" option. Then search the index on the keyword "club."*

# Bulletin Board Systems

Now let's turn to what might be considered the online underground. Which is to say, bulletin board systems or BBSs. At its most basic level, a BBS is nothing more than a phone line, a modem, and a computer running BBS software that lets the machine automatically accept incoming phone calls, prompting the caller for name and

password. In fact, many communications software programs these days include a *host mode* feature that lets you set your own system to automatically answer the phone.

Turn your computer and modem on, load your comm software, activate host mode, then take off for the weekend. Regardless of where you are, if you've got access to another computer and a modem, you can call up your desktop machine at the office and run it as if you were sitting right at its keyboard.

Naturally, no one who runs a BBS is going to give that kind of access to the public at large. That's why callers are prompted for their names and passwords. Or, if they are first-time callers, they are taken through a registration process, during which they can specify the password they want to use. Many boards charge subscription fees to callers who want full access.

Sometimes these fees are set merely to help the board's sysop cover expenses. But a growing number of boards are profit-making enterprises, charging as much as $75 a year for perhaps 10 hours of access per week. Any number of these enterprises have purchased small satellite dishes to enable them to receive things like the text from all Internet newsgroups, news, weather, and sports, plus the feed from *USA Today*.

In any case, whether the board is commercial or totally free, once callers are admitted to the system, there is no telling what they will find. The one thing we can say for certain is that the types and general design of the features will be very similar to what the Big Three systems offer.

## Who knew?

And that is very much our point. You can be on a BBS and truly not be able to tell whether you're logged onto a multimillion-dollar system like CompuServe—or some guy's Macintosh or IBM-compatible computer. As for graphics, take a look at Fig. 6-4.

Figure 6-4

*Graphics can make a BBS look like America Online!*

These graphics appeared instantly on our screen, thanks to the Remote Imaging Protocol (RIP) created by TeleGrafix Communications, Inc. RIP graphics were introduced for DOS/Windows and Macintoshes in 1993, and more and more communications programs and BBSs are offering them. The point being that "working the boards"—as using BBSs is called—doesn't mean giving up pleasing visual screens.

According to our friend Jack Rickard, editor and publisher of *BoardWatch Magazine*, there are approximately 60,000 BBSs in North America alone. They offer a wide range of features, starting with electronic mail. Though its articles cry out for editing, *BoardWatch* is the single most important publication to have if you are interested in this field. For more information, call 800-933-6038.

## BBS-based "networks"

The least sophisticated boards let you exchange mail only among other users of the board. You sign on on Tuesday and leave a private message for John. John signs on over the weekend, picks up your message, and sends you a reply. Simple. But many boards are part of

one or more special networks that have been created for the transfer of mail.

The most famous such network is FidoNet, a system that makes it possible for you to call your local FidoNet board in, say, Miami, and send a message to someone living in Portland, Oregon. You make a local call to your board and your friend makes a local call to her board. Both of you send and receive messages as if you lived only a few blocks apart. The magic occurs late at night—as all the best magic does—when all the BBSs on the FidoNet system stop taking callers and instead call each other to exchange messages. This is called *mail time*, and it lasts for about an hour.

Created by Tom Jennings, FidoNet is a technological wonder. But that's not why we bring it up. The fact is, many FidoNet "node" BBSs are connected to the Internet. So you could send an e-mail message to anyone whose FidoNet address you know, using your preferred Internet e-mail connection.

No one's saying it's necessarily simple or easy. But there can be no denying that there are one heck of a lot of links *from* anywhere *to* anywhere. That's why it doesn't take long to spread the word about almost anything—whether it concerns some wonderful special deal you're offering or some problem with your product.

## Other BBS features

Most BBSs also offer *conferences* of some sort, which are very much like the SIGs, clubs, and roundtables found on commercial systems in that they make it easy for people to ask questions and discuss specific topics of interest to them. BBSs also usually have large file libraries packed with public domain and shareware software. Sometimes these libraries actually exist on CD-ROM, instead of on the board's hard disk drive.

It's not unusual for a multi-line BBS to offer real-time CB-radio-like chat among users. Often there are games to be played once you pass through the "door" leading from the BBS software to some other location on the host system. Some BBS sysops also sell products of one sort or another. Many offer real-time interactive games. And many are devoted to some particular interest, whether it is saving the whales or the glories of eating red meat.

## Corporate applications

More to the point for our purposes here, any number of companies have set up their own bulletin board systems to make it easy to support and interact with their customers. Naturally, they tend to be computer-related companies.

Recently, for example, we needed a printer driver (a small but essential piece of software) to make XyWrite work with our H-P LaserJet printer. We called the company, and its voice-mail system notified us that there was a XyWrite BBS we could call. We did so and had the needed file located and downloaded in about three minutes. In another five minutes, it had been installed and tested, and we were on our way.

Yes, this required a level of knowledge most of your customers do not have. But that doesn't mean you can't use the same technique. All it means is that you or someone you trust is going to have to design everything for the lowest common denominator. That means including step-by-step instructions for accessing the BBS in your voice-mail message. (You can't just provide your BBS phone number and expect your customers to know what to do.)

It means very carefully designing the system that they will see when they do call. And it certainly means making sure that whomever you hire to prepare this system anticipates the questions and needs of your typical customer.

# Using BBSs as marketing tools

Whether you're a caller, a subscriber, or a businessperson, the big problem with BBSs is not only the diameter of the pipeline, it is the number of pipelines that are available. Most bulletin boards are

connected to a single telephone line. That line may or may not be shared by other human beings in a home, but let's assume that the BBS sysop has agreed to pay the phone company $8 a month for a separate, second phone line.

The common practice these days is to allow a given caller to remain connected to a BBS no more than one hour a day—although many boards cut that to half an hour a day. Since there are 48 half hours in a 24-hour day, the maximum number of people such a board can service each day is 48.

Yes, a sysop can add more communications cards to his or her computer and pay for more phone lines and modems. The sysop can add more computers. And those computers can be configured as a network. But now we're getting well beyond the scope of the typical bulletin board system.

## Setting up your own BBS

We absolutely adore BBSs. We love their sysop-imposed personalities. We love their anything-goes anarchism. But we do not suggest that most businesspeople spend their time trying to market to BBS users. This game is not worth the price of the candle.

Instead, you might consider setting up your own BBS to serve current and potential customers. You'll have to reserve a phone line for your BBS, connect it to a computer with a modem, and then load some sort of BBS software. This is not tough to do. What requires the thought is designing the screens and the features callers will encounter once they are logged on. Your best guide to BBS hardware and software is *Boardwatch* magazine.

The main focus of this book is the Internet and the World Wide Web, of course. But the main point of this chapter has been to alert you to the millions of other people on the Big Three systems and how you might reach them. "Rule out nothing," in other words!

# How to get connected

AS a businessperson or entrepreneur interested in making money on the Internet, your needs go beyond those of the average person. The typical Net or Web "surfer" is interested primarily in low cost, high convenience, and good customer support.

Those things are important to you as well. But there are many other considerations. Including questions like, "Can I have my own domain name?" and "How easily can I change and update my Web page?" But this is a lot to take on all at once. So here's what we suggest.

## A three-step program

Use America Online to get your feet wet. Then, once you're comfortable using the Web and the Net, get an account with an Internet service provider (ISP). This will save you money and allow you to register your own *domain name* (a custom online address about which we'll have more to say later in this chapter). Then and only then should you begin thinking about putting up a Web page.

In this chapter, you will learn the hardware and software basics of getting connected, regardless of your level of experience. Next, you'll be introduced to the steps you should take to rapidly bring yourself up to speed if you've never been online or on the Net before. Finally, you'll learn how to locate and open an account with an ISP.

We're going to assume here that you're a complete novice and that you have already read Chapter 3, "Crucial concepts made simple: How the online world works."

## What it takes to go online

You already know a great deal about going online. You know about modems, bit-per-second rates, the ASCII code set, and lots of other things.

Now let's get more specific. In addition to a phone line, you will need a modem and a communications software package. If you bought your

personal computer relatively recently, it is entirely possible that it came with these two items as part of the deal. (Check the back of your machine to see if there is anything that looks like a telephone jack—it could be an internal modem.)

If not, we recommend that you buy a *28.8 kbps/V.34 external data/fax modem*. The cost will be about $170, possibly even less as you read this. You want a 28.8 modem because that's the fastest speed available. Units that claim speeds of 57.6 kbps use proprietary techniques that can deliver that speed only when modems of the *same* make and model are used at both ends of the connection—which isn't likely to be the case most of the time.

Don't be lured into buying a *V.FAST* unit claiming 28.8 kbps. Such modems were manufactured before the V.34 standard became official in June 1994. As such, they represent the manufacturer's best guess on the final standard, and may not be 100 percent compatible with all other true V.34 modems.

## Why external?

There are several reasons why we recommend that you buy an *external* modem. For one thing, it can be used with *any* computer system. With the right cable, you can use the same external modem with a PC, a Mac, or a laptop computer of any type.

An external modem is also easy to control. If it starts acting up, just reach over and turn it off and then on again. This comes in handy when you get hung up on a Web page and your software won't let you break the phone connection.

Finally, external modems have lights to show you what's happening. When you're running a communications program, for example, the SD (send data) light will flash each time you hit a key. That can be reassuring when you're trying to find the source of a problem, because it tells you whether or not your information is "getting out the door." If it is—if the light flashes—then the problem lies with the phone line, the packet-switching network, or the online system you're trying to connect to.

The data lights on an external modem are also useful when you are on some Web page staring at the hour-glass symbol and wondering if anything is happening. Is the site sending you the image or not? Or has the thing just gone into the Twilight Zone? If you see the RD (receive data) light flashing, you know that the connection is still good and that the data is indeed arriving, albeit slowly.

## When to go internal

The alternative to an external modem is an *internal* unit, which is basically a modem on a circuit board. These boards fit into your Mac or PC just like any other add-on board, but, of course, they're system-specific. They are neat and clean and occupy zero desk space, but having tried both over the years, we still prefer external units.

In our opinion, the only good reason to buy an internal, card-mounted modem for a desktop system is that your computer is not equipped with the high-speed UART chip necessary for using a fast external modem. (See the nearby sidebar called "Checking your UART.") Before the data bits whizzing around inside your machine can be sent to the modem, the parallel, eight-abreast formation they normally use must be changed. Eight-at-a-time parallel must be changed to one-bit-at-a-time serial.

### Checking your UART

*Computers manufactured as late as 1993 may have difficulty working effectively with today's high-speed (28.8/V.34) modems. The bottleneck lies with a little chip called a UART. That's short for Universal Asynchronous Receiver/Transmitter. This is the chip that is at the heart of your computer's communications port or serial card.*

*Older chips can handle a top speed of 9.6 kbps, far less than a speed of 28.8 kbps. So how can you find out what kind of UART you've got? The answer is to run the Microsoft Diagnostics program that comes with MS-DOS 6 and above. Select "C" for "Com Port" and see what the program has to say.*

*Look for an item labelled "UART Chip Used." If the chip number is 8250, you have an old, slow UART. What you want is a chip with a number beginning with 165 or higher, like 16550AF.*

*In general, the higher the chip number, the better. Computer dealers can sell you a high-speed serial card for about $25. But if you're a real speed fan, consider a souped up card like the Lava-650 card for Windows users. Built around the zippy new 16650 UART and equipped with a 32-byte buffer, the Lava-650 lists for $59.95. For more information, contact Lava Computer Manufacturing at 416-674-5942.*

*The alternative to buying a high-speed serial card and an external modem is to buy an internal 28.8 modem, since you can be sure that such cards will contain a UART able to operate at that speed.*

## PC Cards for notebooks and laptops

Most notebook and other portable computers come with a serial port, so you can plug in a conventional external modem if you want to. You would not want to lug such a unit around, however. Alternatively, you might be able to equip your notebook with an internal modem. No muss, no fuss. Just plug in the phone line whenever you want to communicate. It's neat, but then you are always carrying your modem with you as part of your computer.

*PC Cards* solve both problems, however. These devices used to be called PCMCIA cards (Personal Computer Memory Card International Association) until someone got smart and realized how difficult that is to remember. PC Card modems are light, self-contained, and detachable. They're also more expensive than comparable internal or external models.

Two other things to keep in mind about PC Cards: First, you may have to pay a bit more for a notebook that's equipped with a PC Card/PCMCIA socket. Second, internal modems and PC Cards draw the power they need from your computer. If the computer is plugged into an electrical outlet, no problem. Otherwise, expect a real drain on your battery.

##  Making the physical connections

The manual provided with your modem is likely to be your best guide when making the necessary physical connections. But a brief overview might be helpful. Basically, you connect the computer to the modem and the modem to the phone line. Make sure all the plugs are firmly seated in their sockets. Make sure that your modem is on. Then load your communications program. Most of the time, it's just that simple.

So where are the land mines? Well, you could encounter a plug/socket incompatibility. If you have a Macintosh, your external modem is connected by plugging a round plug into the receptical labelled with the telephone handset icon on your machine. So when buying your modem, make sure that you get a Macintosh modem cable. (It may be packed with the modem itself, but be sure to ask.)

If you're using a PC with an external modem, you need to be aware that your machine's serial RS-232 communications port may offer you a *DB-25* or a *DB-9* connector. These plugs and sockets are shaped like an elongated capital *D*, hence their name. The first type has 25 pins or sockets, the second has nine. Many computer-to-modem cables these days include both DB-25 and DB-9 connectors, but you might want to check your system before you order your modem.

Look at the back of your computer's system unit. If you see a connector offering 25 *sockets*, it is almost certainly your parallel printer port. If you see a connector offering 25 or nine *pins*, however, it is probably your computer's RS-232 serial communications port. Or one of them, at any rate.

##  Mind your comm ports!

Excuse me? You mean computers can have more than one comm port? Yes, in the PC world, they can. And this fact leads to the last major land mine you might encounter. All DOS/Windows machines are designed to support at least four communications ports, typically COM1 through COM4. Each port has a separate address. If your

software and your internal modem or serial card are configured for different addresses, nothing will work.

This is where it can pay, for once in your life, to read the manual. Most communications software comes configured to talk to COM1. Yet we once had an internal modem that came configured to be COM4. We knew to check these settings because we've been doing this for a long time. But you might not. So, before you install an internal modem or a new high-speed serial card, make sure you know which comm port address it is set for.

You can change the setting by flipping one or more DIP (dual in-line package) switches (the tip of a ballpoint pen works well for this) or getting out a pair of tweezers and resetting the board's jumpers. All of which will be explained in your manual.

You can check on your comm ports using the Microsoft Diagnostics program mentioned earlier in this chapter. Be aware that serial ports can be used for mice and printers as well as modems. Finally, for technical reasons having to do with *shared interrupts* or *IRQs*, if you have more than one serial port, you should avoid configuring those ports to be COM1 and COM3, or COM2 and COM4.

## All about communications software

Now let's move to the software side of things. We've spoken at length of Web browser programs like Netscape. But browser programs are really only a small part of the overall comm software picture. So here's what you need to know.

During all those years that the Internet was closed to most of us, people still communicated via computer. But they did so using a technique called *terminal emulation*.

This is based on the old mainframe-and-terminal model: You've got a big, expensive, powerful mainframe computer located in a climate-

controlled "glass house" somewhere, and you've got any number of dumb terminals scattered about.

## Dumb terminals and TTY communications

The dumb terminals consist largely of a keyboard and a screen and have very little processing power of their own. But each does have certain characteristics. That's why you'll hear of the DEC VT-100 terminal or the IBM 3101 or 3270. Most communications programs, like ProComm for DOS/Windows machines or Microphone for the Mac, can be set to emulate a wide variety of terminals.

But the terminal protocol that is the lowest common denominator is that of an old teletype machine (TTY). This is simplest of all, for it assumes that you will be sending text to a host computer one line at a time and that the host will send text to you in the same manner. There are no graphics other than those that can be created using ASCII codes. And you can't "mouse" all over the screen selecting this and that.

The only real complication in TTY communications is that your comm program's settings must match those of the remote host. But only two sets of settings are involved: 7/E/1 and 8/N/1. Translated, that means "7 data bits, Even parity, and 1 stop bit" and "8 data bits, No parity, and 1 stop bit." If one setting does not work, try the other.

CompuServe, MCI Mail, Dialog, NewsNet, Dow Jones News/Retrieval, Delphi, and most of the world's bulletin board systems can be tapped using a plain communications program set to operate in TTY mode. When you are using such a program, you can record incoming text on disk by *opening your capture buffer* or *logging to disk*.

You can quickly dial a favorite number by selecting its entry in your *dialing directory* or phone book. You can prepare *auto-logon* and other *scripts* in many cases. And you can *upload and download files* using protocols like ZMODEM, XMODEM, and the like. (These are all key phrases to look for in your comm program manual.)

## Connecting to the Net

The one thing you won't be able to do is to connect with AOL or Prodigy, or with the Internet and the World Wide Web—at least not in the conventional sense. Prodigy and AOL require you to use the software they supply. And the Internet requires you to use a special *protocol*. A protocol is nothing magical. It is simply an agreement among parties on exactly how certain things will be done.

The reason we can fire up Procomm Plus for DOS, log onto CompuServe and pick up our mail, and sign off again in the twinkling of an eye is that Procomm and CompuServe follow the TTY protocol we've been telling you about.

Netscape Navigator and other Web browsers and Internet programs follow a different protocol. Theirs is a protocol designed for *networks*. It is a protocol of *clients and servers* instead of *terminals and hosts*.

Thus, while you are connected to Web Server A using Netscape, you can tell Netscape that you'd also like to contact and set up a connection with Web Server B. Then you can switch between sessions. All this, using the same single phone line and the same single Internet connection. You cannot do this with a TTY connection.

There's no need to rehearse the technical details. The protocol that makes the Internet possible is called TCP/IP—Transmission Control Protocol/Internet Protocol. As you may recall from Chapter 5, to use the Net and the Web, your computer will need not only a Web browser program or other TCP/IP client, but also a file called WINSOCK.DLL and a program to get the modem to dial the phone and log you on.

## Bringing yourself up to speed

Now let's move to the second major topic of this chapter, namely, how to quickly bring yourself up to speed about the online world. If you have little or no online experience, you really should start with America Online (AOL). You've probably got one or more AOL free-

subscription-offer disks lying around. And if you don't, simply call 800-827-6364 and ask for one.

Each disk is good for 10 free hours on the AOL system. After that, you will be billed $9.95 a month and receive five hours of connect time. Additional hours are billed at $2.95.

CompuServe has long been our favorite consumer system, but, while the breadth and depth of information it offers has no rival in America Online, AOL is much more user friendly, especially for brand-new users. Among other things, AOL offers round-the-clock online customer support via its "chat rooms." Just log into a room, key in your question, and an AOL support rep will respond in less than a minute.

For its part, at this writing, Prodigy is more than a little iffy. Long a product of a partnership between IBM and Sears, Sears has announced that it wants out and would like to sell its stake in the online service. Things may have stabilized as you read this, but at this point, we simply cannot recommend the system to brand-new users.

### Free trial offers

*The Big Three systems all offer free trial subscriptions which you can find out about by calling their toll-free numbers. You might also check with Microsoft Network (MSN) to see what they have to offer.*

| | |
|---|---|
| *America Online* | *800-827-6364* |
| *CompuServe* | *800-848-8199* |
| *Prodigy* | *800-776-3449* |
| *Microsoft Network* | *800-386-5550* |

## Exploring via AOL

We own no stock in America Online and have no financial interest whatsoever in recommending it. But over many years we have become intimately acquainted with all of the leading online systems, and AOL is definitely the one we would recommend to someone who is just starting out.

Here's what you should do. Read this book from cover to cover, underlining the Net and Web addresses you want to try. Activate your AOL subscription and get yourself a kitchen timer. Set your timer for one hour and sign on to AOL. When stuff has stopped appearing on your screen after you have logged on, hold down your Ctrl (Control) key and hit your K key to bring up the "keyword" box. Type in internet and hit your Enter key to get to the AOL Internet feature.

Then use the knowledge and addresses you've found in this book to roll up your sleeves and explore the Net and the World Wide Web. When the timer sounds, exit AOL by clicking on the "File" item at the top left of your screen and then clicking on "Exit" on the menu that will drop down. This will stop the connect-time clock. Once you're offline, take a deep breath. You might be ready for another 30 minutes or a full hour, but at least you will know how much time you have spent.

This may sound silly to you. But be aware that AOL bills of $200 or more per month, charged to your Visa or MasterCard, are not uncommon among those who lose track of time while online. So, a word to the wise—get the darned kitchen timer and use it!

In fact, we'll go even further. If your goal is to learn about the Internet and the World Wide Web, before you pay big bucks to some seminar company, decide that you're going to use this book, your kitchen timer, and $100 to explore things on your own via America Online, or, if you insist, via CompuServe, Prodigy, or the Microsoft Network.

## Make a little list

Create a list of the sites you want to visit, the things you want to do, and the Internet features you want to explore. Then stick to it—regardless of the temptations you will encounter along the way. When you have a question or a problem, take full advantage of AOL's customer support facilities, both online and on the phone, or similar facilities offered by other systems.

If you follow our advice and visit the sites covered in this book, you will find that your $100 has been well spent. You may still want to

attend a seminar, but you will get a heck of a lot more out of it when you do. The bottom line is this: Seminars, books, lectures, radio and TV shows, and all the rest are great, but none of them can substitute for real, live, hands-on experience.

So use this book, use AOL (or some other system), and your kitchen timer to get that experience and to get up to speed. Then consider the alternatives.

# Moving to an Internet service provider (ISP)

We're going to assume that you have indeed brought yourself up to speed this way. You've got a sense of what's going on and a feeling for what your competitors are doing. (See Chapter 11 for information on using Internet *search engines* to locate your competitors on the Net.) In a word, you've spent hours exploring and have at least a basic sense of what this stuff is all about.

Now what? Well, it's "childhood's end," isn't it? It's time to flap your wings and fly on your own. The trade-off is this: You can continue with AOL, CompuServe, Prodigy, or MSN and pay $20 or so for about 8.5 hours of connect time. Or you can pay $20 to an Internet service provider (ISP) for virtually unlimited usage. The catch being that ISPs typically do not offer much in the way of customer service.

# Domain name advantages

Certainly a prime advantage of getting an account with an ISP is the low cost. But from a businessperson's perspective, there are many others. The one you should be most interested in at this point is the opportunity to have your own *domain name*.

The Internet's *Domain Name System* is explained in more detail in Chapter 8. For now, think of a domain name as your own custom e-mail address. Let's say your company is Widgets, Inc., so on a system like America Online, your e-mail address might be **widgets@aol.com**. Once

you have an account on an ISP's system, however, you can have an address like **tom@widgets.com**. And your partner can be **barbara@widgets.com**.

But what's the advantage to that? Isn't it rather like getting a vanity license plate?

In fact, the benefits of having your own domain name go well beyond sheer vanity. The first has to do with establishing your corporate identity. Having "aol.com" in your e-mail address is a little like having "care of" in your land-mail address. It makes you seem like less than a full-fledged organization.

A second and even more important benefit to having your own domain name is *uniformity*. You don't want your customers to have to remember that your electronic mail messages go to **widgets@aol.com**, while your Web page is located at **http://www.sprynet.com/widgets**.

It's far easier for them if your e-mail address is **tom@widgets.com**, and your Web page is located at **http://www.widgets.com**, and anyone who wants instant information about your company can send a short note to your auto-responder at **info@widgets.com**.

Another benefit to having your own domain name is that it gives you flexibility in your choice of Internet service provider. Domain names are transportable. That means that if you become dissatisfied with your ISP or discover another service that can better serve your needs, you won't have to throw out all your letterhead and business cards. You can simply move your domain name to the new system.

## A SLIP/PPP connection

For the sake of simplicity, we can say that in addition to connecting via a system like one of the Big Three consumer systems, there are basically two kinds of Net connections available to most people: Dedicated, hard-wired, high-speed connections and SLIP/PPP dial-up connections. Eventually ISDN (Integrated Services Digital Network)

connections will become widely available as well, but it will be a while before such hook-ups become a major alternative.

If you work for a large company or university, you may very well have access to a hard-wired, high-speed connection. Ask your data processing manager or computer center supervisor. Dedicated T1 or T3 connections, as they are called, are available to individuals and small companies. But they carry hefty installation fees and high monthly costs.

It makes much more sense to let an ISP bear those costs and pay that company to give you access to its Internet connection. Most ISPs offer SLIP/PPP connections on a dial-up basis. The acronyms stand for Serial Line Internet Protocol and Point-to-Point-Protocol. All you really need to know, however, is that a PPP connection is the faster, more advanced option.

Your service provider will almost certainly supply the communications software you will need to use a SLIP or PPP connection. That software will consist of at least three components: a phone dialing program, its associated WINSOCK.DLL file, and Netscape Navigator or some other browser. There may also be special programs for FTP, Telnet, e-mail, newsgroups, and the like, but you can now use those and most other Internet features directly from your browser program.

## How to find an Internet service provider

The best way to find an ISP is to use the Internet itself. For example, you can use your account on America Online or some similar system to tap into the newsgroup **alt.internet.access.wanted**. There you will find lots of tips, advice, and requests from Internet users around the world. It's easy to post a question like, "Can anyone recommend an ISP in the 609 area code?" and check back in a day or so to see if there has been a reply.

The only trouble with the newsgroup approach is that you're taking pot luck that someone will see and be able to answer your request, or that the answers you need have already been posted. Still, this newsgroup offers a good way to ask if anyone has had any experience with an ISP you may be considering.

## POCIA and The List

Fortunately, coming up with a list of ISPs to consider has never been easier, thanks to two Web sites: POCIA and The List.

POCIA stands for Providers of Commercial Internet Access. Maintained by the Celestin Company of Port Townsend, Washington, the POCIA List is based on a regularly updated text file that has long been one of the authoritative lists on the Net. To get to POCIA, point your browser at **http://www.celestin.com/pocia.**

You can also get the text version of the POCIA List using e-mail. To do so, send a blank message to **cci@olympus.net**. Or, if you're not online yet, contact us at Glossbrenner's Choice and we can send it to you on disk for a small charge. (See the Glossbrenner's Choice appendix at the back of this book.)

The second site, The List, is a product of Mecklermedia Corporation, publisher of *iWorld*, *Internet World,* and other books and magazines. It claims to be "the world's most comprehensive list of Internet service providers." To reach The List on the WorldWide Web, aim your browser at **http://www.thelist.com**.

Both of these sites are worth checking. There's some duplication, of course, but for a thorough search of your ISP options, visit both sites. You can search POCIA and The List by area code, or you can look for just those ISPs that offer nationwide service. The List automatically gives you the details about all the ISPs that serve your area code. (See Fig. 7-1 for a sample.) POCIA, on the other hand, presents you with a list of ISPs, and you have to take the extra step of clicking on the name of the ISP to get information about it.

Figure 7-1

```
COMCAT INC.
  Area/Country Codes:        215
  Automated email:           info@comcat.com
  Human email:               info@comcat.com
  Phone:                     (215) 230-4923
  Fax:                       (215) 230-4923
  URL:                       http://www.comcat.com/
  Services:                  SLIP, CSLIP, PPP, Web Server Services
  Fees:                      SLIP/CSLIP/PPP: $19.95/mo, $49.95/quarter, or
                             $89.95/6 mos

DelNet (Internet Delaware)
  Area/Country Codes:        215, 302, 410, 610
  Automated email:           zimm@delnet.com
  Human email:               zimm@delnet.com
  Phone:                     (302) 737-1001
  Fax:                       (302) 737-1567
  URL:                       http://www.delnet.com/
  Services:                  PPP, Windows, Windows NT and Windows 95 dialup,
                             pricing plans, small business/organizational
                             programs, classroom training/workshops. Check
                             our web page for complete details
  Fees:                      Basic Personal: $14.95/mo for 5 hrs/mo
                             Standard Personal: $18.95/mo, $25/setup
                             Standard Commercial: $74.95/mo for 40 hrs/mo
                             $100/setup
                             Preferred Commercial: $94.95/mo for 80 hrs/mo
                             Direct-connect accounts (T1/FT1/56Kb), ISDN
Internet-Gateway
  Area/Country Codes:        215, 609
  Automated email:           Sales@net-gate.com
  Human email:               Sales@net-gate.com
  Phone:                     (609) 983-0066
  Fax:
  URL:                       http://www.net-gate.com/
  Services:                  Shell, SLIP/PPP, WWW, dedicated/leased lines to
                             T1,
                             Web hosting, DNS registration. Full T1 feed
 Fees:                       Setup: $25
                             SLIP/PPP: $20/month (or $200/year) unlimited
                             Commercial prices vary. Please call.
Surf Network, Inc.
  Area/Country Codes:        215, 302, 609, 610
  Automated email:           info@p3.net
  Human email:               info@p3.net
  Phone:                     (215) 784-7010
                             (800) 787-3212
  Fax:                       (215) 784-7016
  URL:                       http://www.p3.net/
  Services:                  Shell, SLIP/PPP, ISDN, fractional/full T1, WWW,
                             Web page hosting/design/consulting/authoring
```

*A sample from Mecklermedia's The List*

Figure 7-1

```
Fees:                 Shell:          $25 setup, $15/month
                      SLIP/PPP:       $25 setup, $18/month
                      Dedicated 28.8K SLIP/PPP: $275 setup,
                      $125/month
                      Dedicated 56K: $1100 setup, $290/month
                      ISDN, fractional/full T1: Call
```

*Continued.*

##  Choosing an ISP

The detailed information you will find about each ISP using these two Web sites will probably include an *automated e-mail* or *auto-responder* address. If so, send a blank or one-sentence e-mail message to that address and then check your mailbox a few minutes later. More than likely, you will find that your mailbox contains the ISP's electronic brochure.

You will probably see confusing technical terms like *shell*, *UUCP*, *frame relay*, and *asynch*. Don't worry about them. Look for *PPP* and for the fees or prices. Also look for a Web site address. Use your account on AOL, CompuServe, Prodigy, or some other system to hit the auto-responders and to visit the Web sites.

Remember, your goal at this point is not to find the ultimate Internet service provider. Your goal is to establish an account with an ISP, get your chosen domain name registered, and basically get comfortable working without the safety net of AOL-quality customer service and tech support.

So what *do* you look for? Well, first of all, you look for competence. It's important to understand that there are lots of people with the technical skills to set up an ISP company. And it's not too expensive—someone can get into the business for as little as $10,000.

##  The same, yet different

For example, the ABC and the XYZ companies may charge the identical rates and offer the identical services. But the ABC company

may be able to handle only 50 callers at a time, while XYZ can handle 250. To add a further twist, ABC may have a high-speed T1 (1,544 kbps) connection to the Net, while XYZ has only a 56 kbps connection. (That's right, the ABC company's T1 connection is nearly 30 times faster than 56 kpbs.)

On the other hand. . . No, let's not take this any further. Our point is that on the surface, two ISPs may appear to offer identical services at identical prices—but still differ considerably in the number of callers they can handle and the speed of their connections to the Internet. To say nothing of the quality of their customer and technical support, the hours that support is available, the other services they offer, and so on.

In a word, shopping for an ISP is not like shopping at the large department stores at your nearest mall. Those stores carry essentially the same products and sell them at essentially the same prices. The market is settled and mature, so we all know what to expect. Not so in the ISP market.

Not only is the entire ISP business brand new, it is also subject to changes that are as rapid as they are enormous. At this writing, for example, there are nearly 2,000 ISPs across the country. Yet, AT&T's WorldNet has announced that beginning in March 1996 it will give five *free* hours of Internet access a month to its 80 million residential customers, with each additional hour billed at $2.50. Or customers can opt to pay $19.95 a month for unlimited access and 24-hour, toll-free customer service.

SprintNet, MCI, and other major players are moving into the ISP market, too. So, as you read this, it seems inevitable that the number of ISPs will have contracted. This is one more reason to proceed with caution. You don't want to invest a lot of time and effort in a Web page and pay for an ad campaign promoting your e-mail and Web site addresses, only to have your ISP suddenly go out of business.

Still, we've got to start somewhere, so let's begin with the basic criteria you should look for in any ISP:

- Reachable via a local phone call
- Connection speed of 28.8 kbps

- ➢ Free access software
- ➢ PPP connection (rather than the slower SLIP connection)
- ➢ Customer service and technical support by phone
- ➢ A cost of $20 to $30 a month for unlimited access
- ➢ Sufficient incoming lines to minimize busy signals
- ➢ A T1 or faster connection to the Net
- ➢ Domain name registration

Only the last three of these points require further explanation, starting with sufficient incoming lines. When you dial up an ISP, you place a phone call to its location. This means two things. First, the ISP must have enough phone lines to be able to take your call, along with many of its other customers. Second, each of those lines must be connected to a modem. Phone lines and modems can be a considerable expense, so some ISPs tend to skimp.

Still, "unlimited access" to the Internet is worthless if you get a busy signal every time you call. So, as part of your selection process, get the ISPs dial-up number or numbers and test them during the early evening hours. If you constantly hear a busy signal, cross the ISP off your list.

As for the T1 connection requirement, you can cut through the technical details and simply visit the ISP's World Wide Web home page. Give the page a good workout, click here and there, and ask yourself if the connection seems relatively fast or slow. Certainly all kinds of other factors can have an effect. If you're using AOL to do this and AOL is heavily loaded, the response time will be slower.

Sad to say, just because an ISP says it has a T1 connection doesn't mean that it really does. The firm might be using the much cheaper, much slower 56 kpbs connection option.

Finally, domain name registration. As you will discover in the next chapter, a centralized organization called the InterNIC keeps track of and implements domain names. It charges $100 to register a name for the first two years, and $50 a year after that. You can handle the

registration yourself, using forms provided on the Net (**http:// | rs.internic.net/rs-internic.html**), but it's really not worth it. Far better to let your ISP take care of the registration process for you. Most will do so for a small, *one-time* fee of $25 to $50 (over and above the InterNIC fees).

# Conclusion

In our opinion, if you're a businessperson, the most important things to look for in an ISP are domain name registration, cost, competence, and customer service. So if POCIA or The List turn up, say, a dozen ISPs in your area code, start the selection process by visiting each ISP's Web site. Look for competence. Collect each ISP's list of offerings and prices, either via the Web site or via auto-responder.

Rule out anyone who charges much more than $20 to $30 a month for unlimited access. Then call the voice numbers of each remaining ISP. Ask them to send you their information packet or brochure or other literature. (If the ISP has nothing it can mail you, that may be a sign that it's operating on a shoestring.) Ask them if they mail a monthly newsletter to their subscribers. And what are the hours for technical support?

In short, try to get a sense of each ISP's operation. After all, you've been on AOL and have explored the Net and the Web as we suggested. You are thus not a completely naive customer. Plus, as a businessperson, you can tell when you're dealing with someone who really knows what he or she is doing. So use your instincts. Or, what the heck, if the ISP's shop is located nearby, pay a personal visit!

Again, don't worry about your Web home page or auto-responder or other things right now. Concentrate on finding someone who's good! That will make your life online so much easier.

## Leading nationwide Internet Service Providers

*Adapted from the POCIA List, here are many of the leading* national *ISPs. These companies provide service to more than a single geographical area.*

| Provider | Phone | Contact |
|---|---|---|
| *AGIS (Apex Global Information Services)* | *313-730-1130* | *info@agis.net* |
| *ANS* | *703-758-7700* | *info@ans.net* |
| *AT&T WorldNet* | *800-967-5363* | *http://www.att.com* |
| *BBN Planet* | *617-873-2905* | *net-info@bbnplanet.com* |
| *Concentric Research Corporation* | *800-745-2747* | *info@cris.com* |
| *CRL Network Services* | *415-837-5300* | *sales@crl.com* |
| *DataXchange Network, Inc.* | *800-863-1550* | *info@dx.net* |
| *Delphi Internet Services Corporation* | *800-695-4005* | *info@delphi.com* |
| *EarthLink Network, Inc.* | *213-644-9500* | *sales@earthlink.net* |
| *Exodus Communications, Inc.* | *408-522-8450* | *info@exodus.net* |
| *4GL Corporation* | *713-589-8077* | *info@4gl.com* |
| *Global Connect, Inc.* | *804-229-4484* | *info@gc.net* |
| *Information Access Technologies (Holonet)* | *510-704-0160* | *info@holonet.net* |
| *Institute for Global Communications* | *415-442-0220* | *igc-info@igc.apc.org* |
| *Liberty Information Network* | *800-218-5157* | *info@liberty.com* |
| *MIDnet* | *800-682-5550* | *info@mid.net* |
| *Moran Communications* | *716-639-1254* | *info@moran.com* |
| *NETCOM On-Line Communications Services* | *408-554-8649* | *info@netcom.com* |
| *Netrex, Inc* | *800-363-8739* | *info@netrex.com* |

| | | |
|---|---|---|
| *Network 99, Inc.* | *800-638-9947* | *net99@cluster.mcs.net* |
| *Performance Systems International* | *800-827-7482* | *all-info@psi.com* |
| *Portal Information Network* | *408-973-9111* | *info@portal.com* |
| *SprintLink - Nationwide 56K - 45M access* | *800-817-7755* | *info@sprint.net* |
| *The ThoughtPort Authority Inc.* | *800-477-6870* | *info@thoughtport.com* |
| *WareNet* | *714-348-3295* | *info@ware.net* |
| *Zocalo Engineering* | *510-540-8000* | *info@zocalo.net* |

## Toll-Free Service Providers

*The ISPs listed below are among those that can be dialed via a toll-free 800 number. If you're travelling and need to get to your Internet account, this feature can save you money on long-distance phone charges.*

| | | |
|---|---|---|
| *Allied Access Inc.* | *618-684-2255* | *sales@intrnet.net* |
| *American Information Systems, Inc.* | *708-413-8400* | *info@ais.net* |
| *Association for Computing Machinery* | *817-776-6876* | *account-info@acm.org* |
| *CICNet, Inc.* | *313-998-6103* | *info@cic.net* |
| *Cogent Software, Inc.* | *818-585-2788* | *info@cogsoft.com* |
| *Cyberius Online Inc.* | *613-233-1215* | *info@cyberus.ca* |
| *Colorado SuperNet, Inc.* | *303-296-8202* | *info@csn.org* |
| *EarthLink Network, Inc.* | *213-644-9500* | *sales@earthlink.net* |
| *Global Connect, Inc.* | *804-229-4484* | *info@gc.net* |
| *Internet Express* | *719-592-1240* | *info@usa.net* |
| *Mnematics, Inc.* | *914-359-4546* | *service@mne.com* |
| *Msen, Inc.* | *313-998-4562* | *info@msen.com* |
| *NeoSoft, Inc.* | *713-684-5969* | *info@neosoft.com* |

| | | |
|---|---|---|
| *NETCOM On-Line Communications Services* | *408-554-8649* | *info@netcom.com* |
| *New Mexico Technet, Inc.* | *505-345-6555* | *granoff@technet.nm.org* |
| *Pacific Rim Network, Inc.* | *360-650-0442* | *info@pacificrim.net* |
| *Rocky Mountain Internet* | *800-900-7644* | *info@rmii.com* |
| *Synergy Communications, Inc.* | *800-345-9669* | *info@synergy.net* |
| *VivaNET, Inc.* | *800-836-8649* | *info@vivanet.com* |
| *VoiceNet* | *800-835-5710* | *info@voicenet.com* |
| *WLN* | *800-342-5956* | *info@wln.com* |

# Part 2

# The tools at hand

# Making the most of e-mail

# CHAPTER 8

THINGS have changed since we discussed e-mail in the first edition of this book. At that time, when Web pages cost thousands of dollars, we suggested that you ignore the idea that "you've got to be on the Web" and let your competitors spend their time and money pursuing business that way while you craftily focus on e-mail and auto-responders.

Today, Web pages cost a few hundred dollars (if that) to create and involve monthly fees as low as $50. There is also the fact that today it is simply expected that any company worth its salt will have a Web page. It's a matter of image, not a matter of need or effectiveness.

This doesn't mean, however, that e-mail has been unseated as the single most *useful* feature on the Net. After all, how are all those visitors to your Web page going to ask you questions or request more information? Through e-mail, of course. Indeed, every business's Web page should contain a clickable icon that lets visitors quickly and easily send an e-mail message to the page's owner.

## The big payoff

But it gets better. As you'll see in Chapter 9 when we talk about auto-responders, you can easily set things up like this:

> Prospective customers *anywhere* in the world see your special "info" address in an advertisement. They want to know more. So they log onto the Internet, tap a few keys to send a blank or one-line message to your special auto-responder address. And within minutes (sometimes within *seconds*!) they receive in their mailboxes your product descriptions, price lists, company "backgrounder," press releases, or whatever other information you want to provide.

Talk about instant gratification! Talk about customer interaction! And no human intervention is required, thanks to the *mail robot* or *mailbot* or *auto-responder* software provided to you by your Internet service provider or someone else for as little as $10 a month.

You can also put an auto-responder icon on your Web page. The prospective customer need only click on it, and your brochure—in plain ASCII text—will be sent automatically to the person's mailbox.

This frees your customers from having to absorb all your information right away. They can continue browsing the Web without having to read, print, or save to disk all the pages presented at your site. The information that's of interest will all be waiting in the mailbox to be read at the customer's convenience.

There's a lot more you can do as well, all without straying very far from the essential e-mail concept. But let's get basic Internet e-mail down first. Then we'll look at how to set up an auto-responder in the next chapter.

## Basic e-mail, all systems

The best way to *send* e-mail is to prepare the text of your message while you are offline. Use your favorite word processor and spell-checker. Then save the message as a plain ASCII text file using the "Save as" option and then selecting "nondocument," "unformatted," "ASCII," or whatever other term your software uses to refer to plain text.

Then, if you are using a Big Three system, sign on and get to your system's mail feature. Tell the feature you want to send mail, upload your previously prepared text file at the appropriate point, and key in the e-mail address of your correspondent.

On AOL and Prodigy, you will have to send your prepared message as an *attached file*, so you key in a brief note like, "Hi, Bob, take a look at this attached file, please." On CompuServe you can indeed prepare everything offline and upload it using the "Create new message" option.

With AOL and Prodigy, you're locked in to using their e-mail software. And, frankly, it is pretty weak. Suitable for short, ad hoc notes, perhaps, but definitely not "industrial strength." On the other hand, there are a dozen or more front-end programs for CompuServe, each of which includes powerful features to collect, send, and manage

e-mail messages and SIG/Forum postings. One of the most popular is the shareware program TAPCIS. (Key in go tapcis on CompuServe.)

## Moving to the Net

When you move to the Internet and your ISP connection, however, things change. What you must understand is that each of the Big Three systems has a built-in software module that handles electronic mail. These modules were originally designed for e-mail sent between fellow subscribers using the same service.

There was no provision for accepting messages from some outside network. Still, when Internet e-mail became important, the Big Three extended their respective e-mail modules to include it.

This has never been the case on the Internet itself. Basically, the Net's Simple Mail Transport Protocol (SMTP) routes the mail to your ISP's Post Office Protocol (POP) server, where it is stored under your name. The next time you sign on, your mail will be sent to you when you or your software ask for it.

There are no fancy features, like attaching files to messages or forwarding messages to someone else, or even replying to a given message. None of these things are built in the way they are when you use your Big Three account.

Instead, you are expected to supply your *own* e-mail software, and it is expected to be "aware" of the POP protocol and the Internet and everything else. It's not a great analogy, but ISP-based Internet e-mail is like being able to use your own go-cart at an amusement park instead of being forced to use the go-carts supplied by AOL or Prodigy. The features and the power are up to you, not the online system.

## How Internet e-mail programs operate

There are numerous ways to send and receive e-mail via the Internet. Our focus here is on the options and opportunities available when you use an ISP connection. At this writing, there are two major options. You can log onto your ISP using Netscape Navigator and use that program's built-in abilities to send and receive e-mail. Netscape can even be set to automatically check for mail at intervals you specify.

Alternatively, you can use a dedicated mail program like Eudora or Z-Mail. When you sign on to your ISP with programs like these, your mail will be picked up automatically, and you will then be signed off. Internet e-mail programs are like that. They nip into the Net to pick up your messages and then quickly sign off.

Once you are offline, you can prepare your replies to those messages, including any instructions to attach files to them, and then tell the program to log on again, blast your replies into the Net, and quickly sign off again.

In other words, the composition of new messages from you, or of your replies to messages you have received, takes place offline. Which makes a heck of a lot of sense. There is absolutely no reason why anyone needs to be physically connected to the Net or to an online system while reading mail or preparing replies. (E-mail programs can also be set to automatically sign on and check for mail at regular intervals.)

## E-mail software features

As you might expect, Internet e-mail programs are loaded with features, many of which you'll probably never use. But there are some basic ones to zero in on. When you're preparing a reply to a message, for example, you will be able to "quote" all or part of that message. The quoted lines will show up in your reply set off by angle brackets.

You'll be able to *attach* binary and other files to your outgoing messages, and you can usually arrange for a program to automatically tack your *signature* or *sig* file onto each message. (More on both attachments and sig files later.)

You can create your own mailing lists and use a person's real name to address a letter instead of his or her e-mail address. The e-mail

program will automatically substitute the e-mail address when it sends the letter. And, of course, you can file your correspondence in different *folders*.

## Canned replies: The most important business feature

In our opinion, if you're using e-mail for business, the single most important feature to look for in an e-mail program is the ability to reply to an incoming message with a previously prepared file. The file might be your standard cover letter, price list, order form, or something else.

This is not the same as attaching a file to a message. You want to be able to click on an incoming message, personalize your reply by keying in "Dear Ms. Smith," then tell the program to load your standard cover letter.

You'd think the need for this feature would be obvious to the people who write e-mail software. But it isn't. Not even the commercial version of Eudora, probably the best known package in this area, currently offers it.

The only package we've found that allows you to personalize form letters and use other previously prepared text is Z-Mail from NCD Software Corporation. Our experience with both the program and NCD's tech support has been fantastic. We can see why Z-Mail was a recent *PC Magazine* "Editor's Choice." For more information, call 415-898-8649 or visit them at **http://www.ncd.com/z-code/zcode/html**.

## Internet e-mail quirks

The key thing to remember about electronic mail on the Internet is that it was designed decades ago, and it is aimed at the lowest common denominator. Over the years, the Internet community has added its own little twists and quirks, all while staying faithful to the lowest-common-denominator concept.

Although we have never attempted it ourselves, we have it on good authority that there is no physical reason why an 8-bit binary file can't be sent via Internet e-mail. The trouble is, even if you know for a fact that your own ISP's system can handle it, you can't always be sure that the same is true of your correspondent's system.

Thus, for all intents and purposes, you can use only the 128 characters that form the standard 7-bit ASCII code set for Internet e-mail. In addition, each message can be no larger than 64K. That's the equivalent of about 35 double-spaced pages. Plenty of room for a message, but not for the text versions of most binary files. (Yes, *text* versions, as we shall see!)

## E-mail tips & tricks

*There's no question about it: E-mail is an entirely new means of expression to most people. Certainly it is also a powerful business tool—or can be, if used properly. So, in no particular order, here are our tips on how to make the most of this incredible tool.*

**1** *E-mail should be checked regularly, otherwise you might as well be using the Post Office's* snail mail, *as Net denizens call it. Either you or someone you designate should check e-mail a couple of times a day. But don't overdo it. Checking for mail every hour looks like work, but amounts to procrastination.*

**2** *Don't send "thank-yous" in response to every message you receive. ("Thanks for the info." "Thanks for getting back to me.") Reply only when you actually have some new information to communicate, or need to make an additional request. And don't "copy in" everyone and his brother. As Internet users would say, "conserve the bandwidth."*

**3** *Begin each message with a salutation like "Dear Mr. Smith," just as you would do in a paper business letter. To simply start typing the body of the letter with no greeting is boorish and rude.*

**4** *Prepare a* signature *or* sig *file that contains all the information about you or your firm that would normally appear in letterhead stationery (land address, phone, and*

*fax numbers), along with your e-mail and Web addresses. Make sure that it gets attached to the end of every e-mail message you send.*

**5** *Don't include the entire original letter in your reply, and use the option of quoting lines from that message sparingly.*

*Instead, take the extra effort needed to follow the time-honored convention of letter writing and say something like, "I noted your concern regarding implementing the Forbin Policy. I must say that, in my opinion, we should . . ." Electronic mail, after all, is not online* chat *frozen in time. It is correspondence, which is something else quite again.*

**6** *Compose replies in anger or passion, if you must. But let that puppy cool before you blast it off to* flame *somebody. In many ways, e-mail makes it far* too *easy to communicate. And, of course, once sent, there is no way to recall a message. To quote Virginia Shea, author of* Netiquette *(Albion Books), "Never send a message you wouldn't want to receive yourself."*

**7** *Use* smilies *and other e-mail shorthand at your peril—once you start, it's hard to stop. Sad to say, we find ourselves including the canonical smiley— :) —in messages these days without even realizing it.*

*Worse still, in normal person-to-person speech we find ourselves saying things like "OTOH, you could go with the red blazer." Or "IMHO, you should buy the blue cardigan." These terms are pronounced "oh-tee-oh-h," and "im-ho," and they are pernicious. They stand for "on the other hand" and "in my humble opinion." Both are e-mail/chat shorthand.*

**8** *Don't feel that you have to respond to every piece of e-mail you receive. Although it may go against your grain, in this world of downsized corporations with fewer and fewer secretaries and support personnel, executives don't even respond to paper letters much of the time.*

**9** *When you are preparing your message, use 65-character lines with no left margin. A 65-character line is standard in business letters and much easier to read than the 80-*

*character lines that computers permit. As for a left margin of 0, you should know that this makes it much easier for your correspondents to reformat and print your letter. The only time we would suggest using a left margin of, say, 10 spaces, is in preparing the text for an auto-responder. (See Chapter 9 for more on this subject.)*

**10** *Finally, don't use all capitals unless you intend to SHOUT at someone. If you want to italicize a word, frame it with asterisks, like *this*.*

## E-mailing binary files

Internet e-mail programs include a text editor or word processor for preparing messages offline. They're also smart enough to prompt you for the subject line and e-mail address you want to use. They may even include a spell-checker.

But what if you don't want to have to learn to use yet another word processor? What if you want to use WordPerfect, Microsoft Word, or some other favorite? You can do that, but don't make the classic beginner's mistake of assuming that your wonderful font-filled document will be displayed properly on your correspondent's screen.

For one thing, that person may not use the same word processing program. So, unless the program your correspondent uses can *import* your format, the results are likely to be a lot of garbage characters on the screen. To be safe, be sure to save any file created with your word processor as plain ASCII text.

If you *must* send someone a WordPerfect or similar document with all its special codes and formatting intact, you must send it as a *binary file*. That means it will first have to be converted into 7-bit ASCII text.

Binary files also include spreadsheets, graphic image files (.PCX, .TIF, .GIF, etc.), sound files, and compressed archives (.ZIP, .SIT, etc.), all of which must be converted to standard ASCII text if they are to be sent via Internet e-mail. There is less to this than meets the eye. After all,

binary files consist of nothing but numbers, so suppose you just express each number using the hexadecimal numbering system?

## MIME, UUENCODE, & BinHex

You can express any number in hexadecimal using the digits 0 through 9 and the letters A through F. These 16 symbols are all plain ASCII text. And this is exactly the technique that has been used for years. In the Macintosh world, in fact, BinHex encoding is the most popular technique.

There is also a technique called MIME (Multi-purpose Internet Mail Extensions) protocol. And another called UUENCODE, versions of which are available for most computers. The "UU" in the name is short for Unix-to-Unix, but such programs are available for DOS/Windows users on the Net or from Glossbrenner's Choice.

The text version of a binary file can be quite large, to say the least. Thus, given the Net's 64K-per-message size limit, a binary file may result in several separate text files, all of which must be transmitted to your correspondent. When the text files arrive, your correspondent can decode them, to reproduce the binary file.

## Complications & problems

Fortunately, the e-mail programs we've told you about can handle all of this coding nonsense automatically. All you have to do is attach the binary file to your outgoing message. America Online does the same thing when you attach a file to a message sent on that system. (AOL automatically converts attached files into MIME format before sending them over the Net.)

Unfortunately, there are complications. If both you and your correspondent use the same e-mail program, then everything should go swimmingly. Your program encodes the binary file on the way out, and your friend's program decodes it when it is received.

But suppose you use different packages. Suppose your program uses UUENCODE and your friend's uses BinHex. Or what if some other friend on America Online sends you an attached binary file, which AOL has converted into MIME format? You can overcome such incompatibilities if you own the necessary decoding programs, but what a nuisance.

Frankly, if you must get a binary file to someone, it's best to send it on floppy disk via a courier like Federal Express, or use one of the Big Three consumer systems instead. If you need to regularly exchange binary files with a good customer, you might even want to consider providing the customer with a CompuServe, America Online, or Prodigy account.

# Addresses on the Net

Now let's consider those crazy Internet mail addresses that you're starting to see in company ads and in magazine and newspaper articles. The tip-off that it's an Internet e-mail address is the "at" sign (@). These addresses consist of two parts: the stuff to the left of the "at" sign and the stuff to the right.

As an example, consider the address **grendel@beowulf.heorot.com**. (Mail addresses are not case-sensitive.) If Grendel were giving you his address, he would say, "I'm Grendel at Beowulf dot Heorot dot Com." But Internet routing computers read this kind of address from right to left. So the address tells them (and us) that the location is a commercial system called Heorot on a computer called Beowulf that's part of that system. And Grendel is the *logon* name of the individual person.

The information to the right of the "at" sign is called the *domain*. Internet addresses all follow the *Domain Name System* of addressing. Most addresses you'll see end in one of the following *zone* name extensions:

| | |
|---|---|
| .com | U.S. commercial businesses |
| .edu | U.S. college and university sites |
| .gov | Governmental bodies |

| | |
|---|---|
| .int | International bodies, like NATO |
| .mil | Military organizations |
| .net | Companies or organizations that run large networks |
| .org | Nonprofit organizations and others that don't fit anywhere else |

Moving to the left, following the zone is the organization's name—in this case, Heorot. If the organization is a large one, it may have several computers or network servers, each with its own name. In this case, the computer at the Heorot organization where Grendel hangs out is called Beowulf.

The Internet mail system effectively "reads" these addresses from right to left. The computers that route and transport the mail know that it is their responsibility to deliver a message to the "highest" subdomain in the full domain name, in this case, the Heorot system. After that, it is the responsibility of the subdomain name system to take over routing and transport within its own network.

## International e-mail

*E-mail addresses for users outside the U.S. typically end in a country code. For example, .AU is Australia, .KH is Cambodia, and .NP is Nepal.*

*If you expect to send and receive a lot of international e-mail, you might want to get a copy of the International E-mail Accessibility FAQ. (FAQ stands for "frequently asked questions.") In addition to the complete list of country codes, this FAQ includes information about the level of service available in each country (full Internet access, e-mail only, etc.), and where to find further country-specific information if you need it.*

*You can request a copy of the FAQ by sending e-mail to **mail-server@rtfm.mit.edu**. Leave the subject line blank, and in the message area key in this one-line message:*

*send usenet/news.answers/mail/country-codes*

*A similar document with clickable links to additional information is available on the World Wide Web:*

***http://www.ee.ic.ac.uk/misc/country-codes.html.***

# The InterNIC & domain name registration

The InterNIC (Internet Network Information Center) is the organization that keeps track of and registers domain names. Once fully-supported by the National Science Foundation, the InterNIC now supplements its operations by charging a registration fee for domain names: $100 for the first two years, and $50 for each successive year.

The process takes about three to four weeks. You can do it yourself using the forms and instructions provided at the InterNIC Web site (**http://rs.internic.net/rs-internic.html**). But why bother when most Internet service providers will handle it for you for a small, one-time fee of about $25 to $50 (in addition to the InterNIC fee, which is usually billed separately).

Once your domain name is registered, you own it. Should you ever decide to change providers, you can take your domain name along with you by having your *new* provider update the information on file with the InterNIC.

For more on the domain name registration process, contact the InterNIC at these locations:

- Registration Services Home Page
  **http://rs.internic.net/rs-internic.html**
- InterNIC Questions via E-mail
  **question@internic.net**
- Registration Help Line
  **703-742-4777**

## Choosing a domain name

*Your domain name should be relatively short, easy to remember, and directly related to your business name or the product or service you offer.*

*As you can imagine, many of the most obvious single-word domain names have already been taken. So instead of* ***cars.com****, you may have to consider a name like* ***cars-online.com*** *or* ***netcars.com****. The maximum number of characters allowed is 24, including hyphens, but you'll want to keep your domain name well below that.*

*The fastest and easiest way to find out whether a particular domain name is available is to use the InterNIC's WHOIS query function at* ***http://rs.internic.net/cgi-bin/whois****. Here's the result of our search on the word "cars":*

```
CARS Information Systems
 Corporation (CARSINFO-DOM)             CARSINFO.COM
Cars & Things
 Ltd. (EARNHARDTS-DOM)                  EARNHARDTS.COM
Cars And
 Trucks On-Line (CATOL-DOM)             CATOL.COM
Cars On Line (CARS-ON-LINE-DOM)         CARS-ON-LINE.COM
Cars Online,
 Inc (ONLINECARS-DOM)                   ONLINECARS.COM
Cars and Cars (CARSNCARS-DOM)           CARSNCARS.COM
Cars at Cost (CARSATCOST-DOM)           CARSATCOST.COM
Cars at Cost (CARSCOST-DOM)             CARSCOST.COM
Cars, Inc. (CARS2-DOM)                  CARS.ORG
Demaree, Mark (MD864)                   cars@CARCLUB.COM   +1 415 399 6616
Martin, Joe (JM1834)                    cars@INDIRECT.COM  (602) 390-6561
Smith, Ernie (ES553)                    cars@BLARG.NET     206/634-3322
Tronco, Carlos (CT60)                   cars@ROSS.COM      (512) 892-7802
                                                             ext. 231
Will, Rob (RW875)                       cars@BLARG.NET     206/634-3322
```

# IP addresses & when to use them

The Domain Name System is actually a mask that hides the *numerical* addresses the Internet Protocol (IP) actually uses. Somewhere along the way to our friend Grendel, one or more Internet *nameserver* computers will convert the Domain Name System address **grendel@beowulf.heorot.com** into something like **Grendel@123.45.67.89**. This might translate as "network number 123.45, and computer 67.89 on that network."

For computers, it's easy. For humans, it's not. So the Domain Name System was invented to let us use plain English to specify the same thing.

Most of the time, you will have no problem using the domain name version of an e-mail address. But if a letter gets "bounced back" to you as undeliverable, it may be necessary to use the numerical IP address instead. Before resending, check the address on the bounced-back letter to make sure that you did indeed type it correctly in the first place. If you did, then it's a sure sign that some nameserver system along the way does not yet have that domain name mapped to the proper numerical IP address.

Send the letter again using the IP address. If it still comes back, phone to let your correspondent know that the address does not appear to be working.

## Encrypt your text for privacy

*Electronic mail is* not *private. At least not theoretically. In practice, so many messages flow on the Net each day that it is highly unlikely that anyone is reading yours.*

*Technically, though, someone* could *read your stuff. After all, if the National Security Agency has the ability to pluck a single phone conversation out of thousands taking place on a microwave link, and if the Central Intelligence Agency can determine what people in a room across the street are saying merely by monitoring the diaphragm-like vibrations of the window panes, how can anyone assume that the Internet is secure?*

*In point of fact, no one does. That's why it's best to assume that if something* can *be done, it* will *be done, eventually, by someone, somewhere. The way to play it safe is to encrypt any truly sensitive e-mail messages you send to colleagues via the Net. And it is so easy to do, once you and your correspondent have the right program. Here are several you might consider if you are a DOS/Windows user. (Similar programs exist for the Mac.)*

- *PGP (Pretty Good Privacy) is the famous "public key" RSA encryption program written by Phillip Zimmermann.*
- *PC-CODE by Richard Nolen Colvard includes a version of what he calls* super-encipherment, *in which "each character of plain text is both scrambled (transposed) as well as substituted for some random 'other' character."*

- *The Confidant by Stan W. Merrill encrypts files so thoroughly that a National Security Agency supercomputer might be needed to figure it out. Yet your recipient will find the text simple to restore because you have supplied the program and the key.*

*All three of these programs are widely available on the Net, or you can order them on a single disk (Encryption Tools) from Glossbrenner's Choice.*

# Sending mail to other networks

No discussion of the basics of Internet e-mail would be complete without highlighting one of its often overlooked benefits: Namely, that it lets each subscriber to one of the Big Three consumer online systems communicate with every other subscriber. CompuServe subscribers can send messages to America Online users, who can send messages to Prodigy users, who can send messages to your mailbox at your Internet service provider.

This really is a big deal. The interconnectivity of systems is something the United Nations has been striving to get established for nearly ten years! But for most of those years, the *X.400* concept, as it was called, got nowhere. It wasn't until public pressure literally forced virtually every online system to offer Internet e-mail that the interconnectivity dream was finally realized.

You will also hear of an *X.500* standard. This is the foundation upon which people hoped to build a master directory of e-mail addresses. That hasn't taken place, either. Instead, there are numerous privately maintained directories that offer basic listings free of charge. See the nearby sidebar for a couple of examples.

## Finding e-mail addresses

*The best tool for finding the e-mail address of a particular person or company is the telephone. That's right. Just call up and ask. But if that's not an option for some reason, try one of these online directories:*

- ***Four11 Directory Services*** *Four11 is a commercial online directory service that claims to have over 5 million listings. All Internet users are provided free basic access, which includes a free listing and free searching. For more information, send e-mail to* ***info@four11.com,*** *or try the service yourself by visiting the Four11 Web site at* ***http://www.four11.com****.*
- ***LookUP!*** *This is another online directory that you can search with your Web browser. They don't make any claims at the site about the number of listings in the directory, but based on our test searches, it's not as extensive as the one maintained by Four11. Test it yourself by visiting the Web site at* ***http://www.lookup.com****.*

*For a thorough treatment of all the various ways to find e-mail addresses on the Net, you might want to consult the Finding-Addresses FAQ written by long-time Internaut David Alex Lamb. You'll find it on the Web at this address:* ***http://www.qucis.queensu.ca/FAQs/email/finding.html****.*

# How to do it!

Many subscribers to the Big Three systems, MCI Mail, and most Internet service providers are still not aware of the connectivity that exists today to allow the exchange of e-mail among the various systems. Here's a quick primer.

## America Online (AOL)

To send mail to someone on AOL, remove any spaces from the person's AOL user name and add **@aol.com** to get an address like **jsmith@aol.com**. (If you don't know the user name, your best bet is to call the person and ask.)

To send mail from America Online to someone on the Internet, just put the person's Internet address in the "To" field before composing your message.

## CompuServe

CompuServe users have numerical addresses in the form **12345,678**. To send mail to a CompuServe user, change the comma to a period and add **@compuserve.com** to get an address like **12345.678@compuserve.com**.

To send mail from CompuServe to someone on the Internet, use an address in the form **internet:jsmith@company.org**.

### ⁂ MCI Mail

To send mail to someone with an MCI Mail account, add **@mcimail.com** to the end of the person's name or numerical address. For example: **555-1234@mcimail.com** or **jsmith@mcimail.com**. (You're better off using the numerical address if the person has a relatively common name, since there can be no doubt about the John Smith at 555-1234, but considerable doubt about JSMITH.)

To send mail from MCI Mail to an Internet address, at the "To:" prompt, key in the person's name and (EMS). At the resulting "EMS:" prompt, key in internet. At the resulting "MBX:" prompt, key in the recipient's Internet address.

### ⁂ Prodigy

To send mail to a Prodigy user, add **@prodigy.com** to the person's Prodigy user ID. For example: **jsmith@prodigy.com**.

To send mail from Prodigy to an Internet address, you'll need Mail Manager software, which is available for download from Prodigy. After composing your message offline using Mail Manager, send it to the person's normal Internet address, like **jsmith@company.org**. No special punctuation is required.

## E-mail signatures

Earlier in this chapter we spoke of e-mail *signatures* and *sig* files. These are simply short text files that you append to most of your messages. Typically they contain the kind of information that would normally appear in your letterhead: name, land address, voice phone, fax number, e-mail address, and so on.

E-mail programs like Eudora and Z-Mail let you prepare sig files that will be added automatically to every message you send. For example, here is the signature file we use:

```
=-=-=-=-=-=-=-=-=-=-=-=-=-=-=-=-=-=-=-=-=-=-=-=-=-=-=-=-=-=-=-=-=-=-=-=-=-=-=-=-=-=-=-=-=-=-=-=-=-=-=
Alfred and Emily Glossbrenner  Voice:  215-736-1213
699 River Road                 FAX:    215-736-1031
Yardley, PA  19067-1965        E-mail: gloss@gloss.com
      "We write the best computer books in the world!"
For more information, send a short message to books@mailback.com.
=-=-=-=-=-=-=-=-=-=-=-=-=-=-=-=-=-=-=-=-=-=-=-=-=-=-=-=-=-=-=-=-=-=-=-=-=-=-=-=-=-=-=-=-=-=-=-=-=-=-=
```

## Keep it simple

If you are using the Net for business, creating an e-mail signature is a really good idea. But a number of cautions are in order. In general, you don't want your signature to run much beyond nine or ten lines. As long as you don't try to be cute, that's plenty of space to convey the essential "letterhead" information.

Think in terms of two columns—one on the left for your land address and one on the right for your e-mail, phone, and fax numbers. If there's room, you might include an advertising tag line or motto. The key thing is to avoid going overboard and thus irritating your correspondents.

### Signatures on parade

*Here are three signatures files from people we know. Ralph Wilson offers reasonably priced Web pages for small businesses and publishes an excellent Internet marketing newsletter. John Rosenberg is a professional database searcher and friend who can find out anything you care to know. And Holiday Links is one of our consulting clients.*

```
===============================================================
Dr. Ralph F. Wilson, Editor             rfwilson@wilsonweb.com
WILSON INTERNET SERVICES                        (916) 652-4659
Web Design & Consulting for Organizations and Small Business
P.O. Box 308, Rocklin, Calif. 95677 USA    Call before faxing
===============================================================
```

```
John S. Rosenberg   703-533-9292  800-678-9393  703-538-6135  (Fax)
Online Resources, Inc. 200 Little Falls St., #G-201, Falls Church, Va.
22046
john@onliners.com   * * * *    "We Cover All The Bases..."    * * * *
```

```
0=0=0=0=0=0=0=0=0=0=0=0=0=0=0=0=0=0=0=0=0=0=0=0=0=0=0=0=0=0=0=0=0=0=0=0=0
      HOLIDAY LINKS -- International Home Exchange Holidays
3 College Road                     Tel/Fax: 01904 702693
Copmanthorpe, York Y02 3US         E-mail:  gi46@dial.pipex.com
England, UK                        World Travel at Minimal Cost!
0=0=0=0=0=0=0=0=0=0=0=0=0=0=0=0=0=0=0=0=0=0=0=0=0=0=0=0=0=0=0=0=0=0=0=0=0
```

*For more examples of signature files (good, bad, and ridiculous), visit the Yahoo! directory at **http://www.yahoo.com** and click on "Arts," then "Computer Generated," then "ASCII Art," then "Signature Files." You'll find several collections of sigs, quotations, ASCII art, and other information that will help you create your own sig file.*

## E-mail marketing & direct mail

Now you've got the tools and the knowledge needed to really fly using Internet e-mail. So, of course, we know what you're thinking. You're thinking, "What a great, cheap, promotional tool! Why spend money on direct mail when I can blast my sales message to thousands of people on the Net for next to nothing?"

Well, think again. Any number of our consulting clients have come to this same, erroneous, conclusion. There are companies out there that are trying to make a business of collecting, say, the e-mail addresses of people who have posted messages to certain newsgroups. So they go to the newsgroup **alt.hotrod** and collect all the e-mail addresses of everyone who has posted messages to that group and then try to sell the list to companies that market car products.

### The me-approach, again

The car product company, taking the me-approach, of course, says "Great! Let's send them all an e-mail message about our new framitz converter. It'll cost us next to nothing, and just think of the sales!"

Big mistake. With the right software, all of this can indeed be done very cheaply. Trouble is, Internet and online users don't view their electronic mailboxes the same way they view the mailboxes at the end of their driveways. Part of this is long tradition and culture and part is dollars-and-cents practicality.

Online users view unsolicited e-mail they way most of us view unsolicited telemarketing phone calls. It's an invasion of privacy and a misuse of a medium that is reserved for private communication. And it requires much more energy and interaction than a piece of junk mail.

But at least with junk mail, the recipient is not forced to *pay*. Not so with junk e-mail. Robert Raisch of The Internet Company (**info@internet.com**) has long been one of our favorite commentators on the Net and the Web. Recently, Mr. Raisch coined the term *postage-due marketing* to describe the practice of sending unsolicited sales messages to someone's e-mail mailbox.

##  Postage-due marketing

You can get the complete text of Robert Raisch's "Postage-Due-Marketing" white paper by visiting the Internet Company's Web site at **http://www.internet.com/marketing**. He begins by recounting the Net-infamous case of the Arizona "Green Card" lawyers, Laurence Canter and Martha Siegel and their *spamming* of the Net.

Depending on who's talking, the practice of sending the identical message to thousands of newsgroups or e-mail addresses is called spamming because it is similar to what happens if "the Spam hits the fan," or because of a Monty Python sketch in which a diner orders Spam repeatedly, "well past the point of absurdity."

Here's part of what Mr. Raisch has to say:

> As most professional marketers realize, effective marketing is never cheap nor easy.
>
> The media has chosen to paint this as an issue of culture clash between the idealistic Internet old guard and a pragmatic new

> breed of online marketeer without understanding the economic or social realities of the situation. Upon a little research, this characterization lacks any real substance.
>
> In essence, Canter & Siegel's actions were economically irresponsible, demanding that the public shoulder the cost of their marketing tactics—without any possibility of refusal.

Mr. Raisch continues to elaborate on why he came up with the term *postage-due marketing*:

> In the physical world, advertisers bear the entire cost of distributing messages to the consumer. The only cost the consumer shoulders is the time it takes to consider a solicitation and either embrace or discard it.
>
> In the online world, the costs of distribution are shared between advertiser and consumer. Consumers pay a measurable fee to receive information via the global Internet—from a shell or SLIP account to a high-speed dedicated connection. Some pay hourly charges for information and some pay per message, but each Internet subscriber pays in some way for the information they receive.
>
> To fully appreciate why Postage-Due Marketing raises the ire of the global Internet community, ask yourself whether you would accept a collect call from a telemarketer or an advertising circular that arrived postage due. Or, if you spent an entire evening consumed with calls from telemarketers while you waited for an important call.

# Conclusion: A new paradigm

One of the biggest mistakes businesses make when trying to market electronically is to assume that what works in other media will also work online. As you explore the Web, you will see pages that are as gorgeous as any full-page ad in the *New Yorker or Martha Stewart Living*. Trouble is, two to ten minutes of connect time are required for the user to receive such a huge amount of data. And few will sit still for that.

Similarly, you will encounter "e-mail list brokers" who will try to sell you on the idea of doing an electronic direct mail campaign. Don't listen. Direct marketing or "junk mail" does not work on the Net. In fact, it is likely to generate extremely negative feelings toward you and your company.

There are ways to use e-mail as an extremely effective marketing tool—as you will see in the next chapter. But always bear in mind the you-approach. The Internet and the online world present an entirely different marketing challenge than anything you have experienced to date. The techniques you have been using for years in other media don't work here. So you've got to adapt and "market smart!"

# Auto-responders

## The secret marketing tool

# CHAPTER 9

IMAGINE being able to instantly bounce a description of your product or service to anyone who sends an e-mail message to an address you've put into one of your print ads . . . or included in one of your radio ads. That's exactly what an Internet auto-responder does.

This kind of feature goes by many names. But, while *mail daemon* (pronounced "demon") may be the most poetic, *auto-responder* is the most descriptive, so that's the term we'll use. The nearest equivalent in the non-online world is a *fax-on-demand* (FOD) system. FOD can be implemented a number of ways, but in its simplest form, a customer dials the phone and requests a fax by talking to a human being or by using the keys on a TouchTone phone.

FOD is a wonderful marketing tool that can nicely complement your Internet auto-responder. But it also calls for an investment of several thousand dollars. An auto-responder, in contrast, can be set up for as little as $10 a month.

And why not a Web site? Well, why not? Auto-responders and Web sites are not mutually exclusive. On the contrary, they are quite complementary. After all, the idea is to make it as easy as possible for a prospective customer to obtain information about your product or service.

The neat thing about an auto-responder is that customers don't have to make the effort to visit your Web site. The can fire off a simple e-mail message and receive your information and order form as an e-mail reply in less than a minute.

In a nutshell, World Wide Web home pages are pretty and sexy, but they require your prospect to make the effort to come to you. Auto-responder messages consist of plain, 7-bit ASCII text, but they *go directly to the customer*! Your prospect doesn't have to key in your Web address, wait while the Net makes the connection, and then search for the information that's of interest. Sending a simple e-mail message is all the prospect has to do.

In the best of all possible worlds, you would have not only a Web page but also an auto-responder and a fax-on-demand system, and they would all reference each other. But Web pages and fax-on-demand take time to implement. An auto-responder, on the other hand, can be set up today and you can include its e-mail address in your newspaper ads tomorrow.

# Geared to information distribution

The reason auto-responders are so exciting is that they perfectly mesh with the design of the Net. The Internet, after all, is not really a *transactional* medium. It's an *informational* medium. Yes, that sounds like a lot of technobabble. But think about it for just a minute. The Internet was established by the U.S. government to facilitate the flow of information among the Pentagon, defense contractors, and research labs at the nation's colleges and universities.

Once established, the Net was *developed* largely by people in the academic world. They're the one's, after all, who had the time to create and expand concepts like Archie, Gopher, and FTP. Good souls that they are, these people tend not to think in terms of capitalism and the transactions needed to make it work. Many are on record, in fact, as saying that all information should be free.

As a result, the Internet that has developed over the last 20 years is very much geared to information distribution. There are lists—and lists of lists—of informational items. There are file collections, Campus Wide Information Servers (CWIS), Veronica and Jughead search tools, and lots of other stuff—all of it designed to help you find and obtain *information*.

Not that transactional services and security measures cannot be overlaid onto the Net. But these things are really just beginning to be implemented today. In our opinion, it will be years before these issues are resolved and a universally convenient solution has been agreed upon.

##  In the LISTSERV tradition

You'll sometimes hear auto-responders referred to as *mailbots* (short for *mail robots*). As such, they are part of a long tradition on the Internet of letting computers do the work.

For example, when you want to be added to an Internet mailing list, you typically send a message to a *list server*. This is a computer running a program called LISTSERV (no final *E*). The trick is to include in the body of the message the word "subscribe" or "sub" followed by the name of the mailing list and your name.

Thus, if you were to send a message to **listserv@rmii.com** containing the line subscribe HTMARCOM Jerry Fowler, the list server at a company called Rocky Mountain Internet, Inc., would add Jerry Fowler to a mailing list called HTMARCOM so that he would be automatically sent information about High-Tech Marketing Communications.

##  And mail servers, too

Similar programs called *mail servers* also exist. Their purpose is to automatically send one or more files to your e-mail mailbox in response to your request. Sometimes, you must be sure to include some special word in the message's subject line. Sometimes you are supposed to leave that line blank and key in send followed by the directory path and exact name of the file you want.

Different mail servers support different commands, so it's important to pay attention to the specific instructions on how to use a given mail server to retrieve a particular file. (As an experiment, try sending a message to **mailserv@ds.internic.net**. Leave the subject line blank, and key in help as your message.)

##  Finally, something usable!

Mail servers like this are clever. And long-time Internet users don't mind the complexity. Frankly, many of them *thrive* on it. But

complexity of this sort just won't play with the general public. Fortunately, auto-responders represent simplicity itself. Businesspeople can now put a line like this in your ads: "To learn more, send e-mail to **info@mailback.com**."

That's it. No detailed instructions. No special "magic" words. Just a blank or one-line message (something like "Please send info" is fine) sent to an Internet e-mail address. And what will your prospects see? Often within *seconds* they will get a message back from your auto-responder containing whatever information you want them to have. The response from QuoteCom Data Service shown in Fig. 9-1 is a good example.

Figure 9-1

```
This is an automatic response to your request for information about
QuoteCom.  More extensive information may be found using:

  ftp.quote.com                  in the directory /pub/info
  email to services@quote.com    with Subject of "help"
  http://www.quote.com/
...................................................................
                     QuoteCom Data Service

QuoteCom supplies financial market data to Internet Users.  There are
four primary aspects to the QuoteCom service:

    1)  Intraday price quotes (15 minute typical delay from exchange)
        Available on demand for stocks, commodities, mutual funds,
        and other financial instruments.  Includes simple balance
        sheet data for stocks.

    2)  Portfolio tracking and reporting via email.
        Users can receive an email message at the close of each
        trading day detailing the performance of a portfolio.
        Limit alarms may be set which, when triggered, will generate
        an email message advising the user.

    3)  News and analysis.
        QuoteCom has licensed trading-oriented business news from
```

*Here's part of the first page of an auto-responder message from QuoteCom Data Service. To receive a copy yourself, send a blank message to* ***info@quote.com****.*

It could be a corporate "backgrounder" or press release. It could be your price list, plus a ready-to-print order form. Just ask yourself: If I could instantly send, say, three pages of text to any prospective customer, anywhere in the world, what would I say? (We'll share some ideas with you in a moment.)

And the cost? How does $10 a month sound? That's $120 a *year*. At those prices, you can afford to set up several auto-responders and use them to track how each individual ad is pulling.

Excuse, me—track? That's right. Different companies offer different features, but the company we use (for $10 a month) automatically sends an e-mail notification to us each time someone sends a message to our auto-responder (**books@mailback.com**).

If we were so inclined, we could use this information to develop a mailing list of people who have expressed an interest in our books. Though, as we noted in Chapter 8, you must be very careful how you use any e-mail mailing list. If we were to advertise our books and consulting services in different media, we could easily track how specific ads are pulling by using a different auto-responder address in each one (**books-wsj**, **books-nyt**, **books-pw**, etc.).

## Auto-responders to try

*Listed below are a number of auto-responders you may want to try. Just send a blank e-mail message to any of these addresses. As you review the responses, think about how you might be able to use a service like this. Also, notice that some responses contain additional auto-responder addresses you can use to obtain more specific information on some product or service.*

| | |
|---|---|
| *books@mailback.com* | *Books written by Alfred and Emily Glossbrenner (catalogue and order form)* |
| *cruise.vacation.station@reply.net* | *Cruise news, reviews, and commentary from Free Spirit Cruises and Tours.* |
| *demo@cexpress.com* | *Demonstration programs available from Computer Express.* |
| *gold@pgr-gem.com* | *Information about buying and selling gold from PGR Gems and Minerals.* |
| *info@cexpress.com* | *Hardware/software catalogue from Computer Express.* |

| | |
|---|---|
| *info@digital.com* | *Product information from Digital Equipment Corporation (DEC).* |
| *info@infomagic.com* | *Catalogue and order form for the InfoMagic CD-ROM company.* |
| *info@quote.com* | *Investment and financial news from QuoteCom Data Service.* |
| *info@stoli.com* | *Designed to whet your appetite for visiting Stoli Central, the "Web site with a twist."* |
| *info@telebase.com* | *Information about EasyNet Service (access to 250 databases).* |
| *tapes@mailback.com* | *Great deals on blank cassette and DAT tapes from Cassette House.* |

## But more than a little hard to find

Once again, the truly new development in this area is the opportunity to deliver information to your prospects **instantly** in response to a simple, blank or one-line message sent to your auto-responder address.

It's entirely possible that your Internet service provider can set you up with this option. But we've found that most ISPs are so bedazzled by the World Wide Web that they aren't even aware of the auto-responder feature. More fools they, since we've been by told programmer friends that the coding for auto-responders is extraordinarily simple.

# How to pick an auto-responder vendor

So what do you do? You might want to start by contacting directly or visiting the Web sites of several companies that specialize in offering auto-responder service. (See the nearby sidebar for some suggestions.) Read their materials. Test some of the auto-responders they've set up

for their clients to see how fast the information arrives in your mailbox.

Make your first stop the Mailback Auto-Responder Service operated by DataBack Systems and use it as your benchmark. This is the system we selected for our own auto-responder after researching the field. We've been with them for over a year, and they are truly excellent.

We should note that although DataBack Systems has a policy of crediting a free month of service for each new customer who mentions your name upon signing up, we have asked them to suspend that policy in our case. So when we extol the virtues of their Mailback service, it's not for financial gain.

Mailback really is a good system. To see for yourself, point your browser at **http://www.mailback.com** and spend 10 to 15 minutes exploring. Print out the pages you encounter that detail the services offered and prices charged, and use them as your yardstick for judging other auto-responder services.

## Auto-responder companies

*These companies all offer auto-responder services. Visit the Web sites shown here to explore each company's offerings in detail. Or try the auto-responder addresses to see how quickly each company gets its product and pricing information to you.*

*Cuenet Systems*
*Interactive Internet E-mail Solutions*
*P.O. Box 1134*
*Ben Lomond, CA 95005*
*408-867-5374*
***cuenet-info@cue.com***
***http://www.cuenet.com***

*Cybercon, Inc.*
*149 Glenbarr Court*
*St. Louis, MO 63088*
*314-861-0270 (voice)*
*314-861-2175 (fax)*
***info@CyberconInc.com***
***http://www.CyberconInc.com***

*Electronic News Network (ENN)*
*6711 Glenray Drive*
*Houston, TX 77084-1067*
***enn@phoenix.net***
***http://www.phoenix.net/~enn***

*Mailback Auto-Responder Service*
*DataBack Systems*
*13230 S.W. Thatcher Drive*
*Beaverton, OR 97008*
*508-817-2379*
***info@mailback.com***
***http://www.mailback.com***

*ReplyNet*
*Box 7607*
*Gaithersburg, MD 20898*
*800-210-2220*
*301-930-3011*
***info@reply.net***
***http://www.reply.net***

# Other considerations

Certainly there's an explanation somewhere. But you would think that—with the open and easy access to information offered by the Internet—a "perfect" market would quickly develop in which all consumers are aware of all vendors' prices. And that, as a result, prices and offerings would rapidly converge around a rather narrow range. But that has not happened with Web pages, nor has it happened with auto-responders. At least not yet.

We have looked, and as far as we're concerned, you can confidently use the prices and policies offered by DataBack Systems as your guide. DataBack, for example, does not levy a *metering charge* under which you agree to pay a fee for each quantum of characters transmitted.

This kind of charge is justifiable only when you're sending out large documents to thousands of people each day. If your auto-responder is mailing out a response of 10K or less to one or two hundred people a

day—we all should be so lucky—there is no justification for a metering charge.

To put 10K in perspective, assume 65-character lines and 56 lines per single-spaced page. At one byte per character, including spaces, that works out to 3,640 bytes per page. So you will need between 9,000 and 10,000 bytes (9K to 10K) for messages equivalent to two-and-a-half single-spaced pages.

That may well be enough. You don't want to overwhelm your prospect, after all. In any case, a 10K maximum on message size is quite workable.

## FireCrystal tips on preparing your message

*Through FireCrystal Communications, your co-authors offer a consulting service to businesses interested in making money on the Internet. You may think you can prepare and format an effective auto-responder message on your own, and of course, you can.*

*That is exactly what most current auto-responder users have done—and it shows. As more people discover this technique, the competition for a customer's attention will grow. After all, an auto-responder can easily deliver your message—the trick is in getting the recipient to read it!*

*This is something we're pretty good at. Over the years, we've helped clients ranging from Michelin to Merrill Lynch. If you need our help, by all means contact us. We'd be delighted to explore the possibilities with you.*

*Meantime, here's our advice for creating a truly effective auto-responder piece:*

***Step 1**. Make your message visually appealing. Good copywriting is important, but visual appeal in this medium is even more so.*

*We recommend keeping your text to no more than five pages. Indent the copy 10 spaces on each side, with margins set at 10 and 75. Use the business-letter style of single-spaced paragraphs separated by a single blank line. (See Fig. 9-1 for an example. The folks at QuoteCom Data Service do it right!)*

*Try to think in terms of points you can set off with bullets (lowercase o), and indent and align for attractiveness.*

***Step 2****. If you haven't already done so, get yourself a really good advertising copywriter. Take the time to meet with the writer. Present your current print materials (brochures, catalogues, press releases, etc.), and explain which products, features, and benefits you feel are most important.*

*The copywriter may or may not agree with you. But that's okay. There's nothing like a disagreement to help you take a fresh look at something.*

***Step 3****. A fresh look is so important, we've made it Step 3. Don't make the mistake of simply transcribing your current print materials. As your copywriter will tell you, every medium is different.*

*Long, detailed letters may work with direct mail, but they're not appropriate for e-mail responses. On the other hand, you're not laboring under the space constraints of a magazine ad. And you can assume that since the customers are coming to you, they really want some solid information.*

***Step 4****. Insist that your auto-responder text end with an order form. Include the traditional Internet "cut here" line, and make the form the kind of thing someone can easily print out, fill in, and then send to you via regular mail.*

*And don't forget to include your land address, toll-free phone, regular phone, fax number, and regular Internet e-mail address. You want to make it as easy and convenient as possible for customers to get in touch with you.*

***Step 5****. Test it yourself. When you've got your message prepared, e-mail it to your auto-responder provider. Then, when you know for certain that your provider has activated your responder, sign on to a system—any system—and send a blank message to your auto-responder address.*

*Take the you-approach once again and pretend that you are a customer who has responded to an e-mail address in one of your company's print ads. If you don't like what you see, make sure that corrections and modifications are made.*

# Conclusion: Tell the world

We think you will find an auto-responder to be the single most effective marketing tool on the Net because it makes the fewest demands on your prospect. It comes to them! They don't have to drum their fingers waiting for a connection to your Web site. And, of course, you're not limited to just one auto-responder. The cost is so low that you can easily afford to set one up for each major product category.

But, whether you've got one auto-responder or a dozen, none of them will do you any good until you spread the word.

All of your print, radio, and TV ads should include a line telling people to hit your auto-responder. And if you don't currently do any advertising, maybe the introduction of your auto-responder would be an effective focus for an ad. You'll also want to take maximum advantage of Internet *search engines* and the free listings available in various Internet directories. Plus you should plan on regularly posting discrete announcements in the appropriate Internet newsgroups and Big Three SIGs or forums.

As it happens, telling the world is precisely what we're going to show you how to do as we cover these and related topics in Part 3. But first, we'll show you how to set up your "point of presence" on the World Wide Web in the very next chapter.

# 10

# Setting up your web site

# CHAPTER 10

NOW we come to it. Now we all take on the incredible task of putting up a World Wide Web home page and establishing a "point of presence" on the global Internet. E-mail, auto-responders, and the rest are fine, but this—this is the big leagues.

Perhaps. But if putting up a Web page is such a big deal, how is it that huge numbers of high school students—and many kids in elementary school—already have their own, personal World Wide Web home pages? And don't say "Oh, well, kids these days were brought up with computers . . ." as if that implied the existence of some kind of special knowledge that one can no longer absorb past the age of 14.

The fact is, Web pages are simple. They are far less complicated than the information you have already absorbed in reading this book. Remember: A World Wide Web page is nothing but a text file that contains not only informational text but also pointers or references to graphic image files and instructions on how both text and images should be displayed. (For a refresher, turn back to Figs. 5-1 and 5-2).

## There is no "magic"

The "magic" of a Web page is solely in the hands of the browser software a person uses to access it. Indeed, we almost hate to burst the bubble, but think about this for just a moment. The Macintosh and Microsoft Windows have long been able to display graphic image files. And they have long had the ability to display text using different fonts, typefaces, point sizes, and all that.

So what's the big deal about some browser program that runs under the Macintosh or Windows system and displays images and text in various fonts pumped in from a remote online system?

The answer is that there *is* no big deal. You log onto a Web site and that site begins sending you text and individual graphic image files. Your browser program does the rest. It basically assembles the various text and image components of a given Web page and displays them on your screen.

That's really all there is to it. Where the game is won or lost is in the decisions you make about how many images you include and how big they should be, and the text you choose to present, and the hotlinks and other features the page contains.

## Three considerations

Entire books are devoted to putting up a World Wide Web page. But in the end, it all boils down to three main points: First deciding how you are going to create the page. Second, what the page will contain. And third, how you will make the page available to Internet users.

Running through each of these considerations is the question of whether you pay someone to do it for you, or do it yourself. We'll lay out all the major options here, but we should tell you that our bias is always to "Do what you do best and hire out the rest."

Even if each of us were capable of producing a Web page as dazzling as anything a top consultant could create for us, there is still the cost of our *time*. The time you spend mastering HTML coding is likely to be time that you are not spending growing your business or playing with your kids. All to save a few bucks.

## Options for creating a Web page

That said, we must acknowledge that books about HTML programming have been appearing for months now on the *Publisher's Weekly* list of computer-book bestsellers, right up there with *Open Heart Surgery for Dummies* and titles of that sort. Clearly, a substantial number of people are interested in creating their own Web pages. So that's where we'll begin.

You can create a Web page HTML file with nothing but Windows Notepad and an HTML reference sheet. The only reason to use Notepad is that, like all *text editors*, it automatically saves files as plain 7-bit ASCII text. You can use any word processor to create an HTML file, as long as you remember to save the file as ASCII text.

# Rolling your own

If you decide to create your own page, consider doing things this way: Start by pointing your browser at **http://www.mailback.com** and clicking on the "Painless Web Pages" option at the bottom of the screen. That will take you to a nicely written set of instructions on how to proceed, including the suggestion that you click to obtain one or more sample page *templates*. There is also a link to a "Helpful Pointers" page that offers links to inexpensive Web page design services.

Naturally, DataBack Systems, the creator of this site, would like to sell you on putting your painless Web page on its system. But you can get the templates they offer, fill them in, and put them on some other hosting system. You're under no obligation, in other words.

Or you might use your account on one of the Big Three:

- On America Online, specify the keyword "Personal Publisher."
- On CompuServe, go to WebCentral and select "Home Pages."
- On Prodigy, jump to "Personal Web Pages."

At these locations, you will be given instructions for putting up a Web page on each of these services. Note that, at this writing, AOL is the only system that permits commercial Web sites, but you can certainly practice on any system, and none of the Big Three charges for this service.

## Tips for creating your own HTML code

*It's inevitable that one day everyone will use WYSIWYG ("what you see is what you get," pronounced "wissy-wig") Web-page-creation software tools. But at this writing, such packages are just coming into general use. The typical do-it-yourselfer must prepare the HTML text file first and then switch to a browser program to view it.*

*In Netscape, for example, you would click on "File" and then "Open File" to display your work, leave Netscape running as you switch to your text editor window to make changes, then Alt-Tab back to*

*Netscape and click on "Reload" to bring in the latest version of your file.*

*Fortunately, you are not alone when you set out to create your own page. Not to put too fine a point on it, on the Web, everything is up for grabs. So when you're surfing the Web and you find an image you like, click on your right mouse button (assuming you are using Netscape) to save a copy to disk.*

*Similarly, when you see a page or a feature that you find impressive, "capture the code" by saving the page to disk as an HTML file (click on "File" and then "Save"). Or click on "View" and then "Source" to take a look at the underlying HTML code. In effect, you can use other Web sites to create your own customizable template file.*

## Home Page Construction Kit & other tools

*As you would expect, the Net and the Web are brimful of software, images, and other tools designed to help the average person create a Web home page. One of the best places to start is at the site of the Home Page Construction Kit created by Ellie Cutler and John Labovitz. The site is one of the Global Network Navigator (GNN) offerings, and you'll find it at this address:*

***http://nearnet.gnn.com/gnn/netizens/construction.html***

*At this site you will be able to click on topics like "Publishing a Home Page," "Home Page Template," and "Sample Home Pages." You should definitely download the sample Home Page Template and play around with it. You'll be amazed at how easy it is to modify the template to create your own page, and to give it a totally different look and feel by making relatively simple changes to the template file.*

*You'll probably find just about everything you need for creating your first Web page at the Home Page Construction Kit. But when you're ready to move beyond the basics, pay a visit to one or both of these sites, where you'll find HTML tutorials, editors, graphics, and other resources:*

- *The Web Developer's Virtual Library*
  ***http://www.stars.com***
- *HTML Authoring Tools and Guides*
  ***http://infoweb.magi.com/~eblair/htmlg.html***

*You might also use Yahoo! or Infoseek to locate* A Beginner's Guide to HTML *from NCSA (National Center for Supercomputing Applications). Or work your way through the Yahoo! directory, clicking on "Computers and Internet," then "Software," then "Data Formats," then "HTML," and finally "Guides and Tutorials."*

*You will also find archives and collections of images, icons, flags, graphics, and logos—all of which you can download and incorporate into your page—at these sites:*

- *Images, Icons, and Flags*
  ***http://white.nosc.mil/images.html***
- *WWW Icons and Logos*
  ***http://www-ns.rutgers.edu/doc-images***
- *Terry Gould's Graphics*
  ***http://www.netaccess.on.ca/~kestrel/list.html***
- *Tony's Icon Collection*
  ***http://www.bsdi.com/icons/tonys.html***

## Word processor HTML converters

The latest versions of leading word processors like WordPerfect and Microsoft Word have the ability to save anything you create as an HTML file. The resulting Web page may not be "cutting edge" in its features, but it's a start.

If you have older versions of word processing software packages, you may be able to take a slightly different route. You may find that you can create a document and then run a special program or add-on that will *convert* the document into an HTML file. Here are the programs to look for if you are a Microsoft Word or WordPerfect user:

- Microsoft's Internet Assistant for MS Word
  **http://www.microsoft.com/MSOffice/Word/ia**
- Quarterdeck's WebAuthor for MS Word
  **http://www.qdeck.com**
- Internet Publisher for WordPerfect
  **http://wp.novell.com/elecpub/intpub.htm**

## Non-WYSIWYG HTML editors

Programs designed to convert word processor files work, but they don't give you as much hands-on control over the results as the next step up, namely, HTML editors. HTML editors let you create the text of your page and then add HTML tags selected from a toolbar or drop-down menu.

Many of the programs in this category are either free or offered as shareware. Here's a starter list of programs and where to find them:

- HotDog
  **http://www.sausage.com**
- HoTMetaL Pro (freeware version)
  **http://www.sq.com/products/hotmetal/hmp-org.htm**
- HTML Assistant Pro
  **http://fox.nstn.ca/~harawitz**
- HTML Easy!
  **http://www.seed.net.tw/~milkylin**
- HTMLed
  **http://www.ist.ca/htmled**

And for Macintosh users:

- World Wide Web Weaver
  **http://www.northnet.org/best**
- BBEDit
  **http://www.uji.es/bbedit-html-extensions.html**

## WYSIWYG HTML editors

Unfortunately, HTML editors of this sort usually have no facilities for *viewing* the Web page you are creating. To do that, you must switch to your browser and load the page you are working on as a file. Cumbersome, to say the least.

Fortunately, an entirely new category of software is being introduced as you read this—graphical *Web authoring programs*. These packages let you create pages as if you were painting a picture. You can insert, grab, and move the elements of your Web page and see the effects instantly.

Here's a list of several of the leading programs at this writing:

**PageMill** from Adobe, Inc.
Macintosh available now, Windows coming soon, $99
800-441-8657
**http://www.adobe.com**

**Spider** from InContext Systems, Inc.
Windows, $99
800-263-0127
**http://www.incontext.com**

**FrontPage** from Microsoft Corp.
Windows, $695
800-426-9400
**http://www.microsoft.com**

**Internet Assistant** from Microsoft Corp.
Windows 95, Free
800-426-9400
**http://www.microsoft.com**

**WebAuthor** from Quarterdeck Corp.
Windows, $49.95
800-683-6696
**http://www.qdeck.com**

**HoTMetaL Pro** from SoftQuaid, Inc.
Windows and Macintosh, $195
800-387-2777
**http://www.sq.com**

## Hire a Webmaster!

Certainly all of the tools cited so far work to one degree or another. But, as you know, we feel quite strongly that businesspeople should do

what they do best; advertising professionals should do what they do best; and plumbers, electricians, carpenters, and others should concentrate on their chosen trades.

You might be the smartest person in the world, with vast stores of previously untapped talents for graphic design and computer programming. But there are still only 24 hours in a day. Regardless of your talents, do you really think you should be spending much time sweating over the HTML code for a Web page? Wouldn't it be better to spend your time growing your business and pay an expert to create your page?

And here's a real kicker. HTML can implement the basics of a page. But if you want *forms* for your visitors to fill out, and if you want users to be able to search your database or do other truly cool things, you'll have to learn to write CGI-BIN scripts as well. That raises the bar to an entirely new level.

## How to find a Web consultant

So let's assume that you've decided to follow our advice. Let's assume you've decided that you have no business trying to replace the transmission in your car, install a new high-efficiency furnace in your home, or design your own Web page.

The next question is: Where can I find a qualified Webmaster or consultant? The answer is that finding a competent, compatible, reasonably priced Web design consultant can be a challenge. There are no standards, no official requirements or qualifications. Anyone can claim to be a Webmaster. Anyone can get listed in a directory of consultants.

Fortunately, an old Bible verse can be of help here: "By their works shall ye know them." This is a very, very new profession, but you can bet that the really good Webmasters have put up several pages for clients that you can go visit yourself.

Not that you should rule out people who are just starting—you may well find that your neighbor's teenage daughter or son can create a

page for you that will knock the stuffings out of a professional's best effort. But at least you can start with the pros. In fact, you might even want to start with your local ISP. Call the company's sales office and ask if they can recommend someone who can design a Web site for you.

## Using a consultant directory

One way to come up with a list of potential consultants is to use an online directory. Another, and certainly not mutually exclusive technique, is to visit outstanding Web sites and find out who created them. Let's start with the directory option.

You might point your browser at **http://www.yahoo.com** and work your way through the Yahoo! menus until you get to an entry for Internet consultants. Or you might simply search the Yahoo! index for "consultant" or "webmaster."

But you should probably start with CommerceNet. CommerceNet maintains one of the leading searchable directories of Internet consultants. So point your browser at this address:

**http://www.commerce.net/directories/consultants /consultants.html**

That will take you to a page offering alphabetical listings and other items. But the one to choose is "structured database search" near the bottom of the page under the heading "How to Find What You Need."

The structured database search page that will appear will lead you to believe that you can easily call up a list of all the consultants in, say, your state. Not so. The search engine is very poor, and CommerceNet apparently permits consultants to enter their state names as "Pennsylvania," "Pa.," "PA" and every other variation you can imagine. Unless you search on every possible variation, you won't get all the consultants in your state.

So do this instead: Search on *area code* or *ZIP code*. If you want to find consultants in the 412 area code, key in *412* (the asterisks will

make sure that you get entries for "(412)" as well as "412"). If you want to find people in the ZIP codes beginning with 190, key in 190.

Your search will yield a list of company names. Click on one, and you'll see screens like those shown in Figs. 10-1 and 10-2. Notice that these screens give you contact information first, followed by a discussion of special skills and talents and a list of company references.

Figure 10-1

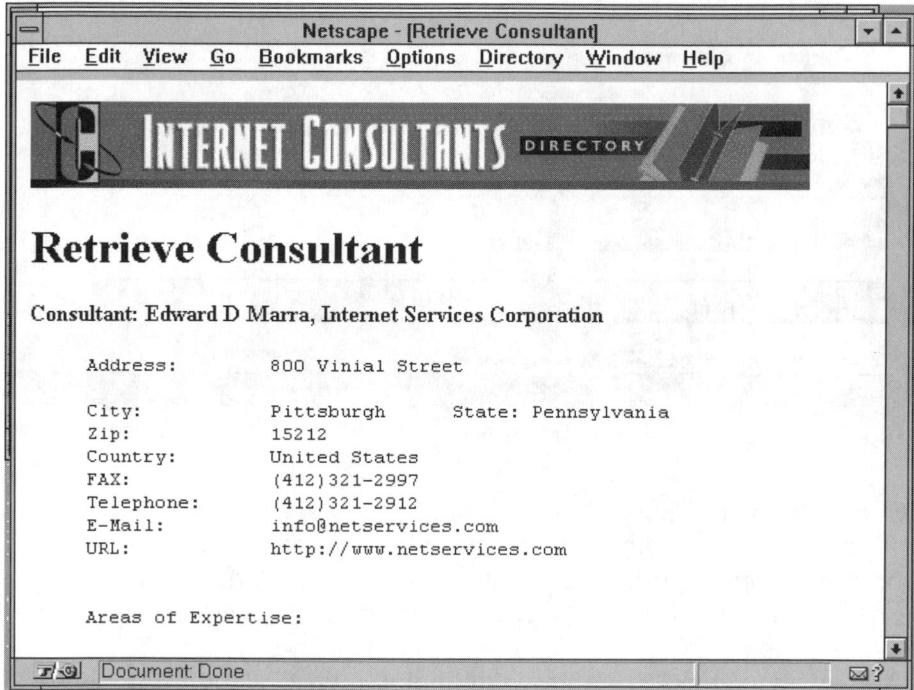


*A consultant in the 412 area code.*

##  Does location matter?

Some readers are undoubtedly scratching their heads wondering why we might suggest that the geographical location of a Webmaster/consultant might matter. It doesn't, of course. There is no reason why you and a Webmaster cannot be thousands of miles apart, never meet in person, and still produce a dazzling Web page.

Figure 10-2

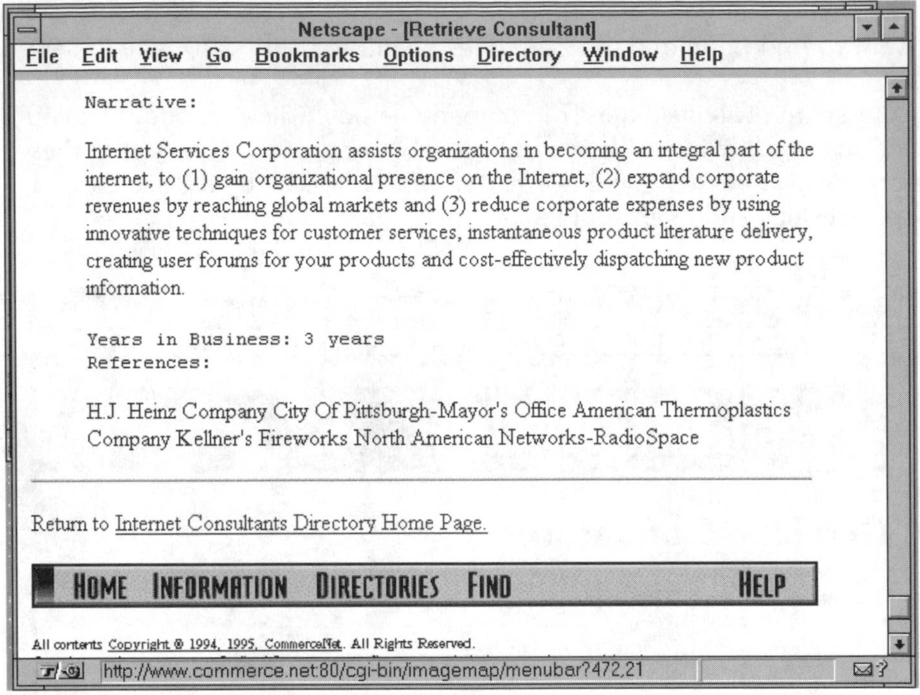


*And the rest of the consultant's story.*

It's just that we have used ad agencies in the past, and we have found that it is so much easier to sit down with an account executive, a copywriter, and a graphic designer, have a cup of coffee, and "brainstorm" an ad. A long-distance conference call just isn't the same.

That's why we tend to lean toward finding a local Webmaster whom you can visit and chat with in person. "No, that doesn't look very good. What would happen if we moved the graphic here?" "Wait a minute, suppose we used a smaller font and highlighted this in color?" You can get to the same place working with a remote consultant, but you'll never be able to do so as fast.

Still, if you live in Tampa and the Webmaster whose work you like is in Chicago, there is no reason why you can't do business. That's why we suggest that you consider searching for your Webmaster by visiting really good Web sites and finding out who created them.

### Where to look for award-winning Web sites

*If you're going to spend time looking at Web sites, it makes sense to zero in on the very best ones. Trouble is, there are so many lists of "best sites" or "award-winning sites" on the Net that it can be difficult to know where to begin. Plus the fact that, in many cases, an organization's list of great sites changes daily, and it's often none too clear just what criteria were used to evaluate the sites.*

*That's why we like the three "best" lists presented here. These organizations present their awards annually, and each is quite clear about who is making the selections and on what basis:*

- *100 Best Business Web Sites*
  ***http://techweb.cmp.com/ia/13issue/13hot100.html***
  *The 100 best business sites, selected by the editors of Interactive Age based on design, content, effective use of hotlinks, and ease of use.*
- *Tenagra Awards for Internet Marketing Excellence*
  ***http://arganet.tenagra.com/Tenagra/awards.html***
  *A small number of awards made annually by a panel of Internet marketing experts to recognize innovation as well as financial and public relations successes in Internet marketing.*
- *GNN Best of the Net Awards*
  ***http://gnn.com/wic/botn/index.html***
  *Global Network Navigator's annual awards for outstanding Web sites in ten categories (Arts and Entertainment, Computers, Food and Wine, Interactive Sites, Internet Navigation, K-12 Education, Literature, Personal Finance, Sports, and Travel).*

## Visiting great sites, and taking names!

We suggest that you start with the "best" lists discussed in the nearby sidebar. Go to each site, and let curiosity be your guide. Remember, you're looking for good, creative Web work, not for pages that apply to your particular business. Almost all Webmasters sign their pages, usually in small print at the very bottom.

For example, we visited the Peachpit Press home page. As you can see in Fig. 10-3, the very last line on the page reads "Site maintained by Point of Presence Company." Since this is a clickable link, we

Figure 10-3

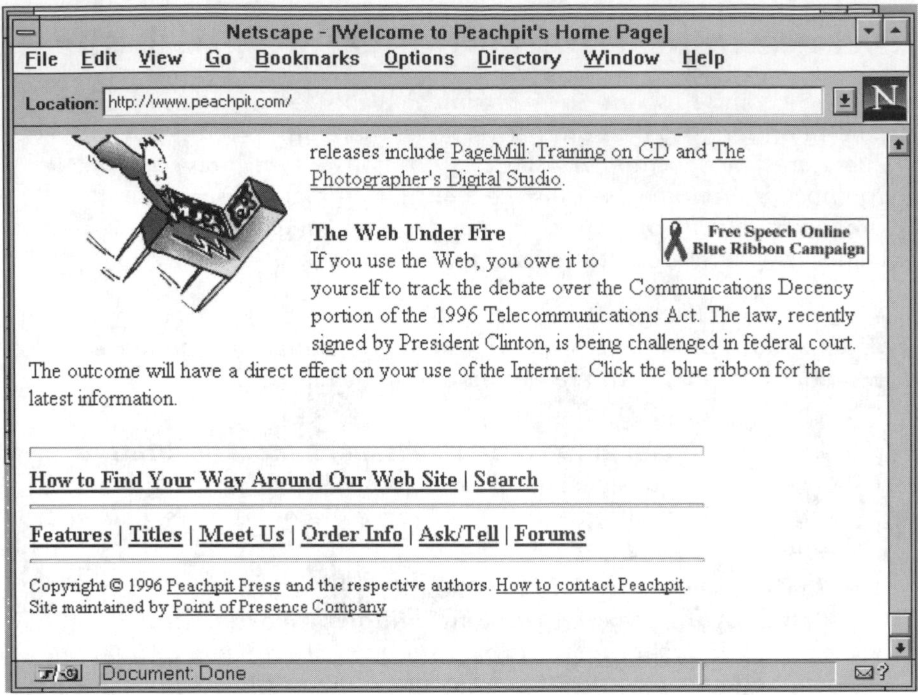


*A page "signed" by the Point of Presence Company.*

clicked, and were taken to the page shown in Fig. 10-4. Notice that the firm makes it easy for you to contact them by regular mail, phone, fax, and e-mail. That's followed by links to "Services," "Clients," "Contact," and "Internet Marketing."

Keep in mind that you can print pages by clicking on "File" and then "Print." Or save them as text files by clicking on "File" and then "Save As." So it's easy to capture the information you need about a given Webmaster. And, whether you are viewing an award-winning page or a Webmaster's own home page, you can make it easy to return the next time if you add the page to your Bookmarks (or Hot Links or Favorite Places, if you use a browser other than Netscape).

When you identify someone you want to work with, you will definitely want a contract. Make sure that, among other things, the contract spells out who owns the material placed at your site; how often the site will be updated and by whom; and how any queries, orders, or

Figure 10-4

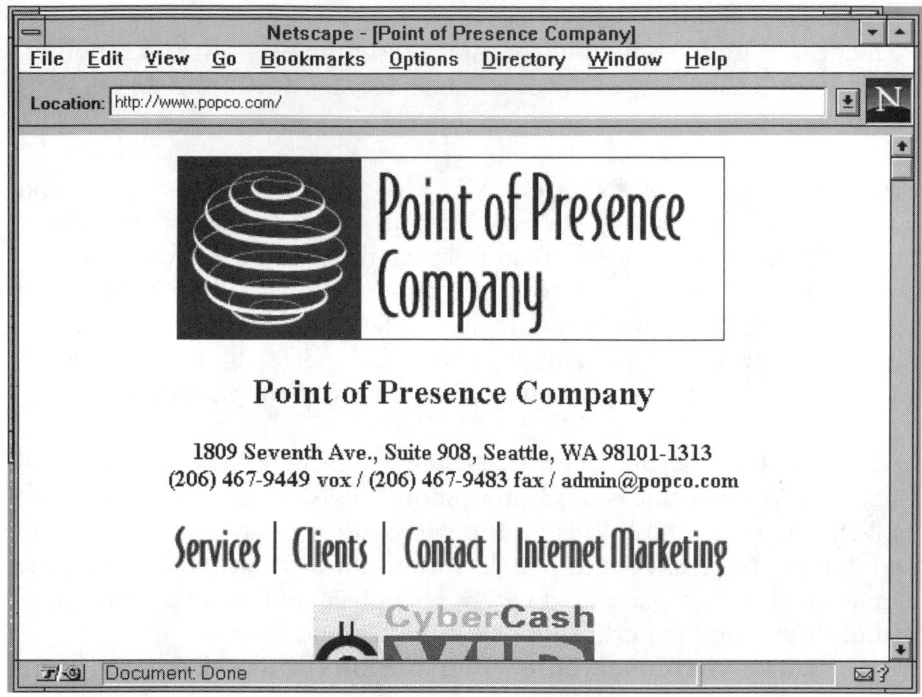


*The Point of Presence Company's home page.*

other traffic generated by the site will be handled. Don't forget that someone is going to have to manage and update the site, so you will probably have an on-going relationship with your Webmaster.

# Wilson Internet Services—a great example

You need to explore good Web sites. And if you're new to the Internet, you need to explore them in-depth. As you visit sites, make a note or two on what you like and might want to incorporate into your own site. And as we suggested, add good sites to your Bookmark list to make it easy to return.

But don't select your Webmaster until you have visited Wilson Internet Services at **http://www.wilsonweb.com** and taken a look at that

company's description of services and price list for "Standard Web Site Packages." The information is clearly presented and offers a range of options for businesses and professionals looking for affordable Web design services.

Prices for creating pages start at $275 for a single "Starter" page and go up to $1,895 for the "Deluxe" 20-page package. These are one-time fees, and of course, they do not include the $50 a month or so you will have to pay an ISP to rent space on a system. We suggest that you print out all of the "Standard Web Site Packages" information and use it as a yardstick for evaluating other Webmaster fees. To reach this page directly, go to **http://www.wilsonweb.com/packages**.

You should also be sure to print and read "12 Web Page Design Decisions Your Business or Organization Will Need to Make." In clear, well-written text, Ralph Wilson, the company's founder, discusses site and domain names, how to handle various kinds of graphics, the basic elements of a Web page, and more. This piece will turn you into an instant Web page expert. To reach it directly, go to **http://www.wilsonweb.com/rfwilson/smallbus/12design.htm**.

# Page design and content

Now let's turn to the second major consideration: What will your page contain and what design features will it use?

Probably the biggest mistake people make here is in not fully appreciating the fact that the Internet and the World Wide Web truly are "new media." This has at least two implications. First, it leads one to conclude that a Web page is just like a page in a printed magazine. So companies, many of whom should know better, load their Web sites with lots of large, lush color photos laced with nothing but conventional advertising. And they wonder why people aren't flocking to their sites.

The second implication of not understanding that this is a new medium is a failure to exploit its features. For example, if you don't make sure that your e-mail address is a clickable link on your home page—so that

your customers can instantly send you mail—then you are not getting all that you should out of your Web page investment. Ditto if you don't include your auto-responder address.

If you're going to make the most of the tools at hand, you've got to get some hands-on experience seeing how others have used them. Which is why we've been urging you to do some major Web surfing throughout this chapter.

## Simplicity, simplicity, simplicity

Developing a sense of the Web will also give you the self-confidence to resist the next major pitfall—complexity. Here's what's happening and what you're likely to find when you set out to hire a Webmaster.

Netscape Communications and Microsoft Corporation are in the midst of a knock-down, drag-out battle to determine who will control the standards that will govern World Wide Web software. One weapon in this war is the rapid introduction of new features that only your company's browser program can handle. Not for nothing do you see messages like "This site looks best with Netscape," on the pages you visit.

Combine this business imperative with the youthful exuberance of most Web site programmers, and the next thing you know, your Webmaster will be pitching you on dividing your screen into *frames* and *ledges*. For the record, a *frame* is a window that can be resized and scrolled. Each frame can display a different URL. A *ledge* is a frame that cannot be scrolled. Think of it as a billboard that remains visible regardless of where a user goes in any frame.

You'll also hear about forms, scripts, embedded Java applets, Live Objects, RealAudio sound files, and QuickTime movies. And someone is sure to suggest using 3-D images and VRML (Virtual Reality Markup Language). To which we say, "Hold it! Full stop and reset to zero."

Certainly you can applaud the enthusiasm from which this flows. And there is no doubt but that folks like these really *can* deliver. But there are at least three reasons for keeping it simple.

First, as with any other project, it is best to start small, work out the kinks, and only gradually add features as necessary. Second, most of these features truly *aren't* necessary. As we pointed out in Chapter 3, most graphic images you encounter convey no information. They exist merely as design elements. Third, as we've also pointed out before, most of today's Web surfers don't have the high-speed connections and powerful computers needed to make advanced features workable.

# Major-league Web page design tips

Yes, it does seem as though we're always telling you to "do this" and "don't do that." But, then again, that's what you're paying us for. Please know, however, that we are well aware of the quantity of information we've sent your way. And no one can blame you if you're feeling a bit overwhelmed and maybe even bewildered.

Hang in there. One of the wonderful features of *this* medium is that you can easily jump backwards and forwards and reread paragraphs, with no need for computers, mice, or software.

## Establish your goal or master plan from the start

Clearly, you have to explore the Web to have any sense at all of whether it is right for you. But having done that, it is crucial to take the time to really think about what you want to accomplish with a Web site. Equally important, you must think about how your site fits in with your other advertising or customer-relations activities.

Putting up a Web page is not life-and-death. As we've said, you can get out for several hundred dollars. But why bother spending even that, let alone your time, if the page is just going to sit there? The days when it was cool to tell fellow cocktail party guests or golfing buddies that, "Oh, yes. We're on the Web," are over.

Today, if your Web site and Internet presence are not part of a grand strategy, if the word *synergy* doesn't appear in your master plan for your site, you're nowhere.

## Plan for frequent updates

You know our rule about "keeping it fresh." Well here's where the pedal meets the metal. Once you've decided that your business can benefit from putting up a Web page, you should focus on how that page will be updated with fresh material. This is an important factor in how your page is designed and coded. You want to make it as easy as possible to update your page as often as you like.

This fact must be conveyed to your Webmaster. And, for your part, you've got to think about assigning someone the job of updating the page. And, by the way, who will be responsible for *promptly* replying to e-mail letters and queries generated by the site? Prompt replies are absolutely essential to making customers feel that they and you really are interacting and participating. A delay of more than a day in getting back to someone is simply unacceptable.

## Give back to the Net!

"Give back to the Net!" is another way of saying both "Take the you-approach" and "Make it worth the trip." No one's going to go to your site to receive a sales pitch. At the same time, no one expects you to put up a page out of the goodness of your heart. Of course they expect you to offer goods or services, but not as part of an "in your face" sales effort.

Keep in mind that a Web site does not have to be a sales site. You might create one to provide customer service, or merely to create goodwill. If you are going to sell, the trick is to create the proper ratio between free "goodies" and your sales message. And the goal, frankly, should be to create a good feeling about your firm in the customer's mind.

For example, how many times have you seen a TV commercial that was so funny or so well done that you rewound your videotape to watch it again? This is a commercial, now, not some delicious bit from *Seinfeld*.

You may or may not be in the market for the product being advertised, but you surely have a good feeling for the company that makes it. And, all things being equal, if you did need whatever was being advertised, you would be predisposed to give that company your business. You might even be willing to pay a few dollars more for it.

That's the kind of feeling you want your Web site to generate on the part of your prospective customers. As you conceive your Web site, forget about sales. Instead, ask yourself, "What would my ideal customers find funny, useful, practical, or amusing?" Give it to them, and then add a link that lets them go to a page with information about you, your company, your business philosophy, your products, and how to order or how to get more information.

In essence, make your main goal to create a page that offers Net users something entertaining, or something of interest or of value, with sales being a secondary concern. Quizzes, contests, trivia, a joke-of-the-day—there are all kinds of creative ways to develop that all-important interactive relationship with your customer that only the Web and the Net make possible.

## Keep it fresh

In our opinion, the very best, most productive use of a Web or Internet presence is the opportunity to quickly, easily, and cheaply build a relationship with your customer. That's a lot of what "giving back to the Net" is all about, of course. But "giving back" is more in the area of projecting a particular image of an open-handed, you-approach company. "Keeping it fresh," in contrast, is about building long-term customer relationships.

Here's the goal: You want your prospects and customers to make your site a regular weekly destination. (Heck, "daily" if you can manage it, but that takes a lot of work.) And you certainly want them to "bookmark" you by adding your URL to their list of Bookmarks or Favorite Places.

To do this, you or someone else must become the Web equivalent of a TV or radio producer or magazine editor. You've got to line up guests or persuade people to contribute articles. You've got to think about adding new, special features. And, most important of all, you've got to *tell* visitors about these coming attractions. You need a button called "Coming Next Week," for example, that will link browsers to a page describing what will be appearing at your site next week, thus giving them a concrete reason to return.

## Test it yourself

Finally, before you allow any kind of public announcement of your site, test the thing yourself. Get your friends, relatives, and business associates to test it, too. Then listen to what they say, for at this point, you are likely to be too close to the project to see it objectively.

Ask your testers if the graphics appear quickly enough. If not, your Webmaster may be able to reduce the "color depth" of each image. Can your testers find their way around intuitively? If not, you might need to think about providing a "map" of your site on the very first page.

Did anyone express a desire to be able to conduct a search of your site? If so, you might want to consider adding a simple search engine designed to help users quickly get to the section of your site of greatest interest to them.

Finally, one can no longer assume that users will enter your site on Page 1 and thus receive your overview and site orientation. With commercial search engines like Alta Vista, Infoseek, and the others discussed in Chapter 11, someone could easily click on a link presented by such features and be transported to your Page 5, instead of Page 1. Therefore, it is a good idea to make sure that each and every page of your site contains a button labelled "Home" or "Home Page" so that visitors can easily find your introductory information.

If you fail to do this, there is no way for someone who lands on your site's Page 5 to get to Page 1. The "Go, Back" sequence in Netscape and similar browsers only tracks the pages you have already visited during a given online session. Thus, if you start at a site's Page 5, there is no way to use this Netscape feature to "go back" to the site's Page 1.

## Putting up the page

Finally, there is the consideration of how best to make your page available to Internet users. There are really just two options. You can either do it yourself or you can pay someone to provide a *hosting service* for you.

We strongly advise against trying to do it yourself, even if yours is a huge company. This is because designing, testing, and creating a Web site is one problem, and setting up the physical connections to make that site accessible is quite another. Both represent major challenges, so start with the creation of your Web site. Only after it is working well, consider setting things up in-house. You may feel differently, but in our opinion, this applies regardless of the resources and talent that reside in your information systems department.

## Doing it yourself

For the record, if you do decide to do it all, all at once, you should expect to hire a consultant who can serve as a general contractor at a rate of $725 to $2,000 per week, plus all travel, lodging, and other expenses. Said consultant will almost certainly specialize in the hardware side of things. The person will probably hire, and bill you for, a Web page designer.

You will need a computer to act as your Web *server*, and that system and a round-the-clock connection to the Internet will cost between $10,000 and $35,000. There are also monthly fees for connecting to the Net ranging from $500 to $2,000, depending on the speed of the line.

You'll also need to buy a DSU/CSU (Digital Service Unit or Channel Service Unit) for about $2,500. And you may need a router to connect the Internet to your local area network (LAN). Add another $2,500 or so.

In short, doing everything yourself is complicated and expensive. And largely unnecessary. That's why our advice is to focus on your Web page design and content first. Get it hosted on some system. And then consider whether it is worthwhile to bring everything in house.

## The role of a hosting system

As we have said before, it is important to grasp the fact that a Web page consists of nothing more than an HTML text file and whatever graphic image files the main HTML summons. If it suits you to do so, you can have the page created by a Webmaster in Vermont and put it up on a system in Texas. In other words, there is no necessary connection between the company that creates the page and the company that runs the hosting system that makes it available to Internet users.

You could have your e-mail mailbox on one system, your auto-responder on another, and your World Wide Web page on a third system. The main reason for *not* doing so can be summarized in the phrase "domain name." This may or may not be important to you, but in the best of all possible worlds, if your company is Widgets, Inc., then, as we have said before, your Web site URL should be **http://www.widgets.com**, and your auto-responder should be **info@widgets.com**, and your e-mail should be in the form **tom@widgets.com**.

The twist is that the domain name address **widgets.com** can be housed at only one specific Internet service provider. This is not a mega-problem. When you run a print ad, you can list Net addresses for your e-mail, auto-responder, and Web page. Probably the same number of characters would be required regardless of the actual addresses.

It's just that Internet users are becoming more sophisticated. If they know that your e-mail address is **something@widgets.com**, they'll assume that your auto-responder address is **info@widgets.com**, and that your home page is located at **http://www.widgets.com**. That's because "info" almost always implies an auto-responder, and because most firms make their home page address begin with "www." followed by their domain name.

This is all a matter of custom. There are no formal requirements. Yet, this is very much the way it is. Therefore, if you can, it is worth centering your e-mail, auto-responder, and Web page on a single hosting system with the same overall domain name.

## Finding the hosting system that's right for you

If you have ever wanted to see the raw edge of market-based capitalism, you have only to delve into finding an ISP who can host your Web site and provide related services at a reasonable price. Your co-authors have moved beyond being astounded and are now merely amused at the variance in prices and services in this marketplace.

One can understand why huge disparities in prices and services might have existed, say, 100 years ago when one side of the country had no easy way of knowing what the other side was doing. But that they can exist today, when every ISP's price list is but a mouse click away, is surprising, to say the least. The Internet and the World Wide Web can indeed create a "perfect market," in which everyone is aware of everyone else's prices.

But this has not happened to date. So the prices of putting up your Web page vary all over the lot. The main cost items you will encounter are set-up fees, monthly rental fees for a certain amount of space on the server, fees for extra space, and possibly some traffic-based charge.

## Costs you can expect

One-time account set-up fees range from nothing to $50 or more. Monthly space rental fees average around $50 for about five megabytes or more of space. Additional space goes for a monthly fee of anywhere from 50 cents to $10 per megabyte. And the traffic component of the basic Web fee varies all over the map, with some providers offering unlimited traffic, others specifying 30,000 hits per week, still others allowing 200 megabytes per month with additional traffic billed at $4 per 100 megabytes.

These figures are taken from an excellent article in the April 1996 edition of *Internet World* called "Web Site on a Budget." The article was written by Steven E. Callihan, and you may be able to find it online at **http://www.iworld.com**, the *Internet World* home page. Mr. Callihan went to the Yahoo! search engine, located a list of some 700 Web hosting sites, and looked at 600 of them. His article cites 14 of the lowest-cost Web presence providers, and nine of the providers who specialize in offering single-page sites on the cheap.

The bottom line is this: Internet service providers and others who provide Web site hosting services have no idea how to charge for what they offer at this point. Naturally, they want to maximize profits. (Who doesn't?) But should there be a charge for the space occupied by the files that comprise your page? Should there be a charge based on the number of times users "hit" your page? (And by the way, what is the definition of a "hit?") Should there be a charge based on the number of bytes of information transferred from the site to the user?

No one knows. What we do know is that an ISP must purchase a hard disk drive, and that one can easily calculate the cost per megabyte of storage on that drive. We also know that an ISP must pay for a connection to the Internet, and that one can calculate the cost of utilizing that connection for a certain amount of time to send a given quantum of data. But what about the hours when that connection is not used to its full capacity?

# Go with someone you know, if possible

So far we've merely sketched the basics. Now you need to know that hosting ISPs also differ widely in other ways. Some offer domain name registration at no charge beyond the $100 that the InterNIC charges for the first two years. Others charge a *monthly* fee for "domain name maintenance," which is Infohighway robbery, plain and simple. Auto-responders may or may not be included in your fees. And you may or may not be able to update the files that compose your page on your own.

So what do you do? We have some very harsh, but effective advice. First, be aware that as AT&T, MCI, SprintNet, and other major players enter the market, local ISPs are going to be under incredible pressure.

There are nearly 2,000 ISPs today, but by July 1997, we'll be surprised if there were 500 left standing. Access to the Internet is rapidly becoming a commodity, and big companies are ideally suited to providing commodities at the lowest possible cost. Local and regional ISPs will survive only if they can find a way to match the prices offered by the AT&Ts and MCIs, and also offer better customer service.

When looking for someone to host your Web page, if you happen to have a really good local or regional Internet service provider in your dialing area, pay them a visit. Explain your plans, and while you're at it, try to get a sense of their operation. If it is less than professional, cross them off your list.

In our opinion, the ideal set-up is to find a really good local ISP who can host your page and provide you with any other Internet services you may need. Including e-mail, auto-responders, listservs, access to all newsgroups, and so on.

But such an ISP should have at least a T1 connection to the Internet backbone. A T1 connection pumps data back and forth at a speed of over 1.5 million bits per second. A T3 line, the next step up, operates at over 43.3 million bits per second. Some ISPs, in contrast, connect

to the Net using a line that operates at only 448 *thousand* bits (56K) per second.

If there are no good local ISPs who can host your page and service your other needs, then the next step should be to look at the national providers on the POCIA List. See the sidebar in Chapter 7.

The bad news is that you may have to try several hosting systems before you find the one that is best for you. The good news is that you can indeed take your URL and domain name with you when you move to a new system, so your business cards will not be rendered out of date, and the hosting function is really quite apart from the function of designing and putting up a Web page. Don't like your host? Simply transfer your files to a different system.

But, a word to the wise: keep back-ups of everything. You don't want to come into work some morning to learn that your hosting system has suddenly gone out of business. How will you get your files back then? It is far better to make copies of everything and to set things up so that all customer requests, e-mail, or whatever come directly to you. That way a sudden shutdown cannot hurt you very badly.

## Conclusion: DigiCash, secure transactions, & more

If there's one thing we have learned in nearly two decades of book writing and punditry it is that we can indeed be wrong. It's a dismaying thought, but there it is. Still, like many a less honest pundit, this has not dissuaded us from telling you as much and then continuing to pontificate.

The one relevant topic we haven't addressed in this chapter is the entire field of *secure transactions*. Specifically, the question of how one makes it possible for someone to purchase an item online using a credit card.

To which we say, "What's the big deal?" We all give our credit cards to strangers at restaurants and rental car counters who take them into

dark corners and do who knows what with them. We dial up L.L. Bean, Talbots, or Lands' End and verbally transmit our credit card numbers over the phone. Heck, someone claiming to be from *TV Guide* calls with a special subscription renewal offer and we give out our name, address, and credit card number without giving it a second thought.

## Who is concerned?

The saving grace is that we as consumers and credit card holders are liable for a maximum of only $50 of fraudulent charges on any given card. So why is everyone apparently so concerned about "secure Internet transactions?" The answer is that most consumers are not all that concerned.

It's the credit card companies that are worried, because after $50, they are left holding the bag. And the companies who see a way to skim off a tiny percentage of each Net- or Web-based transaction are beating the drum. Those companies are the ones who want to force everyone who wants to sell anything on the Web to go through their "secure" systems.

What these firms miss is the fact that, by and large, people do not want to buy things using their computers. Some people will do so, of course. But most will treat your Web site as a wonderful (if you've done your job right) place to visit on a regular basis. "And, when I want to place an order, I'll dial your toll-free number."

Of course we could be wrong. But we're still convinced that most people are not going to be interested in actually making purchases online. And those who do have this interest are not likely to be impressed by elaborate (and potentially costly) software-based security systems.

Sure the Net can be "hacked." Sure some credit card numbers can be stolen. But that doesn't mean that they *will* be stolen. The entire situation turns on the ignorance of both buyers and sellers and on the vigorously pursued interests of certain software firms that stand to benefit.

The closest analogy we can think of concerns all the dust kicked into the air about computer viruses some years ago. Naturally, the firms doing most of the kicking were the ones who sell anti-virus software!

If you are worried about your customers' credit card numbers being siphoned off and misused, then don't take orders online. Offer a toll-free number or an order form that customers can print out, fill in, and mail or fax to you. Just don't get taken in by the hype!

# Part 3

# Spreading the word

# Search engines & free directory listings

# CHAPTER 11

MOST articles we've seen recently about Web site marketing begin with the same question. So why should we be any different? That key question, of course, is this: If you build a Web site, will they come? And the answer, as we have emphasized repeatedly, is "No, not necessarily." People may stumble upon your site by accident, the way a tourist might chance upon some wonderful shop by wandering down a crooked lane in the Casbah.

But you don't want to leave your business to chance. In this chapter we will look at the ways you can get your site noticed by Net users with very little effort or expense. We will start with search engines and then consider the option of free directory listings for companies offering products and services on the Net.

## Search engines & how they work

As the saying goes, "Everything's on the Internet some place; the real trick is in finding it." Thus, while books and directories have their role, when it comes to finding things on the Net, what the world needs is a *search engine*! At least that's what many entrepreneurs have concluded.

That's why it is now possible to point your Web browser program at sites like Alta Vista, Yahoo!, Infoseek, WebCrawler, and other sites and search the Web free of charge. That's right—type in a word or phrase and your chosen search engine will bring you a collection—a large collection—of Web pages that contain that word or phrase.

Sounds great. At last something is being done to make the vast quantities of information available on the Internet manageable and "locatable." Well, yes. And, no. As we will see.

But before going any further, you should plan to conduct some searches yourself. You can start by pointing your browser at **http://home.netscape.com/home/internet_search.html**. This is a location maintained by Netscape Communications that can serve as a jumping off point for almost all of the leading search engines.

Alternatively, you can point your Web browser at the following locations and key in a search term or use the menus presented there to search for a business, service, or product:

- Alta Vista
  **http://www.altavista.digital.com**
- Excite
  **http://www.excite.com**
- Infoseek
  **http://www.infoseek.com**
- Lycos
  **http://www.lycos.com**
- Magellan
  **http://www.mckinley.com**
- Open Text Index
  **http://www.opentext.com**
- WebCrawler
  **http://www.webcrawler.com**
- Yahoo!
  **http://www.yahoo.com**

## Search tips: How to make the most of a search engine

*Online searching is an art. It involves thinking—indeed, outthinking—a given database. It requires you to be familiar with not only the quirks of a given database, but also with the varying tools offered by a given search software package.*

*Add to this the fact that free-text searches, the kind provided by Internet search engines, are the most treacherous of all, and you should not be surprised or disappointed if you are unable to find what you want.*

*Still, a lot of the time you get lucky. Here are some points to keep in mind that can further improve your chances.*

1. *Read the instructions or "hints" or "tips."*
   *Yes, this takes time, but why would anyone expect to be able to*

*step up to a complex tool and use it masterfully without any instruction? So check to see if you can you use* wildcards *like "custom*" to find "custom," "customized," and "custom-designed?" Can you use* proximity operators *that let you search for "custom" within two words of "designed?"*

**2** *Use the most unique word you can think of.*
*Take the time to think about the words that will almost certainly appear on the kind of page you have in mind. Then pick the most unique or unusual word from that list. If that word yields too many hits, consider doing a search using that word and the next most unusual word to narrow things down. Is there a phrase you can search for? How do you tell the search engine that you want it to find "body of evidence," not "body" and "evidence."*

**3** *Spelling counts.*
*Computers are stupid. They can only look for what you tell them to find. So if you misspell "widget" as "widdget" in a mad typing frenzy, you won't find what you're looking for. Also, consider all the many variations that are possible: "custom design," "custom-design," "custom designed," "customized design."*

**4** *Make it a multi-step process.*
*Don't assume that you'll do one search and that will be it. Start by taking your best shot. Then pay attention to the sites that contain the* kind *of information you want. What words are used? Make a few notes and then do another search using those words.*

**5** *Check to see if you can "NOT" out a term.*
*Some search engines will let you use a search statement like "cure and bacon not disease" to forestall the finding of sites that talk about medical cures instead of those of the porcine kind.*

**6** *Use multiple search engines.*
*Every search engine has its own way of doing things. And none can truthfully claim to cover* everything. *So if you need to be thorough, you will have to plan on using several search engines. Everything* is *subject to change, but at this writing, our choices would be Alta Vista, Yahoo!, and Infoseek.*

## Making your site visible

You've set up a Web site offering something of genuine value free of charge, plus a little soft-sell for your product or service. You have created the best of all possible Web sites for marketing widgets on the Internet. So how is someone who is interested in buying a widget going to find you?

More than likely, they are going to use the same search engines you just used. And, unless yours is a very, very specialized business, they are going to end up with hundreds of hits—hundreds of Web pages that contain the specified search word or phrase.

So what should you do? How can you make sure that someone searching for information on widgets finds your page and not that of a competitor?

There are absolutely no guarantees. But the way to give yourself the best chance of success in this arena is to understand how search engines work. And compose your Web page accordingly.

## Hey, spider, over here!

You don't have to worry with all this yourself. As you will see in Chapter 13, it's possible to hire someone to take care of things for you. Still, you had best know what's going on.

Most search engines operate by building an *index* that is stored at the search engine site. The index contains words and pointers to the Web pages that contain them. The search engine site will also contain some information about each page it references, usually the page's title and possibly its initial few lines of text.

So where does the index come from? The answer is that most search engines have deployed robot programs called *spiders* that continually visit Web pages and follow the links they contain. The spider programs capture some or all of the text that appears on each page and add the words to the search engine's index.

Fortunately, you are not at the mercy of a spider program that may not get around to your site any time soon. Most search engines encourage you to contact them directly and provide them with

information about your site so that it can be added to the index. Or you can pay a third party to handle this for you. (See Chapter 13 for information on companies that offer this service.)

## Making sure that your page is found

Now that we know how to get your page into a search engine's index, let's consider the things you can do to make sure that people looking for widgets do indeed find your page when they conduct a search.

Each search engine has its own way of doing things. In some cases, only the first few lines of text on your page are added to the index. In other cases, the spider program will index every single word on a page. Search engines also vary greatly in the amount of detail they present to the searcher about a given Web page.

This means that when you are creating your page, you should carefully consider what keywords will help potential customers find it on the Net. Then make sure you include those keywords in the first few lines of text on your Web page.

Put yourself into your customer's mind and think about the words he or she would use in trying to find a company offering what you offer. The reason you should consider using various forms of the same word has to do with the varying capabilities of search engines. If an engine looks for a complete word instead of a string of characters, it might not find you if your prospect has searched for "custom" and your page contains only "customized."

For example, suppose you're in the business of offering custom-designed gold and silver jewelry. You might then develop the following list of keywords for your Web page: gold, silver, jewelry, custom, customized, design, designed, custom-designed, rings, pins, bracelets, semi-precious. Begin your page with an introductory paragraph describing your jewelry business, working in all of these keywords.

## A matter of weighting

Finally, there is the matter of increasing the probability that someone using a search engine will indeed come visit your page. As you will have noticed, search engines seem to be built on the assumption that "more is better." You search for "widget" and the search engine brings you over 100 hits. Are you going to look at all 100 Web pages the engine has found? Not likely.

What you'll do is concentrate on the first dozen or so. And naturally, every businessperson would like to ensure that his or her page is among that first dozen. How to do it?

Some search engines determine the order in which pages are presented to a user on the basis of a *weighting formula* that determines how relevant each page is to the search. So if you search for "widgets," the first page offered will be the one that contains the greatest number of occurrences of that word.

Of course, you can guess what some companies do. They simply start their Web pages with several lines of the most obvious keyword, repeated again and again. We don't recommend this. It's just plain tacky—like calling your company the AAAA Aardvark Company to make sure that yours is the first listing in the phone book. Not only does it look unprofessional, but it's tantamount to admitting that you are such a poor marketer that you have to rely on tricks to get people's attention.

## Free directory listings

Like the World Wide Web itself, search engines are a very recent invention in Internet history. But, almost from the beginning, Internauts have been keeping and updating lists and directories. That's why you'll hear about lists like the "December List" created by John December, the "Yanoff List" by Internaut Scott Yanoff, and the "Unofficial Internet Book List" by author Kevin Savetz.

We are partial to lists because they offer a particularly efficient way of finding things. When a search engine search pays off, the results can be dazzling. Nothing else like it. But more than likely, achieving impressive search engine results will require considerable time, effort, and thought on your part. With a list or a directory, some other human being has done the thinking for you.

Incidently, this is what makes the Yahoo! service distinctive. It lets you do a free-text search of its contents, but its backbone is its human-created hierarchical topic index.

## An evolutionary process

There are now scores, if not hundreds, of individual directories designed to help Internet users find products, services, and companies. Most offer a free basic listing to any qualified firm. They hope to make their money by selling advertising and by offering "premium" listings to companies.

Naturally, everyone has a somewhat different idea about the most successful format or approach to take. In looking at the various alternatives people have created, you almost feel like you're watching Darwinian evolution in progress. At this stage, Life has only recently rolled out its initial entries. The adaptation stage has not yet begun.

All of which means that trying to get your Web site or business listed in every directory going could add up to a colossal waste of time. Not every directory currently online is going to survive, after all.

## The best strategy

That's why we have a rather crafty strategy to suggest. Well, it's not so much "crafty" as it is "smart." First, the quickest and easiest way to get a handle on what directories are out there is to use Yahoo! Point your browser at **http://www.yahoo.com** and then click on "Business and Economy" and then "Business Directory." You will see a screen like the one shown in Fig. 11-1.

Figure 11-1

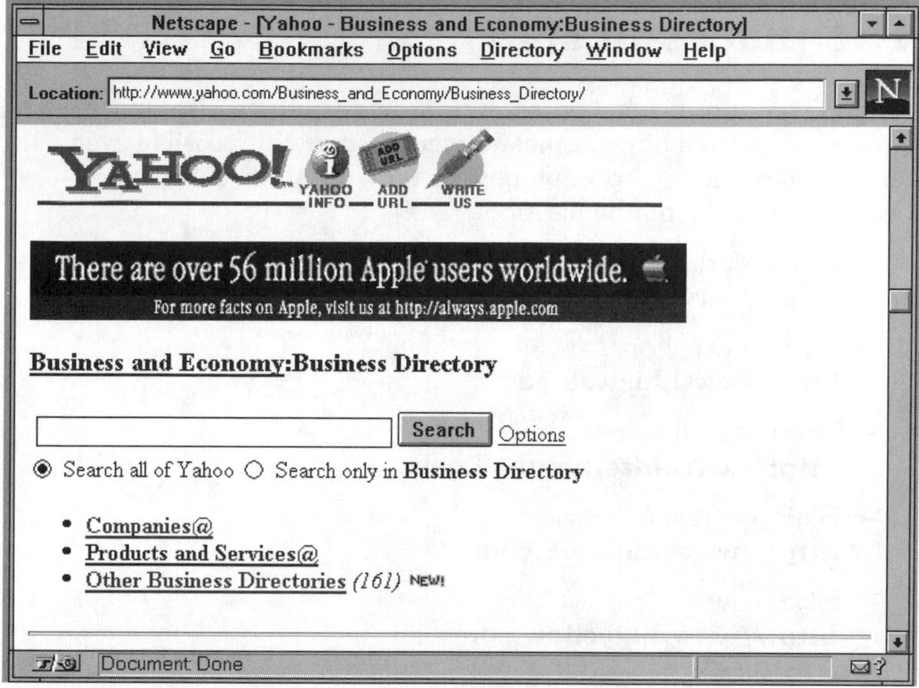


*The Yahoo! directory of business directories.*

Assume that what you find here is as close to "comprehensive" as is possible. After all, if the creator of a directory of businesses or products is not knowledgeable enough to get the site listed with Yahoo!, how good can the site be?

Visit directories of interest. Look at or search for a few listings. If the feature has a good feel to it, go further and pick up the information on how you can get your site listed for free. If not, cross it off your list.

It's very important to take these steps, even if you have no intention of posting a notice about your site yourself. Visiting directory sites will give you a feeling for what's involved and make you a much smarter consumer should you decide to hire someone to spread the word for you.

# The places to start

We don't want to play favorites. But, as in everything else, there are some really outstanding business directory sites. So, possibly even before you consult Yahoo!, point your browser at the following locations. You will not be disappointed!

- Open Market Commercial Sites Index
  **http://www.directory.net**
- BizWeb Directory
  **http://www.bizweb.com**
- Internet Mall
  **http://www.internet-mall.com**
- BigBook Yellow Pages
  **http://www.bigbook.com**
- BigYellow
  **http://www.bigyellow.com**
- InterNIC Directory of Directories
  **http://ds0.internic.net/ds/dsdirofdirs.html**

## What about "malls?"

*One of the very first commerce-related creations to appear on the Internet were the so-called "cybermalls." The term "mall" is used loosely here. You will find it applied to free directories, like the Internet Mall,* ***http://www.internet-mall.com****. But it is also used to refer to sites that create and maintain home pages for clients.*

*The Branch Mall, for example, charges $960 a year for creating and hosting a single page. You don't even have to own a computer. (For more information, call 800-349-1747 or go to* ***http://branch.com****.)*

*The cybermall concept was initially quite appealing. Most were started long before there were search engines, for example. So collecting businesses into a given location (either as a list or as a Gopher) made it easier to find the stores you were looking for. Then, too, Web pages were expensive at the time, so cybermalls offered an affordable way to have a presence on the Net.*

*Today things are different, and we wonder whether cybermalls make sense any more. Prospective customers interested in finding a widget company are probably not going to visit the scores of Internet malls. Instead, they'll go straight to Yahoo! or some other search engine. (Yahoo! really is the best choice here because its indexing scheme makes it easy to focus your search on a particular business or type of product.)*

*There's also the fact that in a cybermall, you are likely to be cheek-by-jowl with one or more competitors. This is great for shoppers because it makes it much easier to locate the kind of stores they want and to easily compare prices. But it is probably not so good for you, the businessperson.*

*Don't forget, being in a mall doesn't eliminate the need for you to promote your site. But how much sense does it make to do so when, once they get to the mall, your prospects will see not only your site but also those of your competitors?*

*To explore online malls for yourself, check the Index of Commercial of Databases and Malls posted by the Multimedia Marketing Group at* ***http://hevanet.com/online/com.html****.*

# 12

# Making the most of newsgroups & mailing lists

# CHAPTER 12

ELECTRONIC mail may be the most used Internet feature, and the Web may (currently) be the most popular. But to those in the know, newsgroups—and to a lesser extent mailing lists—can be the most rewarding. At least from a user's perspective.

Indeed, while newsgroups can be an effective marketing tool, the key is to always keep the user's perspective in full view. You can put up the biggest, most elaborate Web site in the world, and no one will object. That's because by doing so, you are not tramping on anyone's toes. People will visit your site or they won't. The choice is entirely in their hands.

If you try to advertise in most newsgroups, however, people will cut you off at the knees! In fact, you will be lucky if that's all they do. And your co-authors are completely on their side.

UT it this way: Do *you* like telemarketing phone calls, all of which somehow manage to make the phone ring just as you are sitting down to dinner, regardless of when you eat? You can't ignore the call—it could be Mom and Dad or the kids or some other urgent situation. So you set down your dinner plate and say, "Hello," and the voice on the other end says, "Mr. Smith? How are you this evening?"

The phone system may be public, but no one can blame you for feeling that your privacy has been invaded. After all, the telephone salesperson didn't call you on your business line during business hours. The call was placed to your home phone after five in the evening.

Think about the anger and contempt you feel for the caller and the company he or she represents. Then realize that people will feel that way about you and your firm if you dare to place a blatant ad in one of their favorite newsgroups.

You can argue rights and wrongs and legal fine points until your face turns purple, and it will make no difference at all.

Newsgroups (and mailing lists) are de facto *communities*, and you violate each group's standards at your peril.

All of which is not to say that one cannot use newsgroups and mailing lists to do a little gentle selling. But your pitch has got to be soft, it has got to offer something of worth for free, and it has got to take the you-approach instead of the me-approach that is all too common in the business world. And, of course, selling products or convincing people to visit your Web site are not the only opportunities newsgroups offer.

## Finding out what people are saying

For example, newsgroups and mailing lists make it easy to discover what people think of your products or the products produced by your competitors. All you have to do is read the postings to the relevant newsgroups or add your name to the relevant mailing lists.

Better still, use a search engine like DejaNews, Infoseek, or Alta Vista to search the postings to groups for mentions of your product, industry, competitors, or whatever. All three of these sites allow you to limit your search to newsgroup postings:

- DejaNews
  **http://www.dejanews.com**
- Infoseek
  **http://www.infoseek.com**
- Alta Vista
  **http://www.altavista.digital.com**

According to the *Wall Street Journal* (September 15, 1994), Dell Computer Corporation, Packard Bell Electronics, Compaq Computer Corporation, and numerous other companies make a special effort to monitor Internet newsgroups—and their SIG (Special Interest Group) equivalents on such systems as CompuServe, Prodigy, and America Online—for any mention of their products.

Dell has even created an Internet SWAT Team to "peruse traffic for any mention of Dell products, ready to swoop into 'threads' of

conversations to help solve customer problems, change negative perceptions, and protect the company's reputation."

## Taking the time

The information aspects of newsgroups and mailing lists may or may not make sense for your particular business. But it is certainly significant that major companies take these communications forums very, very seriously.

### Why are they called *news*groups?

*Internet newsgroups—or* netnews *as they are sometimes called—are transmitted among sites by a program called* Usenet, *which is a contraction of the words "USENIX" (the name of the large UNIX user group) and "network." The program was designed by Jim Ellis, Tom Truscott, and Steve Bellovin in 1979 at the University of North Carolina. Its original purpose was to automatically transmit news about various aspects of the UNIX world, hence the name "newsgroups."*

*But, of course, things have grown far beyond that. Of some 10,000 groups available today, only about 30 are devoted to discussing matters related to the Unix operating system.*

*Today, there are newsgroups devoted to every imaginable subject. Everything from the TV shows* Beavis and Butt-Head *and* The Rockford Files *to tips on brewing your own beer.*

## Newsgroup essentials

Although the World Wide Web has eclipsed nearly all other Internet features, newsgroups remain such a major factor that one could easily write a book about them alone. Here, however, are the bare facts every businessperson must know:

- Conceptually, newsgroups are merely "player piano rolls" of messages, or *articles* in netspeak. Each group is devoted to some topic. The comments Internet users may want to make about that topic are posted one after the other into a long piano roll.

- No one controls the newsgroups on the Net. The notes that people post circulate like bits of dust in the jet stream. The flow of messages among Internet sites is constant, and that stream encompasses the entire world.
- The only real filtering that takes place is when a given site administrator decides not to accept or make available to users the contents of certain groups. This may be an editorial decision under which the content of a given group is deemed inappropriate. Or it may be a question of limited capacity at the host site.
- However, some newsgroups are *moderated*, which means that a human being reviews each posting and determines whether or not it is appropriate to the group's topic and should thus be made available to all readers.
- Millions of people read the netnews daily. But no one reads every group. The software used to read netnews keeps track of the groups you have chosen to read regularly and which messages in those groups you have not yet read.
- Anyone can post a new article or a reply to an article on almost any group. Taken together, a new article and the replies (and replies to replies) it generates form a *message thread*.

  The only limitations are that the postings be appropriate to the group, that no single posting be longer than the equivalent of about 15 single-spaced pages of text, and that you use plain, 7-bit ASCII text.

## Crucial points

The single most important thing you must know about Internet newsgroups is this: You are not to do any advertising, marketing, promotion, or selling—except in those newsgroups that were created for that purpose.

You might get away with doing it on other groups, if you do so in the right way. If you don't, you'll get *flamed* by group participants. That is, you will receive many a nasty message and word will be spread that you are not a good person, your products stink, and your company should be boycotted.

Flame messages—or just *flames*—should reassure anyone who might be concerned about the death of passionate discourse in this country. For the essence of a flame is *passion*. And without for a moment condoning the crude and obscene flames that are inevitable, one can certainly sympathize with a longtime Net user's desire to keep advertising from intruding into yet another aspect of life.

Besides, the Internet makes it easy to talk back to an advertiser — something most of us would love to be able to do the next time a wonderful movie is interrupted at a crucial point by a commercial for deodorant or floor wax. Truth to be told, many of us *do* talk back to the TV set to no avail. But on the Internet, an advertiser can hear you. And so can everyone else who reads the newsgroup.

## How to get a comprehensive list

The original list of newsgroups was created by Gene Spafford and then taken on by David C. Lawrence. The list is organized into two major parts: one for the ALT groups ("Alternative Hierarchies") and one for everything else ("Active Newsgroups"), with multiple files for each. As a convenience, all of these files are available on the Newsgroup Essentials disk from Glossbrenner's Choice. Or, you can get them via FTP or newsgroup postings:

- To get the files via FTP:
  **ftp://ftp.uu.net/usenet/news.answers/alt-hierarchies**
  **ftp://ftp.uu.net/usenet/news.answers/active-newsgroups/**
- To get the files via newsgroups:
  **news.lists**
  **news.groups**
  **news.announce.newgroups**
  **news.answers**

One thing you will quickly learn about the Net is that there is a FAQ (Frequently Asked Questions) file for nearly everything. In the case of newsgroups, the FAQ is called "Answers to Frequently Asked Questions about Usenet," and it is posted regularly to the newsgroups **news.announce.newusers** and **news.answers**.

The Usenet FAQ and a lot of other helpful information about newsgroups are also available at the Usenet Newsgroups Resource Page maintained by Indiana University:

**http://scwww.ucs.indiana.edu/NetRsc/usenet.html**

## Searching offline

Once you've got the comprehensive list of newsgroups on your disk, the next step is to identify the ones most likely to be of interest. That way, you will be able to tell your newsreader program exactly which group to go to.

So, with your list of newsgroups on disk, it just makes sense to use your computer's power to search it. The program we like for this purpose is Vernon Buerg's famous shareware LIST program, but any word processing program with a search function will do. Just key in any topic that occurs to you, and activate the search function.

For example, we searched the Lawrence newsgroup list for the word "business" and found all of the groups shown here. (Another good keyword to search for is "marketplace.") Check the nearby sidebar for a description of the various newsgroup categories (alt, bit, clari, etc.).

| | |
|---|---|
| alt.business.import-export | Business aspects of international trade. |
| alt.business.internal-audit | Discussion of internal auditing. |
| alt.business.misc | All aspects of commerce. |
| alt.business.multi-level | Multi-level (network) marketing businesses. |
| alt.computer.consultants | The business of consulting about computers. |
| bit.listserv.buslib-l | Business Libraries List. |

| | |
|---|---|
| bit.listserv.e-europe | Eastern Europe Business Network. (Moderated) |
| bit.listserv.japan | Japanese Business and Economics Network. (Moderated) |
| clari.apbl.biz.briefs | Hourly business newsbrief from the AP. (Moderated) |
| clari.apbl.biz.headlines | Headlines of top business stories. (Moderated) |
| clari.biz.briefs | Business newsbriefs. (Moderated) |
| clari.biz.earnings | Businesses' earnings, profits, losses. (Moderated) |
| clari.biz.features | Business feature stories. (Moderated) |
| clari.biz.industry.health | The health care business. (Moderated) |
| clari.biz.misc | Other business news. (Moderated) |
| clari.biz.review | Daily review of business news. (Moderated) |
| clari.biz.top | Top business news. (Moderated) |
| clari.biz.urgent | Breaking business news. (Moderated) |
| clari.nb.business | Newsbytes business & industry news. (Moderated) |
| k12.ed.business | Business education curricula in grades K–12. |
| misc.entrepreneurs | Discussion on operating a business. |
| alt.business.misc | Miscellaneous business topics |
| soc.college.org.aiesec | The Int'l Assoc. of Business and Commerce Students. |

## Newsgroup hierarchies

*To make it easier for people to find what they're looking for, Usenet newsgroups are divided into topics. Each main topic is further divided, and the result is often divided again and again as areas are created for discussions of ever greater specificity.*

*For example, a group called **alt.music** might be formed to discuss music in general. But as people really get into the swing of things, some may decide that they really want to focus on baroque or jazz or* *hip-hop. So **alt.music.baroque** might be formed, along with **alt.music.jazz** and **alt.music.hip-hop**. And so on.*

*Here are the main topic categories of Usenet newsgroups:*

| | |
|---|---|
| *alt* | *Alternative newsgroups. Basically, topics that don't fit neatly anywhere else. Many Usenet sites don't carry these groups.* |
| *bionet* | *Biology, of course.* |
| *bit* | *Topics from Bitnet LISTSERV mailing lists.* |
| *biz* | *The accepted place for advertisements, marketing, and other commercial postings. Product announcements, product reviews, demo software, and so forth.* |
| *clari* | *ClariNet is a commercial service run by Brad Templeton. For a subscription fee paid by the site that carries its feed, Clarinet provides UPI wire news, newspaper columns, and lots of other goodies.* |
| *comp* | *Topics of interest to both computer professionals and hobbyists, including computer science, software source code, and information on hardware and software systems.* |
| *ddn* | *Defense Data Network.* |
| *gnu* | *As in "gnu is not UNIX." The Free Software Foundation and the GNU project.* |
| *ieee* | *Institute of Electrical and Electronic Engineers* |
| *k12* | *Topics of interest to teachers of kindergarten through grade 12, including curriculum, language exchanges with native speakers, and classroom-to-classroom projects designed by teachers.* |
| *misc* | *Groups addressing themes not easily classified under any of the other headings or which incorporate themes from multiple categories.* |
| *news* | *Groups concerned with the Usenet network and software.* |
| *rec* | *Groups oriented towards the arts, hobbies, and recreational activities.* |
| *sci* | *Discussions relating to research in or application of the established sciences.* |
| *soc* | *Groups primarily addressing social issues and socializing.* |
| *talk* | *Groups largely debate-oriented and tending to feature long discussions without resolution and without appreciable amounts of generally useful information.* |

## Get your feet wet!

We've introduced you to the Internet newsgroup concept, told you how it works, and warned you not to risk getting flamed. We've also shown you how to get a comprehensive list of all the newsgroups currently on the Net.

Now we must ask something of you. Before you read any further, take the time to go online and experience what it's like to read one or more newsgroups. This is very, very easy to do. All of the Big Three consumer systems offer access to newsgroups. And, of course, all Internet access providers do so as well.

On many systems, you will be able to choose one or more *news readers* to use in actually reading articles. Our advice is to stay away from newsreader programs with names like "nn" or "trn" and opt instead for the newsreader built into your copy of Netscape or some other browser.

Remember, you can point your browser at the URL of any newsgroup by specifying "news:" followed by the name of the group. Do not use any slashes.

## Now for the payoff!

We're going to assume at this point that you have followed our advice and spent an evening or two exploring Internet newsgroups. If that's the case, you are probably feeling overwhelmed by the breadth, depth, and diversity of this part of the Net. At least we hope so. That way you won't underestimate your task.

We hope, too, that you have started to get a sense of the extent to which each newsgroup constitutes a community. As such, each group has certain unwritten "community standards" on what is acceptable behavior and what is not.

In one group it might be considered bad form to reveal which company you work for, or to ask such a question of someone else. Another group might be more like an industry trade show, where everyone is quite open about corporate affiliation.

How can you determine a given group's standards, mores, and concept of "acceptable behavior"? One way is to read the group's FAQ. (If there *is* one, it will be posted to the group on a regular basis.) But the *best* way to learn about a group is to spend time reading postings in the group. That's why we noted earlier that working the newsgroups can be very time-consuming indeed.

# The *best* way to proceed

There is absolutely no way to know whether your participation in a newsgroup will lead to additional sales. There is no way to know whether your efforts will be worthwhile. What we do know is this: Newsgroups are among the most popular features on the Net, and, with proper care, sensitivity, and an auto-responder you can use them to help get your story out. Here are the steps we recommend.

## Get the Lawrence list

Get the Lawrence list of newsgroups described earlier in this chapter. Put it on your hard disk and search it for words that pertain to your product or business. That will give you a "starter list" of newsgroups likely to deal with or discuss your product or service.

Then take a day—yes, a full day—to explore all of these groups. Capture all of the messages to a disk file and then, once you are offline, read or print out that file. Try your best to get a sense of the group. If an issue is raised or a comment made to which you would like to respond, circle it in red.

You can always broaden the scope later, but you should probably start with just the one or two newsgroups that seem to bear most closely on your product, service, industry, or whatever.

And, don't forget to visit locations like **http://www.dejanews.com** and **http://www.infoseek.com** that let you use a search engine to search the messages posted to newsgroups.

##  Think "town meeting"

Think of each group as a town meeting of a very small town, held in Town Hall, of course. This is the most crucial step of all, for just think about what this mindset means.

Among other things, it means that everybody knows everybody else. (Or almost.) Mr. A knows what Ms. B has had to say in years past on a given issue, and Mr. C can always be counted on to make a curmudgeonly comment on anything. Ms. D is a natural leader who does a pretty good job of keeping the discussion on point, while Mr. E is the proverbial clown who has never met a *bon mot* he didn't like—or utter.

It sounds like Norman Rockwell, and it is probably equally reflective of reality. But that's not the point.

The point is to see yourself as someone entering a town meeting of this sort. If it were a real town meeting and you had any sense at all, you would sit quietly and listen for a while before even thinking about making a comment of your own.

And you would be furious if some boor were to pound on the door, force it open, and toss a flurry of advertising flyers into the room. It would make you so mad that you would absolutely sputter with rage. How dare they!

Yet intrusions of that sort are exactly what some people—in misguided, stupid attempts to somehow make a fortune on the Internet—have attempted. We can only hope that cooler, more sensitive heads will prevail in the future at companies, ad agencies, law firms, and the like.

## Take it slow

Again, think of yourself in a town meeting. Some longtime resident rises to complain about the requirement that sidewalks in front of private homes be shovelled clean within 12 hours of a one-inch snowfall. "What if the homeowner is sick? Or disabled? Or away on vacation?"

If you happen to operate a snow removal service in that particular town—even if it's just a pick-up truck with snow tires and a blade and maybe a snowblower in back—no one's going to flame you for standing up and saying, "Gee, my company can help. We offer really good service at excellent rates. If you'd like to know more details, send an e-mail message to our auto-responder at **info@snowgone.com**. Or hit our Web site at **http://www.snowgone.com**."

A response like that is absolutely excellent. But notice how the fact that you have already set up an auto-responder and a Web site is the key. If you didn't have an auto-responder or Web site, you might be tempted to present all of your services and their prices as part of your newsgroup posting.

Bad move. For that would be seen as exactly what it is—a bold-faced advertisement for your services. You must understand the dynamic. No one will object if you say, "Hey, I can help, and here's where you can go for more information." That leaves it in the hands of each newsgroup reader. They may visit your Web site or hit your auto-responder. Or they may not. Their choice.

"In-your-face" marketing simply does not work on the Internet. The people whose personal, face-space you violate will either ignore you or take action against you. Either way, you lose.

## The best approach of all

At the risk of pushing the town meeting analogy too far, put yourself once again in the bleachers at the high school gymnasium or on a

plastic chair in the basement of the township building. The same long-time resident raises the same questions about the ordinance requiring homeowners to clear their walks after a snowfall.

You stand up and say:

> We'd be happy to help. We will give seniors a 20 percent discount and do the sidewalks of disabled citizens for free. Plus, we have a booklet created by the National Library of Medicine about snow shovelling and heart attacks which we will be pleased to send to anyone who's interested.
>
> For details, just send a blank e-mail message to our auto-responder at **info@snowgone.com**, or visit our Web site at **http://www.snowgone.com**.

## The way to market on the Net

Ladies and gentlemen, *that* is the way to market on the Internet. Set up an auto-responder and a Web page so that only those users who want your information will see it—which is to say, you will not be forcing your information on someone via e-mail or newsgroups. Even to a Net "newbie," sending mail to an auto-responder is quicker than calling an 800 number, though you may want to set up an 800 number as well. Logging onto a Web site is nearly as convenient.

Make the effort to identify the names of groups that might attract people interested in your product. Spend a lot of time exploring and winnowing the number down to a few key groups.

Then spend more time getting to know the "community" that each of these groups represents. Don't be bold. Be meek and mild and timid. At first. Get a sense of the group, just as you would get a sense of the house at a community town meeting.

Try to become a part of the community. Everyone is welcome, but you have got to participate. That means you will probably have to spend some time every week to keep up.

One other tip: Any time you post a message to a newsgroup, make sure that you include a short version of your signature file. Limit your signature to four to six lines when posting to a newsgroup. And make sure it contains addresses for your e-mail mailbox, Web site, and auto-responder.

## Leave your ego behind

As part of your offer, think in terms of *giving something back*. So many businesses are like car dealers. They plaster their last names all over the place and insist that people come in—when in reality no one cares who owns the dealership or who the heck the dealer is in the first place.

When you go online to offer your products or services, leave your ego behind. Take a genuine interest in the "community" and do not pull any punches. If you are honest, if you are sincere, and if you can think of some way to "give back to the Net"—whether it is a senior citizen discount or some useful or funny or otherwise interesting text file—Internet users will *want* to do business with you. And they will tell their friends, which is incredibly easy to do on the Net.

# Hand-crafted selling

In advertising parlance, the men and women who are actively involved in the Internet are the "opinion leaders" and the "early adopters" for a certain general line of products and services. They are very bright, and they have easy access to more information than "Joe and Jane Sixpack" can even imagine exists.

So be honest, be forthright, and be generous in the extra information you offer. Provide genuine value and absolutely superb customer service, and you will have an excellent chance of becoming a vendor of choice in the Internet newsgroup community.

The worst mistake you can make is to allow yourself to become bedazzled by the vision of the pot of gold at the end of the online

rainbow. The "point, click, purchase" vision we have warned you about before.

The Internet and the online world are *not* like radio and television. You cannot simply blast your ad to millions of sets and expect a boost in sales.

It's ironic, but online selling is a lot more like going door-to-door than it is like buying an ad on some top-rated TV or radio program. Yet many a fortune has been made by personal, door-to-door selling.

If you've got a truly good product or service to offer, if you're willing to work, and if you care about your customer, you can do quite well and put every dollar in the bank with pride.

## The Big Three systems, too

Among the Big Three consumer systems, the equivalent of an Internet newsgroup is a Special Interest Group (SIG). That's the generic name everyone uses. But, to be precise, CompuServe calls them "forums," and Prodigy and AOL call them "clubs" or "bulletin boards."

Regardless of the name they go by, the SIGs on the Big Three systems are also worthy of your attention. Since all of these systems support Internet e-mail and Web access, citing your auto-responder and/or Web address in a discussion thread is very worthwhile.

You may want to consider contributing some files to a given SIG's library. Press releases, product descriptions, price lists—and especially, truly cool, free programs—are always appreciated. Just remember that whether you're focused on the Big Three or on the Internet, you must never forget the concept of "community."

Regardless of the system you use, your Internet auto-responder and your Web site will make it easy for you to present your product or tell your story. So you won't be in the position of "advertising" where it is not appropriate.

##  Net Happenings

You'll be happy to hear that there is at least one newsgroup that will actually welcome the announcement of your new World Wide Web site or auto-responder. The group is called **comp.internet.net-happenings**, or Net Happenings for short. There is no way of knowing how many people are likely to read your posting to this group. But, since it doesn't cost anything, why leave this particular stone unturned?

The only caveat is to limit yourself to about 100 lines of text. As you will see when you visit the group before preparing your own posting, the articles put up by some companies are far too long. Keep yours short and sweet. After all, anyone who wants more information can request it via e-mail, or hit your auto-responder or visit your Web site.

##  Mailing lists

Now let's consider Internet *mailing lists*.

These work just like a conventional paper-mail mailing list in that, once your name has been added to a list, messages relevant to the list will begin to appear in your electronic mailbox automatically.

As a businessperson, this can work for you in two ways. First, mailing lists can be a wonderful source of information on a given subject. If you are interested in some technical or theoretical aspect of your industry, for example, you may discover that joining the right mailing list is like becoming a member of a perpetual symposium.

Second, once you've really gotten to know the Net, you may decide that starting your *own* mailing list would be a good idea. But just as not every product or service is well suited for marketing on the Internet, not every company should have a mailing list.

## Just for the fun of it

Let's have some fun and invent a completely fictitious (as far as we know)—yet workable—example. Let's assume your company specializes in reproductions of the world's greatest sculptures, scaled down to sizes appropriate to a suburban garden. Michelangelo, Brancusi, Moore, and many others are well represented in your collection.

Imagine how easy it would be to create a two-page article on each of the pieces by Michelangelo alone. How the Master came to sculpt it, what critics have said about it over the ages, why your reproductions are so meticulous, and so on.

Now imagine that you have created those pieces and that you have set up a free Internet-based mailing list that will automatically send out one of your write-ups to everyone on the list once a month. Your transmissions will simply appear in their e-mail mailboxes. (Along with an order form, of course!)

No cost. No obligation. Anyone on the Internet or on one of the Big Three systems can subscribe or cancel at any time. And everything is automated by a computer running LISTSERV software.

All you have to do is keep the articles and information coming. No small task, of course, for someone trying to run a business. But talk about establishing a personal, interactive relationship with your customers!

Your mailing list is like a magazine (without the pictures). If you like, you can set things up so that subscribers can contribute their own articles and comments. With you serving as "moderator," of course.

# Thinking about mailing lists

Setting up your own automated Internet mailing list is not difficult to do. When you feel you're ready, contact your local Internet access provider and ask about the cost for creating a List Server or

LISTSERV that will automatically add people to your mailing list and automatically send out the files you want them to have.

The LISTSERV software will also automatically send out any article posted by a member of the mailing list—if you want it to. If you would prefer to serve as the list's "moderator" and thus decide yourself which contributions get sent to the entire list and which don't, you can do that as well.

This is cheap. One provider we know, for example, charges $50 to set up a list of 50 names, with a monthly maintenance fee of $25. But there is no message-based charge. You can send members of such a list as many articles as you want. Probably, you can negotiate an even better deal with your own local access provider.

# Essential facts

Here are the key things a businessperson needs to know about Internet mailing lists.

### Getting a list of lists

Two of the most comprehensive lists of mailing lists are the SRI List of Lists by Vivian Neou and PAML (Publicly Accessible Mailing Lists) by Stephanie Da Silva. To get the SRI List, send an e-mail message to **mail-server@sri.com**. Include the line send interest-groups in the body of the message. For PAML, check the newsgroups **news.lists** or **news.answers**, where it is posted periodically. Or look for it at this Web site: **http://www.neosoft.com/internet/paml**.

As a convenience, both of these lists are also available from Glossbrenner's Choice on a disk called Mailing List Essentials. The disk also includes DOS search software to make it easy to find mailing lists of interest. See the Glossbrenner's Choice appendix at the back of the book for details.

### Moderated and unmoderated

Some mailing lists are *moderated*, meaning all contributions go to a single individual who then determines what gets sent to the list as a whole. On an *unmoderated* list, in contrast, whatever any subscriber sends to the list server computer gets sent automatically to everyone.

### ✻ How to subscribe

Subscribing to a mailing list is easy. In most cases, you simply send a request to a *subscription address*, where a human being or a computer reads it and adds you to the list. From then on, you read and respond to messages from the list's *main address*. Be careful not to send your subscription request to the main address. The SRI and PAML lists of mailing lists include subscription instructions for each list.

For example, here are the current instructions for subscribing, unsubscribing, and posting messages to Glenn Fleishman's Internet Marketing Discussion List, whose participants "want to create Internet sites, market products and goods in appropriate ways, develop payment systems, or write about what's going on here."

```
Subscribing

To join this list, send a message with any contents and subject (or none)
to IM-SUB@I-M.COM

Unsubscribing

Send a message with any contents or subject (or none) to
IM-UNSUB@I-M.COM

Posting

Posts to this list should be addressed to:
INTERNET-MARKETING@I-M.COM
```

## Conclusion

Clearly, newsgroups and mailing lists are a wonderful source of information. They are two key Internet features that you will not want to miss. The e-mail addresses we've given you here and the files you will find on the Internet disks you can order from Glossbrenner's Choice will help you get plugged in quickly.

Newsgroups and mailing lists can be used for marketing as well. But as we have emphasized repeatedly, doing so requires time and effort. Above all, it requires sensitivity. Unfortunately, there is really no way to know whether such efforts will pay off for you. But if you do decide to give it a try, make sure you set up your auto-responder and Web site first.

# Announcement services

## Hiring someone to handle it for you

# CHAPTER 13

AS the Web and the Net have grown, the number of sites a business can use to place a link or an ad or other information has exploded. Today, there are so many search engines and newsgroups and directories and electronic magazines that posting information about your site or setting up hotlinks can be a full-time job. That's why you'll be pleased to know that companies have been established that, for a fee, can handle this kind of thing for you. They are usually called *announcement services* or *Web promotion services*, though the terminology is in flux.

## Step back & think for a moment

In this chapter, we're going to tell you about some of the leading announcement services, what they do, and what they charge. We're also going to show you how to locate even more such services. And we've a trick or two to share.

But before doing any of that, let's pause for just a moment to consider what does and does not make sense for you and your company. To put it another way: You do not have to be listed in every search engine's index and in every directory on the Net to successfully attract people to your Web site. The goal, as in all advertising and promotion, is to do your best to make sure that you are seen by the people most likely to buy from you.

So your very first question should be: Are my best prospects the kind of people who routinely surf the Net, participate in newsgroups, and use Yahoo!, Alta Vista, and other search engines? If your best prospects do not normally spend their time doing these things, then it may be a waste of time to devote much effort to getting the word out about your site *on the Net*.

## A counter-intuitive notion

It's counter-intuitive, we know. You think to yourself, "Now that I'm on the Web, I'm just a mouse click away from my customers, so it makes sense to get hotlinks to my page set up in as many places as

possible." That may very well be true in your case. And it is certainly true if you are selling hardware, software, or some other high-tech product likely to appeal to habitual Web surfers.

But what if you're selling, say, kitty-friendly Gutless Wonder violin strings? It's entirely possible that some hard-core Web surfers are enthusiastic violinists. But are there likely to be enough of these prospects to make it worth posting your Web site information to several dozen search engines, directories, and newsgroups?

It may turn out that the best way to attract people to your Web site is to beef up your conventional print, radio, and television advertising, or to expand your promotional activities. You would highlight your Web site, auto-responder, and e-mail addresses throughout, of course. This would help you to reach Internet/Web-enabled customers who realize that there is more to life than the Net alone.

# Free, automated, announcement services

It may well be that the company you hire to design and host your Web page will include announcement services as part of the total package. HMP Systems (**http://www.wp.com/hmpsystems**), the Internet Plaza (**http://internet-plaza.net**), and Wilson Internet Services (**http://www.wilsonweb.com**) do this, we know. And so do many others.

If this is not an option, you can, of course, handle things yourself. Your only cost in registering with the leading search engines and directories is your time. You'll have to go to each site, click on the relevant icon, and key in information about your site.

As time-consuming as this is, it is often the best way to do things, since each feature has slightly different requirements and formats. However, there is, indeed, an easier way. You can use an automated service like Submit It! (**http://www.submit-it.com**) or PostMaster (**http://www.netcreations.com/postmaster**).

##  Think first, fill out forms later

Submit It! and PostMaster present you with a form that requests your site's URL, your name and e-mail address, the name of your site, and a brief description of what it offers. When you're happy with what you've entered, you can tell the system to go ahead and submit your information. (See Figs. 13-1 and 13-2 for the PostMaster greeting screen and submission form.)

Figure 13-1

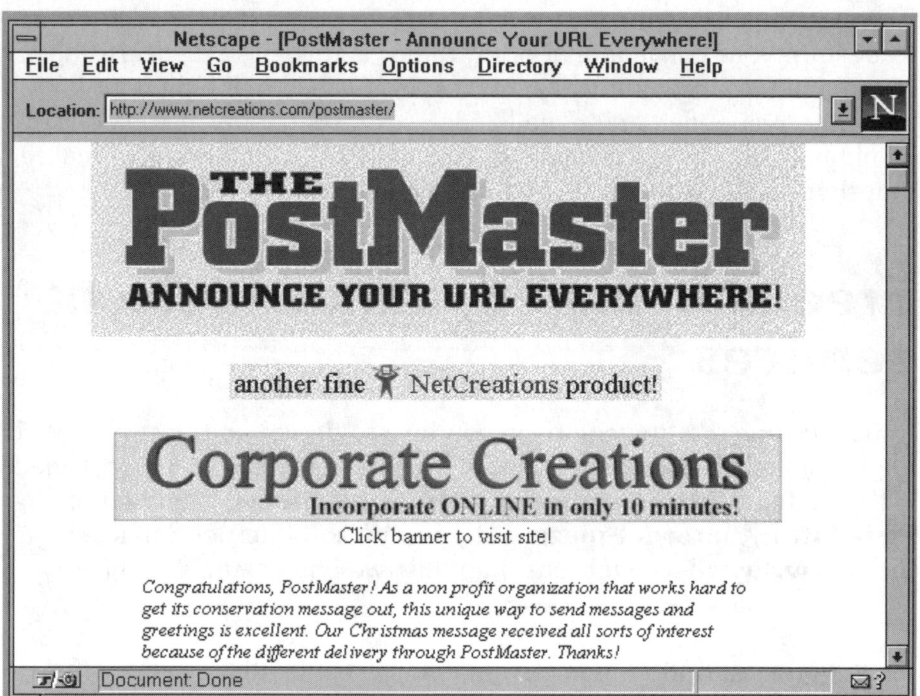


*The PostMaster greeting screen.*

The sites these two services submit to include Yahoo!, WebCrawler, Lycos, Infoseek, Open Text, the Whole Internet Catalog, and Net Happenings. You can control which sites are contacted by checking or unchecking a box by each one.

Our advice is to visit both Submit It! and PostMaster and print out or save to disk the information and instructions they provide. Read this

Figure 13-2

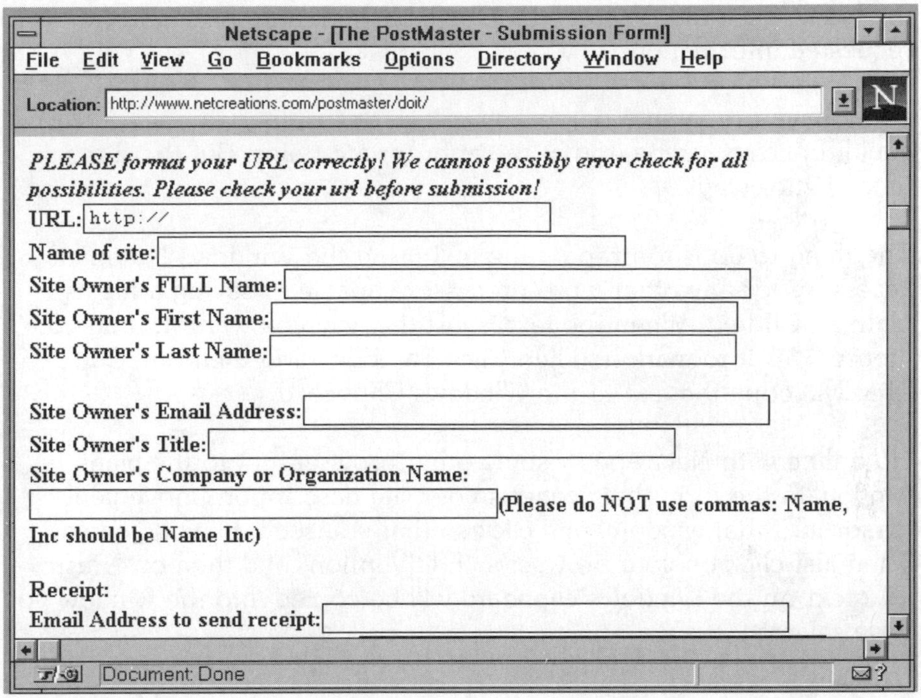

Netscape - [The PostMaster - Submission Form!]

File Edit View Go Bookmarks Options Directory Window Help

Location: http://www.netcreations.com/postmaster/doit/

*PLEASE format your URL correctly! We cannot possibly error check for all possibilities. Please check your url before submission!*

**URL:** http://

**Name of site:**

**Site Owner's FULL Name:**

**Site Owner's First Name:**

**Site Owner's Last Name:**

**Site Owner's Email Address:**

**Site Owner's Title:**

**Site Owner's Company or Organization Name:**

**(Please do NOT use commas: Name, Inc should be Name Inc)**

**Receipt:**

**Email Address to send receipt:**

Document: Done

*The form for submitting your information to PostMaster.*

material, then think about what you want to say about your site. What keywords are your prospects most likely to search for? How can you sum up your site in 25 words or less?

## The old Notepad trick

It's one thing to compose a quick e-mail note to a good friend or relative on the fly. But when you are describing your company's Web site, you want to take more time. The same is true for any text about your business or your services that you plan to put on the Internet. So what do you do when Submit It! or PostMaster or some other services asks you to key in a descriptive paragraph or two?

Well, the first thing to do is to visit the site or otherwise look at the form you will be asked to complete. Print it out and then fill in most of

the blanks by hand. You can then sign back on and quickly key in the requested information.

If you have prepared a paragraph or two describing your site, you could, of course, type it in at the appropriate point. But there is a much better way!

The thing to do is to prepare the text using the Windows Notepad accessory, or any other word processor capable of saving a file as plain ASCII text. When the text is just the way you want it, drag your mouse over it to mark it. Then Click on "Edit" and then on "Cut." That will copy the text to the Windows Clipboard.

Go online with Netscape or some other browser, get to the blank window in the form that requests your site description, move your cursor into that window, and click so that you see a blinking cursor. Then just click on your browser's "Edit" option, and then on "Paste." The text on the Windows clipboard will be copied into the window you have selected.

## Fee-based announcement services

Submit It! and PostMaster are completely automated services. Your information is sent to the various search engines and directories untouched by human hands. That's why the companies can offer the service free of charge.

Their reason for doing so, however, is to get you to visit their sites and give them the opportunity to show you advertising or sell you on additional services. PostMaster's free service, for example, will post your information to about 24 different popular sites. But its main package is the posting of your information to some 260 catalogues, directories, and other Internet resources at a one-time cost of $500. (For more information about the fee service, visit the PostMaster Web site at **http://www.netcreations.com**, or call 718-522-1531.)

Similarly, the Submit It! site is currently sponsored by PostMaster and another Web announcement service called WebPromote (**http://www.webpromote.com**). WebPromote offers three levels of service. The Gold level costs $1,200 a month and includes 24 hours of promotional service. The Silver level is $675 a month for 12 hours. And the Bronze level is $250 a month for two hours. Custom packages are also available. For more information, visit their Web site or call 312-248-6116.

##  Link-placement services

One time-honored technique for building Web page traffic is getting other Web pages to include hot links that will transport their users to *your* page. In the past, something akin to "professional courtesy" has ruled: You put a link to my page on your site, and I'll put a link to your page on mine.

A good example might be a page maintained by one of the professional or business associations you belong to. If the association is smart, it will have a spot where members can place hotlinks to their individual pages at no cost.

However, our sense is that this is changing. In part it is due to the ever-expanding number of relevant links. Pick a topic, and there are undoubtedly several score of Web sites that deal with it. Placing 40 or 60 or 80 links on your page for free is beyond the scope of courtesy. Besides, more and more, a link on a popular page is seen as a valuable commodity.

Suppose, for example, that someone has created a site devoted to the Rolling Stones simply because he is interested in the group. The site is non-commercial. It is not connected with the Stones or any other organization. And it is enormously popular. Tomorrow, the Stones, down to their last $20 million or so, announce that they're going on tour. Don't you think our Webmaster/Stones fan could charge for putting a link on his page?

He could and would. And if he didn't do it, the day after tomorrow, someone would be online with a new Rolling Stones site trying to cash in.

Our point is simply this: Hotlinks on other Web site pages used to be free as part of a reciprocal arrangement. Many still are. But as the Web grows, more Webmasters are going to begin charging for including a link to your page. Not because it costs them anything to do so, but because a link on their page has intrinsic value.

One company that specializes in placing links to your page on other pages is Worldata Services. The firm's brochure and promotional materials are badly cluttered, but they seem to know what they are doing. Basically, for a fee of between $35 and $100 per location, the company's WebConnect service will see to it that you have a hotlink and small graphic-image display ad.

Worldata offers other services as well. For more information, call 407-393-8200, send mail to **mail@worldata.com**, or visit their Web site at **http://www.worldata.com**.

## Personal attention: Eric Ward's NetPost

In this part of the book, we have made a conscious effort to make you aware of the evolutionary nature of the tools we are dealing with. At this stage of the game, no one can stand up and crow that he or she has the perfect solution. Yet, grizzled old online hands that we are, we have some notion of where things *might* be heading. And that's toward *personalized* service of the sort you can expect from a leading advertising or public relations firm.

Automated services like Submit It! and PostMaster are interesting because they demonstrate how cleverness can cut costs. Worldata Services and WebConnect add a human "representative" to the mix. But there is still a higher level of service.

How would you like your own personal "account executive?" No, strike that. At advertising and public relations agencies, account executives tend to be intermediaries, not principal players. They propose. They present. But they don't create. So how would you like to work directly with someone who is not only an Internet expert but also a master of PR and advertising?

And just who might that be? One place to start is with a fellow named Eric Ward, who calls his company NetPost (**http://www.netpost.com**).

No one can know anything for certain, but we think Mr. Ward may represent the future of online marketing. His background includes stints at Time, Inc., Whittle Communications, and R. R. Donnelley. Among his Fortune 500 clients are IBM, Sotheby's, Dole Foods, Stoli Central, and one of our favorite sites, Amazon.com Books.

His unique selling proposition? The best term we can provide is "hand-crafted online marketing." Mr. Ward analyzes your product or service and personally looks for ways to promote it on the Web and in newsgroups and elsewhere on the Net. ("Elsewhere" includes placements in e-zines, Web-zines and other electronic magazine-like publications, print media, and "affinity" pages, about which more, later.)

The cost for a "campaign" will be between $400 and $900. There are no hourly charges, and clients receive an extensive printed report documenting where their links or whatever have been posted.

We have no relationship with Eric Ward at all. But we're not alone in thinking highly of his services. His site won a 1995 Tenagra Award for Internet Marketing Excellence, along with Yahoo!, Federal Express, Ragu, and Virtual Vineyards.

Our instincts are that eventually "online" will come to be seen as one more medium, just as radio is a medium and television is a medium. Eventually conventional advertising and PR agencies will catch up. But right now, the best work online is being done by independents like Eric Ward.

# Finding (& vetting) announcement services

Although we have highlighted some of the best services in this chapter, we have made no attempt to offer a comprehensive list. That's why you should also go to Yahoo! at **http://www.yahoo.com** and search on the phrase "announcement services." Or work your way through the Yahoo! directory by clicking on "Business and Economy," then "Companies," then "Internet Services," then "Web Presence Providers," and finally "Announcement Services."

Once you get there, you will see a screen like the one shown in Fig. 13-3. Your best bet at this point is probably to print the page, sign off, and review the printout for possible sites to investigate.

Figure 13-3

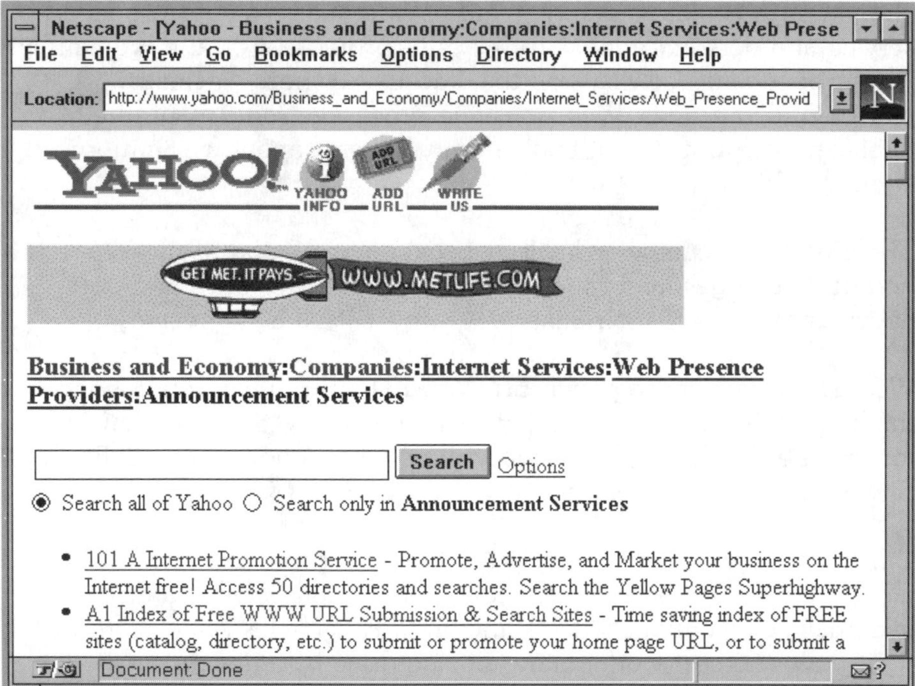


*Check the Yahoo! directory for more Web announcement services.*

## The questions to ask

If you decide to look for someone to take on the responsibility of promoting your Web site, keep in mind that it is very much the wild, wild west out there right now. That's why we are pleased to borrow freely from the advice offered by Eric Ward at his NetPost Web site. Among other things, Mr. Ward recommends the following :

- Demand a printout for every site used.
  Not just a list of the sites supposedly posted to, but actual printouts of your Web page information as it appears on a given site.
- Ask for references.
  And how! It is true that this profession is so new that no one is likely to have a very extensive client list. But the business is old enough that nearly everyone soliciting your business should be able to give you three or four people to contact as references.
- Be cautious of those services that charge by the hour.
  It's one thing to charge an hourly rate for giving advice and otherwise consulting with a client. But when there are clear "deliverables" like a certain number of successful postings to search engines, an hourly charge may not be in your best interests.
- Ask for "category exclusivity."
  There is a clear conflict of interest when a Web site promoter agrees to place links and do other tasks for two or more clients that directly compete with each other. Just as the advertising agency representing Coke would not also take Pepsi as a client, a Web promoter who has agreed to spread the word about your widget site should not have more than one widget maker on his or her list.

## Special interest pages

NetPost's Eric Ward (**http://www.netpost.com**) and Ralph Wilson of Wilson Internet Services (**http://www.wilsonweb.com**) are two of

the sanest, most practical and realistic voices on the Internet when it comes to electronic marketing. We can say that because, most of the time, they agree with us!

In all seriousness, there really is a common-sense, common body of knowledge out there about how to best use this wonderful new medium to market, promote, and sell goods and services. And it has nothing to do with the hype produced by companies with something to gain—hype that is then picked up and disseminated by an ignorant, often lazy press. (Just as the companies pumping this bilge water knew would be the case!)

So we have no compunction about sharing with you here another idea from Eric Ward and NetPost. The concept is so elegant and simple that, frankly, we nearly forgot about it. But here it is.

Scattered all over the World Wide Web are pages created by some individual to celebrate or otherwise bring together resources devoted to a particular subject. Eric Ward refers to such pages as "subject-specific and affinity internet audience sites." But we can simplify that to read "special-interest pages."

## A chocolaty example

As any fan of P.G. Wodehouse knows, the world is filled with eccentrics whose life passion is some rare genus of butterfly or some obscure species of toad. Such people lead a very insular existence, and, on encountering someone who expresses even the remotest interest in their field, tend to grapple them to their souls with hoops strong enough to squeeze the life out of them!

Well, on the Net, people of such passionate interests never need feel alone. Pick a topic, any topic, and there's a very good chance that several thousand other Internet users have already set up a newsgroup, created one or more mailing lists, and put up half a dozen topic-specific Web pages.

As Eric Ward says, special interest pages really are "the hidden treasure of the Net." At least when it comes to marketing. That's because everyone who visits one of these special-interest pages is almost surely interested in its main topic. If you can get a hotlink to your Web site placed on such a page, you're ahead of the pack.

For example, your co-authors happen to love truly fine chocolate. Not the beige, flavored wax that enrobes most common candy bars, but the *real*, exceptionally rich thing. Two single one-inch squares of the "good stuff" and a cup of Mocha Java, and, as Alfred's mother would say, "That's dessert, kids!" Well, it is.

So we used a search engine to look for Web sites devoted to chocolate. And guess what—we found "The Chocolate Lovers' Page" at **http://bc.emanon.net/chocolate**. The first part of this page is shown in Fig. 13-4. It begins with "Chocolate Retailers on the Web" and continues with "Other Chocolate Resources on the Web."

Figure 13-4

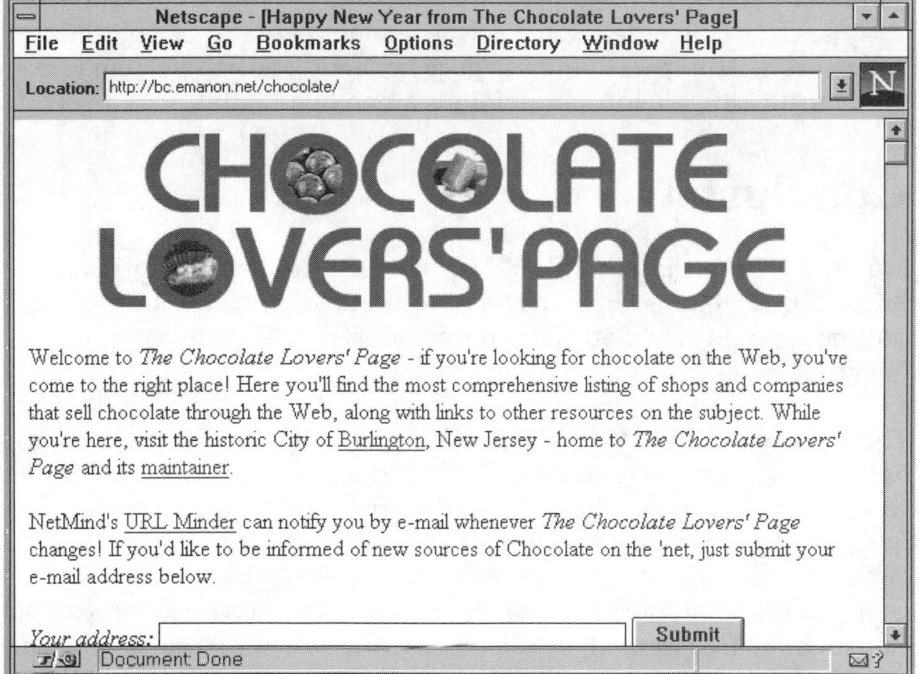


*The Chocolate Lovers' Page.*

If you are a candymaker with any kind of chocolate product in your line, you should have a link on this page. Prospective customers are likely to find the page by using a search engine with the keyword "chocolate." Then they'll go to the page, review the listings, click on your link, and be delivered to your page, at which point you'll have the opportunity to sell them on your offerings.

As is the case on most special-interest pages, posting a link to your page is free. But you've pretty much got to take what you get. Thus, the Chocolate Lovers' Page presents an alphabetical list of chocolate retailers on the Web. Each location gets a single title line. So how is a customer to know whether she should click on "Black Hound" or "Esther Price Chocolates" or "Sweet Seduction?"

The lesson is this: If it's free, you want to have your Web page hotlink/URL listed. But, of course, it's got to be appropriate. You don't want your chocolate shop listed on a page devoted to wild and crazy sex. (On the other hand, maybe you do. None of our business.) In any event, the special-interest page concept is worth pursuing. Even if, in most cases, all you can put up is a one-line hotlink.

## Conclusion

In Part 3, "Spreading the Word," we have covered a lot of ground. We've talked about search engines, free directory listings, newsgroup postings, mailing lists, and announcement services. Now, let's cut to the chase.

The key point is this: World Wide Web sites and auto-responders have become so affordable that if you're in business today, you probably can't afford *not* to use them. This is true whether you are a local florist or pizza shop or an international conglomerate.

Lest you think we have become enmeshed in the hype engine, you should know that in the first edition of this book, we strongly advised *against* putting up a Web site. But now that there are alternatives to the companies demanding tens of thousands of dollars to create a Web site, now that any kid can create a site with a clutch of free software tools, we say, "Sure, why not!"

You have heard this from us many tines before, yet it bears repeating. The Internet in general—and the World Wide Web in particular—offer genuine, revolutionary marketing opportunities. If you make no assumptions, have no expectations, and always, always, always put your customers' needs first—if you take the you-approach at all times—this new medium will pleasantly surprise you.

The essential key is to view it as one more way to help, serve, and answer the needs of your customers. Your co-authors have worked retail. We know how difficult some people can be. But we also know the fulfillment of satisfying a customer's needs.

One thing we have learned is that people like to buy from people they know. And as strange as it may sound, the world-spanning Internet may be your best opportunity to get to know your customers and to have them get to know you. After all, if you don't like—if you don't *cherish*—human beings in all of our humor, pathos, tragedy, and joy—if relationships aren't a major factor in your life, then you probably should not be in sales in the first place.

But if you like people, if you are possessed of the entrepreneurial spirit, as so many of our FireCrystal clients are, and if you've got a product or service to sell, read on! In Part 4, "Online Entrepreneurs in Action," we profile the good, the bad, and the not-so-ugly as we show you the efforts numerous companies have made to exploit the Web and the Net. We guarantee you will find Part 4 both informative and fun.

# Part 4

# Entrepreneurs in action

# 14

# Books & music

# CHAPTER 14

IN this chapter, we'll look at how companies are selling books and audio CDs on the Net. The companies considered here have lessons to offer, even if you are *not* in the book- or music-selling business.

Try to think generically. Books are a known category of product. And specific books by specific authors are known as well, thanks to widely distributed printed reviews, movies based on books, and word of mouth. The same can be said of audio CDs. Books and CDs (in general) are also available from many conventional stores and mail-order outlets.

Much the same could be said of third-party auto parts makers and sellers, sellers of stereo components and video equipment, and anyone else who sells a product or branded product line that is well-known to consumers and is also available from many other outlets.

If that applies to you, then this *chapter* applies to you, even if you don't sell books or tapes and CDs.

## Amazon.com Books

Web address: **http://www.amazon.com**

Alfred spent over a year of his early career as a book salesperson and buyer at the fabled Scribner Book Store on Fifth Avenue in New York City. So we have a special feeling for bookpeople of all sorts.

We know the business. We know that at least 50,000 new books are published each year. That's nearly 1,000 new titles every week. We know that the big chains are making it increasingly difficult for the "mom-and-pop" independent booksellers to survive.

After all, how can an independent offer a standing 20 percent discount on every book on the *New York Times* best-seller list? But the big national chains, with their incredible buying leverage, do this all the time.

The only way independent booksellers can compete is to offer better customer service. For example, we are blessed to live less than a mile from David's Bookshelf in Morrisville, Pennsylvania. Whenever we hear about a book of interest, we pick up the phone and call Bobbie and David Devon, the "mom and pop" who run David's Bookshelf, and ask them to order it.

A day or two later, one of them calls. The book is in. We stop by, pick it up, and say, "Please put this on our account." They don't even ask us to sign anything. They love books, know our interests, and always have a title or two to recommend whenever we ask for suggestions.

The genius of Amazon.com Books (Fig. 14-1) is that it cleverly employs technology to bring customers the kind of selection and discounts they expect from Waldenbooks, B. Dalton, and other big chains, along with the kind of customer service only independent booksellers can offer.

Figure 14-1

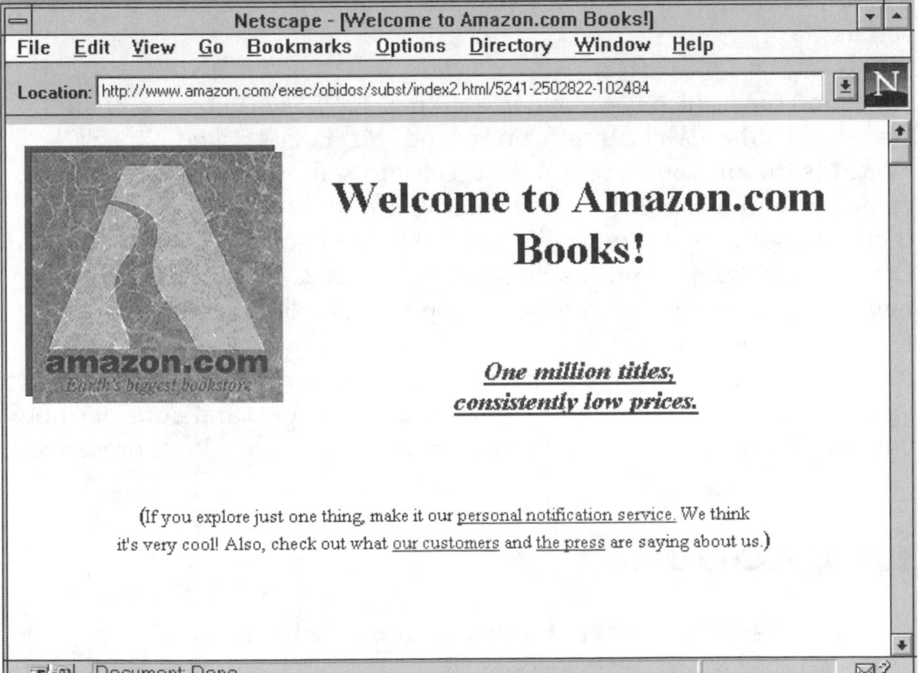


*Amazon.com bills itself as "Earth's Largest Bookstore."*

## All about Amazon.com

Amazon.com offers bestsellers at a 30 percent discount, hardcovers at a 20 percent discount, and most paperbacks at a 10 percent discount. Its catalogue contains over one million titles, and you can search it by author, title, keyword, and more. The typical bookstore at your local mall, in contrast, stocks about 30,000 titles, while "superstores" of the sort Barnes & Noble made famous stock about 120,000.

The folks who run Amazon.com also offer their own suggestions and recommendations. You can even key in a short book review of your own and read what other customers have said.

One of Amazon.com's neatest features is its Eyes & Editors "personal notification service." If you've heard that a book is due out soon in paperback, or have a particular subject or author you like to follow, you can ask Amazon.com to automatically notify you by e-mail as soon as the relevant book becomes available. There is no charge for this service.

Amazon.com, which went live in October 1995, was created by Jeff Bezos, a former Wall Street wunderkind. Mr. Bezos asked himself, "What is the first and best product to try to sell on the Internet?" He came up with a list of 20 possibilities and opted for books because there are so many of them. We point this out because, even though Mr. Bezos didn't come from the bookselling industry, he and his associates have done a masterful job of designing a bookselling feature.

And the way they did it was to take the you-approach. We urge you to visit this site, get a sense of its personality and feel, and consider how you might apply some of the same techniques to your Web presence.

# BookBound

Web address: **http://www.hamptons.com/bookbound**

It's worth noting that Amazon.com Books took nearly a year—and substantial venture capital—to create. A company called BookBound,

"America's favorite bookstore by phone," has taken a much simpler approach. It has created an attractive Web site that explains its service and urges you to place your order by phone.

We discovered BookBound from its little three-inch ad in the *New York Times Book Review*. The ad carried the same drawing of a house you see on the BookBound Web page (Fig. 14-2), and made the pitch, "Call us to order any book in this review." At the bottom of the ad, in small type, was a line reading "Visit our Web site at," followed by the address.

Figure 14-2

*BookBound's storefront on the Web.*

The Web site gives the company the chance to tell you more about its service than it could do in the print ad. And, of course, it makes it possible for people searching for books online to find them.

# Windham Hill

Web address: **http://www.windham.com**

Windham Hill describes itself as an independent record company offering innovative music, hand-selected for its artistic quality. All that's true, of course, but the company is probably best known as the prime purveyor of "New Age" instrumental music.

The point is that Windham Hill is a record company with a difference. It has a distinct personality. And as the firm says, "the unprecedented audience allegiance that was carefully cultivated over the years has been complemented by numerous Grammy Award nominations."

The Windham Hill Web site (Fig. 14-3) has been splendidly designed to foster that kind of audience allegiance. Our sense is that relatively few

Figure 14-3

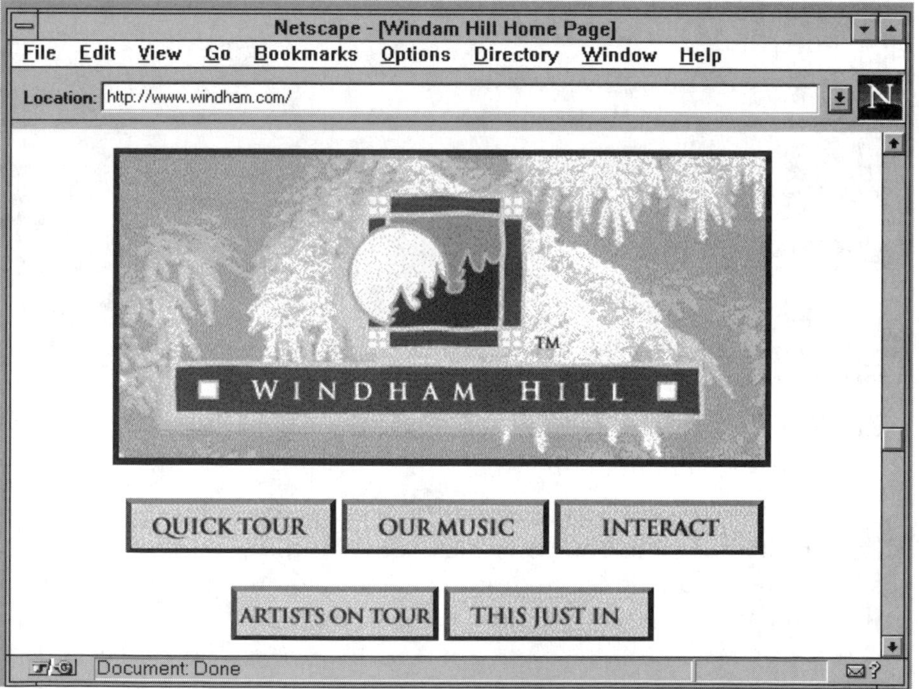


*The Windham Hill home page.*

people are likely to stumble upon Windham Hill, download a sound clip, and order the corresponding CD. But lots of Internet-enabled Windham Hill fans are sure to check in regularly. And, of course, someone who reads a write-up of the company or one of its artists in a magazine might think to look for the firm online.

Even if music is not an interest of yours, visit this site and observe what they've done. There's the usual background on the company and its goals, of course. But there are also lots of opportunities to listen to sound clips, order sheet music and songbooks, check the schedules of "Artists on Tour," read profiles of artists, and learn about their latest releases.

There are also a large number of "chat lines" that allow you to conduct real-time conversations from your keyboard with other fans, and even with Windham Hill artists. The site also makes it easy for you to send e-mail to Windham Hill, but it has avoided the complications of online ordering. Throughout the site, whenever a specific product is mentioned and a price quoted, the toll-free ordering number appears.

# The Capitol Steps

Web address: **http://pfm.het.brown.edu/people/mende/steps**

The Capitol Steps, a Washington, D.C.-based comedy troupe made up of former Congressional staffers, aides, and other self-described layabouts is a sheer delight. You may have seen them on C-SPAN or PBS, or heard them on National Public Radio. (Note that it is indeed "het," not "net," in the Web address.)

Their home page (Fig. 14-4) was created by Paul Mende at Brown University. But Mike Tilford is the "evil genius" behind the Capitol Steps point of presence on the Net. At least, he's the guy who answered (delightfully) when we sent a message to **CapSteps@aol.com** while writing the first edition of this book.

Figure 14-4

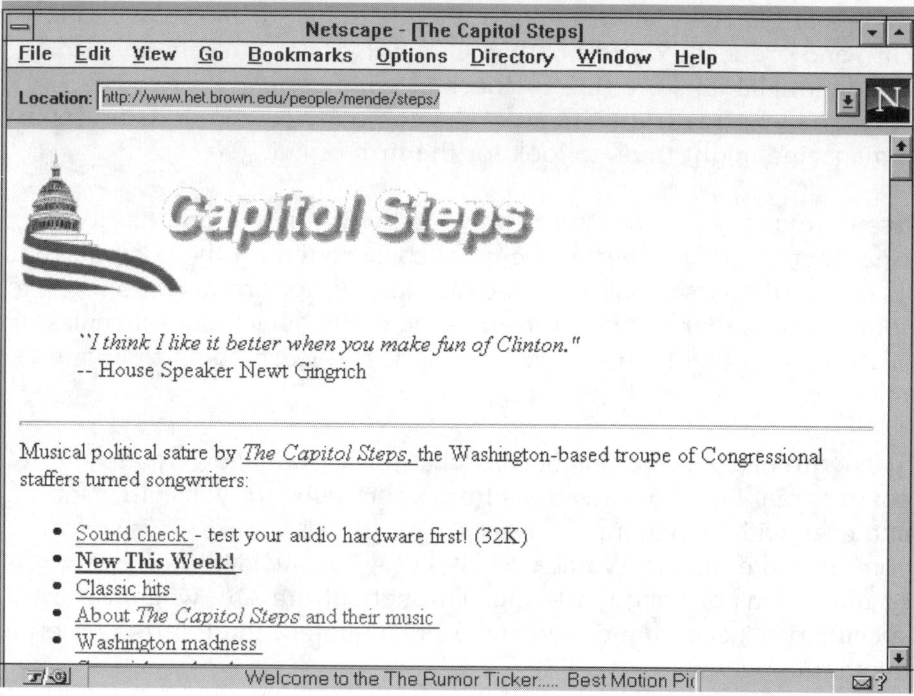


*Welcome to the Capitol Steps!*

When he inadvertently sent us some faulty information, he wrote back: "Sorry for the misdirection. That's what you get for hanging around with politicians—the urge to answer even if you don't know what you're talking about . . ."

We've included the Capitol Steps—think back to Watergate and John Dean and his wife and you'll get the joke—because we like them. But also because this site demonstrates yet another way to do what Windham Hill has done—create a site aimed at your fans and enthusiasts.

You can indeed arrange to purchase Capitol Steps albums at this site. But selling albums is clearly not its main priority. Far more important is to create a sense that "something new is always happening at this site." For each of the most recent six weeks or so, you will find a news headline and a clickable button that will let you download and play some topical Capitol Steps song.

Other links are called "Who are the Capitol Steps?," "What albums have they made?," and "Where can I hear them live?" It's all done with the same kind of genuine non-partisan humor and cleverness that is the group's trademark. So you leave the site with a chuckle or two and a very good feeling about the group.

Among the songs you'll find on Capitol Steps albums are "Good Morning, Starbucks," "Your Son'll Come Out Tomorrow," "Snippity Bobbitt," "I've Taken Stands on Both Sides Now," and "It Don't Mean a Thing if We Trade with Beijing."

One final technical note. Before you go to the site, make sure that the program NAPLAYER is in your Netscape directory. Then do the "Sound Check" that is the first menu item on the greeting screen. If NAPLAYER, one of the programs supplied with Netscape, is indeed on your disk, you will hear the first few bars of "Yankee Doodle" and thus know that you can sample all of the Capitol Steps sound clips you want.

# 15

# Business & financial services

THERE are a huge number of business and financial services in general, and a great many of them have an Internet presence of some sort. But rather than present a roundup consisting of an endless list of places for you to visit, we have decided to focus on just three companies: The Company Corporation, Federal Express, and QuoteCom.

There are at least two threads that link all of these organizations. First, they don't sell a product—they provide a service. Second, each has been quite successful for several years. So they must be doing something right.

# The Company Corporation

Web address: **http://incorporate.com/tcc/home.html**

The Company Corporation is in the business of making it as easy as possible for you to incorporate your business. The cost is $45, plus state filing fees (usually around $75), and you can expect confirmation of incorporation in 48 hours or less.

So what's this got to do with you? Well, first of all, you need to know that this firm routinely takes four-by-five-inch ads in the *Wall Street Journal*. And each ad always includes an 800 number, the firm's address on CompuServe (GO CORP), and its Web address.

The Company Corporation offers a service familiar to many readers—what small-business owner hasn't pondered the pros and cons of incorporating?—and it uses technology to automate the process and thus keep prices to the absolute minimum.

When you arrive at the Web site (Fig. 15-1), you learn instantly that you can incorporate by phone, fax, or online. And you are given a menu that leads to a huge amount of information about why you might want to incorporate, choosing the right business structure, and so on.

The Company Corporation makes it easy to contact them. They give you an e-mail address, toll-free number, international number, fax

Figure 15-1

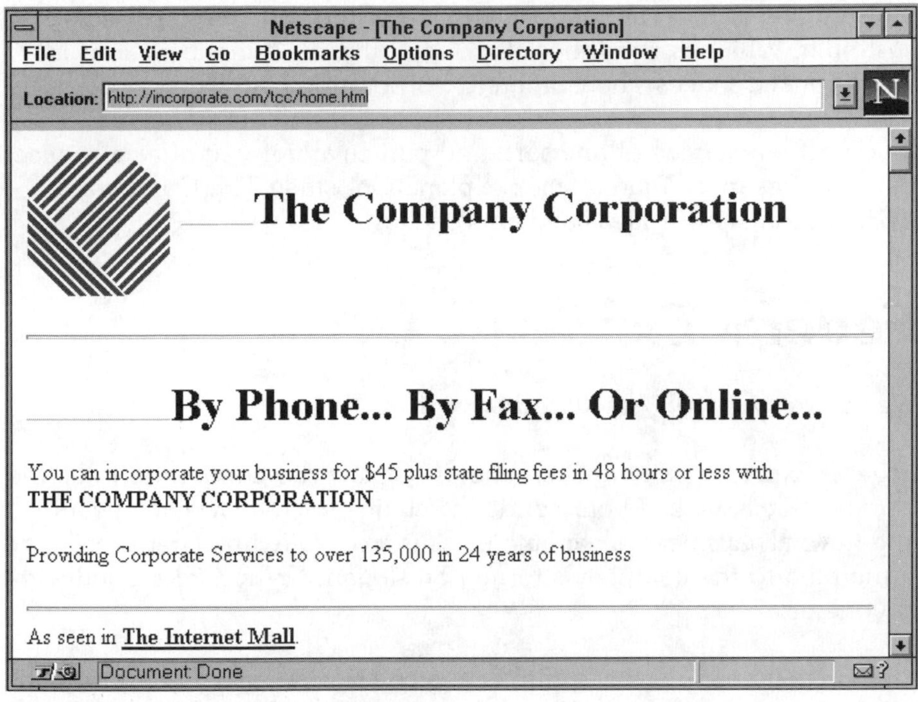


*The Company Corporation home page.*

number, land address, and regular voice phone number. You can click on one link and request that they send you a free guide to incorporating.

Now, think about this. The subject of whether you should or should not change your business from a sole proprietorship to a corporation, and if so into a "Sub-chapter S" corporation or something else, is not something anyone can afford to discuss in a paid advertisement. So The Company Corporation includes an offer in all its print ads for a free printed booklet.

Then along comes the Internet, and bright bulbs that they are, the folks at The Company Corporation exploit it to offer even more information and guidance. Putting up a Web site and referencing it in their ads may save some money on mail-out brochures. But it also lets the firm deliver more information, and it allows them to continually update things.

It also helps to build an interactive relationship with the prospective customer. Which is good, because one of the site's menu options is "Additional Services The Company Corporation Can Provide."

If you offer a service of any sort, and particularly if you offer a service that requires more than a quick explanation, study The Company Corporation site for ideas and approaches.

# Federal Express

Web address: **http://www.fedex.com**

Federal Express has long been one of our favorite companies in all the world. They have been our courier of choice for many, many years and have always been a genuine pleasure to deal with. There really is something to the company's former ad slogan, "Why fool around with anyone else?"

Like any company pushing the technological envelope, they have had some spectacular failures. We well remember FedEx Zap Mail, a service based on high-quality fax technology some 15 years ago. But by all accounts, FedEx's venture onto the World Wide Web (Fig. 15-2) has been a spectacular success. It has become instantly popular with FedEx customers and has saved the company millions of dollars.

The site has a lot to offer, but there are really just two things you need to know. First, for years FedEx has been building and refining an automated, computerized package-tracking function. This allows the firm to offer customers a toll-free voice number staffed by human beings who can tell customers where a given package is at any time of day or night.

The company plugged this function into its Web site, and all of a sudden customers can track packages from their own keyboards. Result: A huge drop in the number of calls placed to FedEx 800 numbers, at a savings of millions of dollars a year.

Figure 15-2

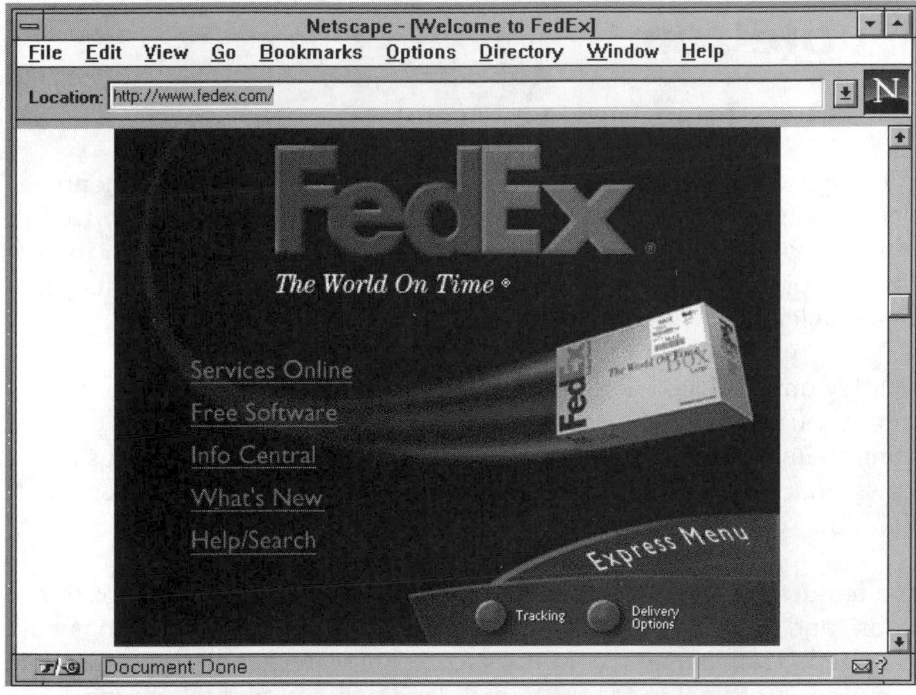


*The enormously popular Federal Express site on the Web.*

Second, the site lets PC and Mac users download a free program called FedEx Ship. The program allows you to print bar-coded shipping documents, on plain paper, using your laser printer. And it thus eliminates the need to type up FedEx airbills.

This is one of the sites most popular features, and we can well understand why. We keep an old IBM Selectric typewriter around solely for the purpose of typing up labels and multi-part forms of the sort FedEx normally uses. What a nuisance!

The Federal Express site is one of the leading Web sites on the Internet, and you absolutely must pay it a visit. It's not likely that you yourself will need anything as elaborate. But it is enormously instructive to see "how it's done" at a truly superior site.

# QuoteCom

Web address: **http://www.quote.com**

Although we know and have written a great deal about investments, your co-authors are not stock traders. Like most people, we try to do our best with limited resources and limited time. But staying on top of things—or even finding the time to read the quarterly statements—is a real challenge.

QuoteCom's mission is to provide "quality financial market data to Internet users . . . [including] current quotes on stocks, options, commodity futures, mutual funds, and bonds. It also includes business news, market analysis and commentary, fundamental (balance sheet) data, and company profiles."

We featured the QuoteCom site (Fig. 15-3) in the first edition of this book, and are pleased to do so again here. However, some things have changed. The company continues to do a wonderful job in making it easy for you to get in touch. E-mail, land address, and telephone numbers are right there, right up front.

But from there, simplicity and clarity take a seat in the "way-back" of the station wagon, right above the spare-tire well. When we checked in recently, for example, QuoteCom offered no fewer than 17 different subscription options. These ranged from free, basic, advanced, pro, ProPlus, Canada, chart, Reuters, and on and on and on.

QuoteCom has always been a leader in using e-mail and auto-responders. But now, the site presents an incredibly complex and elaborate set of instructions on what specific words or phrases you must include in your e-mail subject line and body copy to be sure of getting the specific information you want.

We truly wish that we could be more positive. We singled out QuoteCom in the first edition of this book as a company that really knew how to use the technology. But given what it has become, we offer the QuoteCom site here as an example of technology run amok.

Figure 15-3

*The opening screen for QuoteCom's Web site.*

Please visit the site. Click around a bit. And then see if you don't agree that the folks at QuoteCom have missed the boat when it comes to creating an easy-to-use, logical service. Great potential. Terrible, technology-intoxicated execution.

# 16

# Computer-related products

COMPUTER-related products? Why should I be interested in reviewing that area of the Web? After all, I sell custom-designed jewelry, hand-crafted furniture, or counseling-by-phone. What's that got to do with hard drives, monitors, and DRAM chips?

Nothing, of course. Except that, historically, the most successful online entrepreneurs have been those dealing in computer-related products. Certainly part of their success is due to the fact that Internet users are the perfect audience for those products. But you'll find that such companies may just have something to teach you, even though you are in a completely different business.

## Computer Express

Web address: **http://www.cexpress.com**

Started in 1984 by the husband and wife team of Philip and Lesley Schier, Computer Express established one of the first storefronts on the Net. Since that time, the firm claims to have had over 300,000 satisfied customers for its computer hardware and software products.

This is one online-savvy company. To receive general information, send a one-line note to the address **info@cexpress.com**. For a list of free demonstration programs and instructions on how to download them, send e-mail to **demo@cexpress.com**. For voice contact, call them at 800-228-7449. All of this address information appears prominently on the company's Web page.

The Computer Express home page (Fig. 16-1) is too graphics-heavy for our tastes. But once you're there, you really should explore the links and the demos and the searchable database of products the site offers. Computer Express has developed a winning strategy for attracting and keeping customers. So learn from them.

## Dell Computer Corporation

Web address: **http://www.us.dell.com**

Figure 16-1

*The Computer Express Online Superstore.*

Dell Computer Corporation was started by Michael Dell in his dorm room at college. The firm represents a huge mail-order success story. But, of course, it faces enormous competition from the likes of Gateway, Compaq, and Hewlett Packard.

As you would expect, you can get information about Dell products from its Web site (Fig. 16-2). But you can also check the status of your order. And you can read corporate press releases, locate information for investors in Dell, and check out the monthly specials.

Perhaps most amazing of all, you can get technical support. There's a form to fill out on which you ask your question. (If your browser doesn't support forms, you can submit your query by e-mail.) Dell will do its best to respond within two working days. If your need is urgent, there is a toll-free number to dial.

Figure 16-2

*The Dell Computer Web site.*

This is a fast, well-designed site that really does take the "you-approach." Check it out and see if you don't agree.

# Scandinavian Computer Furniture

Web address: **http://www.scanc.com**

The first thing that impressed us about the ScanCo site (Fig. 16-3) operated by Scandinavian Computer Furniture was the speed with which the large opening-screen graphic loaded. This may be due to the speed of their server and connection to the Internet backbone. But we suspect it is also because the page designer took the time to reduce the color depth (the number of colors used) in the image, a sure sign of a company that knows what it's doing.

Figure 16-3

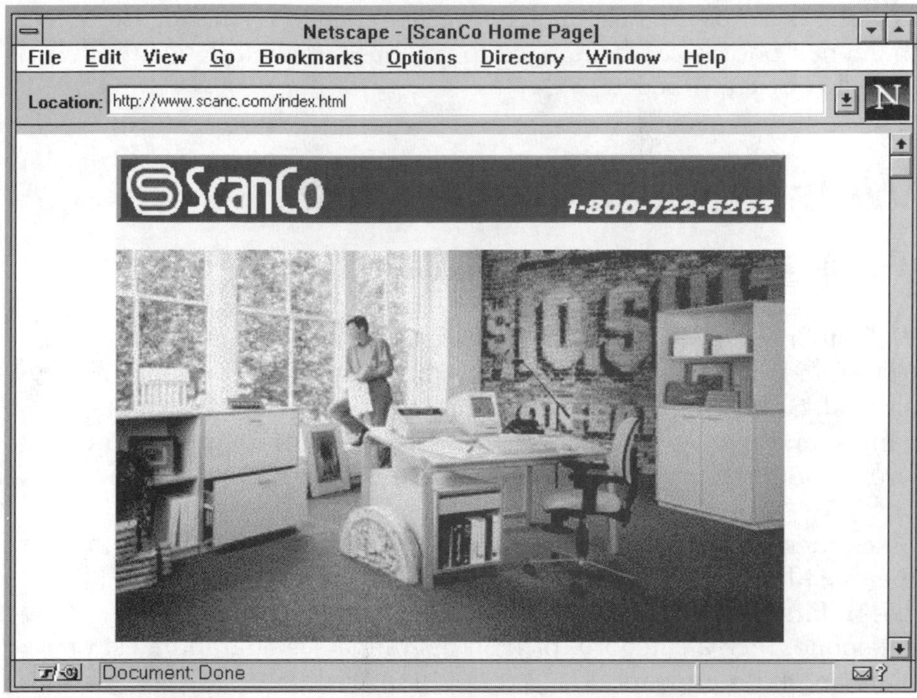


*Scandinavian Computer Furniture's ScanCo home page.*

We discovered ScanCo from its small display ads in the *New Yorker* and the *Wall Street Journal*, each of which always carries the firm's Web address. When you go to the page, you will see that you are given all kinds of ways to reach ScanCo (land address, phone numbers, fax numbers, e-mail).

Select a product category, like "Computer Tables," and an attractive series of "thumbnail" photos appears. Each thumbnail is large enough to give you a good look at the product, but, at about two inches on a side, not so large that they take a long time to transmit.

Click on a thumbnail, and a three-by-five-inch version of the photo appears, along with the product specifications, prices, and packaging and shipping information.

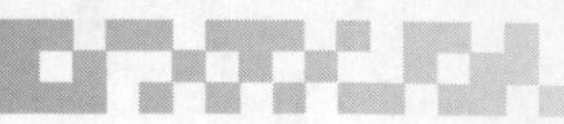

The site is simple and clean, yet visually appealing. And its use of thumbnail photos can be applied to any business with a need to actually *show* a product.

# Walnut Creek CDROM

Web address: **http://www.cdrom.com**

Walnut Creek CDROM is one of the leading creators and purveyors of CD-ROM-based shareware, text files, and Internet information. They also sell commercial CD-ROM-based products like clip art, fonts, games, and the like. We have always liked this company and, indeed, wrote about them in the first edition of this book.

Since then, Walnut Creek has been busy building what may be one of the most Internet-integrated Web sites you will ever encounter (Fig. 16-4). First, the company makes it easy for you to search its catalogue. Pick a category, pick an operating system, and a list of matching titles appears.

We have long felt that more companies should go the extra mile and make their catalogues *searchable* at their Web sites. This makes it so much easier for users to find what they want. (Of course, Walnut Creek also gives you the option of viewing its entire catalogue.)

Second, Walnut Creek "gives back to the Net" with a link to the company's FTP site—offering 52 gigabytes of public domain and shareware software—and links to other major collections.

But FTP and the Web are only two of the Internet tools the company uses. It provides auto-responders to make it possible for customers to request any of nine different e-mail files (catalogue, FAQ, ordering, etc.).

And it uses a mailing list to automatically notify customers of special deals, new products, and so on. You can subscribe by sending a message to **majordomo@cdrom.com** containing the words "subscribe announce" somewhere in the body of the message.

Figure 16-4

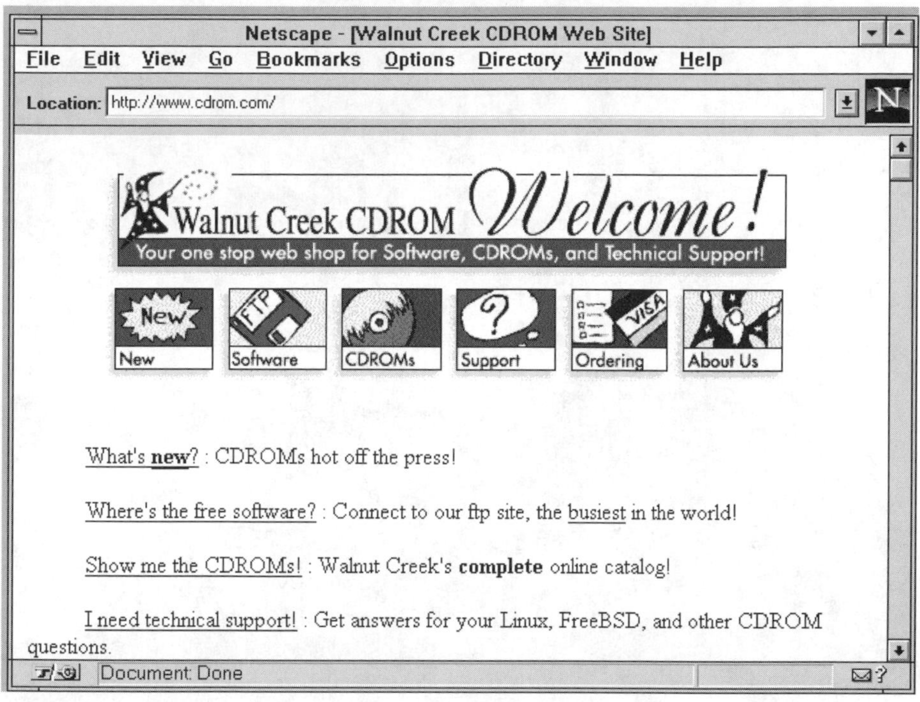


*Walnut Creek's greeting screen.*

Conventional contact information is provided as well, including not only fax, e-mail, and land address information, but also a toll-free number for the U.S. and Canada, and a number for international customers to dial. The sales and orders department is open 24 hours.

Just as you may not need to put product photos on your Web site the way ScanCo does, you may not need to employ as many Internet tools and features as they do at Walnut Creek. But if an FTP site, mailing list, searchable catalogue, and one or more auto-responders are appropriate, you will find that no one has woven such features into a Web site more effectively than Walnut Creek.

# Consumer electronics

REMEMBER the term "transistor radio?" If you do, then you were alive at the birth of the modern consumer-electronics industry. It was in the late 1950s, and transistor radios were a big deal because they had no vacuum tubes, were portable, and ran on a 9-volt battery. We've come a very long way since then, of course.

And, naturally, given the upscale demographics of many Net surfers, consumer-electronics companies are a major presence on the World Wide Web.

## Shoppers Advantage

Web address: **http://www.cuc.com**

We can start with what is probably the most successful online shopping feature of all time. Although it is now known as Shoppers Advantage, it began in 1973 as Comp-U-Card. The original goal was to make it possible for people to shop via their home computers. Something of a radical notion back then. Remember, the IBM/PC didn't appear until October 1981.

A bit too radical, as it turned out. Only by transforming Comp-U-Card into a discount shopping club able to take orders by voice phone could founder Walter Forbes hope to have his dream survive. He did. It did. And in fiscal 1995, CUC International posted revenues of $1 billion.

CUC/Shoppers Advantage solicits price quotes on over 250,000 brand-name items from manufacturers, wholesalers, and retailers all over the country. The information is entered into a computer, and whenever a customer requests a price quote on a given product, the lowest priced option is displayed.

The display may be the one attached to your own computer, if you are using Shoppers Advantage online. Or it may be one that's being used by one of the firm's 4,000 telephone operators. Either way, prices are typically 10 to 50 percent lower than the manufacturer's suggested retail price. You must first join Shoppers Advantage ($49 a year) before you can place an order, but special membership deals are sometimes offered.

CUC International has always aggressively pursued online selling. Its service has been available on CompuServe for over 17 years. You'll also find them on America Online, Prodigy, and other commercial services. Interestingly, as of the first quarter of 1996, only three to five percent of the company's three million members contact the company online.

It's been awhile since we've used Shoppers Advantage, but we *have* bought things from them and have been very pleased with the experience. We have also used the service's product search function many times without being members. And that is what we suggest you do to start.

Think of a product you might be interested in, like, say, a new fax machine. Then visit the Shoppers Advantage Web site (Fig. 17-1),

Figure 17-1

*The Shoppers Advantage home page.*

where you will be taken through the process, answering questions about the fax machine features you want, price range, manufacturer, and so on. You will then be presented with a list of matching products from the Shoppers Advantage database. Click on an item and you will receive a detailed description, including the price and cost of shipping.

Now set yourself the same task using your favorite Internet "mall." No comparison, right? The point being that Shoppers Advantage is a *very* sophisticated operation. So ask yourself, "Why would any customer who knew about Shoppers Advantage bother fiddling around with the typical Internet mall?" Would you?

There are at least two lessons here. We've placed Shoppers Advantage in this chapter because if there was ever a need for customers to be able to retrieve product specifications, it is in consumer electronics. But Shoppers Advantage offers all kinds of products. The first lesson is that *this* is the way to sell products online. Your site doesn't have to be as sophisticated, but, at the very least, you should make it possible for visitors to search your product catalogue.

Second, maybe the best way to sell your product via the Internet is to contact Shoppers Advantage and ask them to include you on their list of companies from whom price quotes are requested. At the very least, you can use Shoppers Advantage to find out what your competitors are selling a given product for.

Regardless of what you want to sell, don't miss Shoppers Advantage. Pretend to be a consumer, visit the site, and give it a real workout. We know you will be impressed—and inspired!

# Cassette House

Web address: **http://www.tape.com**

Art and Robin Munson are one of the best success stories we know of when it comes to marketing and selling on the Net. Songwriters and musicians by trade, they started Cassette House in 1981 to sell blank audio cassettes, DAT tape, instructional books, videos, and various music supplies.

With two or three record stores on every floor of every mall in the country, you wouldn't think this would be such a great online business. But the Munsons do quite well, thank you very much, with a minimum investment and monthly cost.

As you'll discover at their Web site (Fig. 17-2), satisfied customers include Walt Disney Feature Animation, MIT, Sony Pictures, Carnegie-Mellon University, National Public Radio, and many other firms and organizations. Why? The quick answer is "highest quality, lowest price, broadest selection."

Figure 17-2

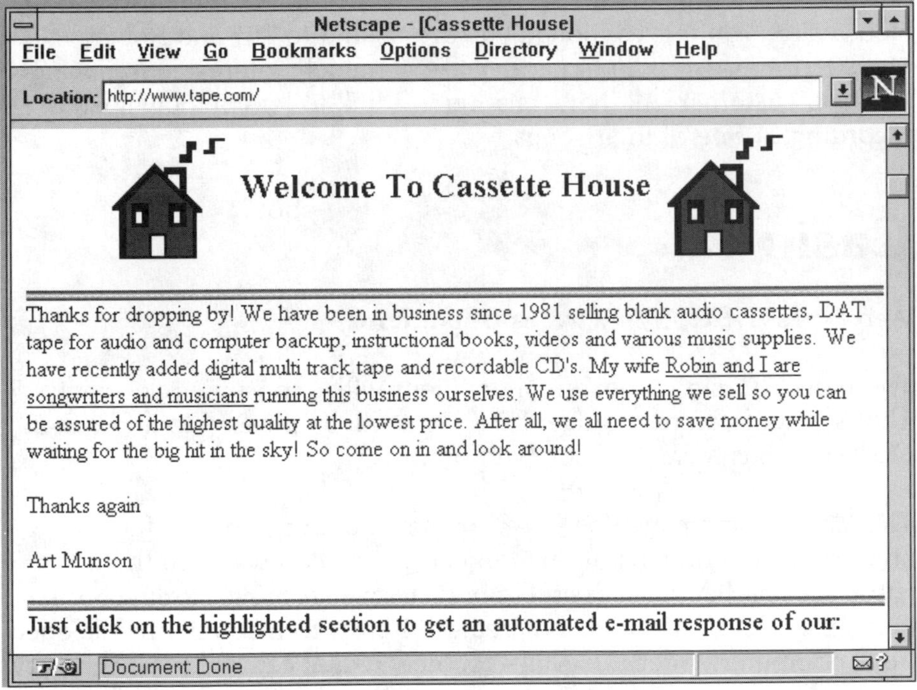


*The Cassette House greeting screen.*

We are not qualified to judge tape quality, and frankly, we did not check prices. But we were intrigued by the fact that Cassette House can sell you a 10- or 20-minute tape in the case of your choice, as well as all of the standard lengths you will find at the stores. Not to mention labels in a wide variety of colors, tape mailers, and "J-cards"

(those cards in a cassette box you can use to note what the tape contains).

These folks clearly know their main business and their customers' needs. And they know the Net. We were pleased to discover that, at our suggestion, the Munsons added auto-responders to their page. But they improved on the suggestion. In addition to offering their product catalogue via auto-responder, they also offer "Latest News and Sale Specials," "A Beginner's Guide to Audio CD Recording," and information on "Live Taping to DAT."

Finally, notice the personality that comes through at the Cassette House site. You feel as though you are talking to Art and Robin Munson themselves, and that they are genuinely interested in having you as a customer. All that's missing is a link to let you download a recording of one of their songs!

## Casio

Web address: **http://www.casio-usa.com**

The name "Casio" is nearly synonymous with "consumer electronics." That's why if you're a gadget freak, you will be pleased to know that Casio Inc. has a cracker-jack Web site.

The Casio home page (Fig. 17-3) presents both a sense of fun and interesting options. In the fun category when we were there is the "Second Annual Casio G-Shock Extreme Snowboarding Championships." But of even greater interest to a certain middle-aged, male computer writer were links to "new digital camera at CES," "new color label printer," and "digital piano with full-size keyboard."

Now, here's the thing. If consumer electronics is about anything, it's about *glitz* and *specifications*. The glitz is in the concept and the product design. The specs, however, are *text*. What better way to convey both than by using the World Wide Web?

Figure 17-3

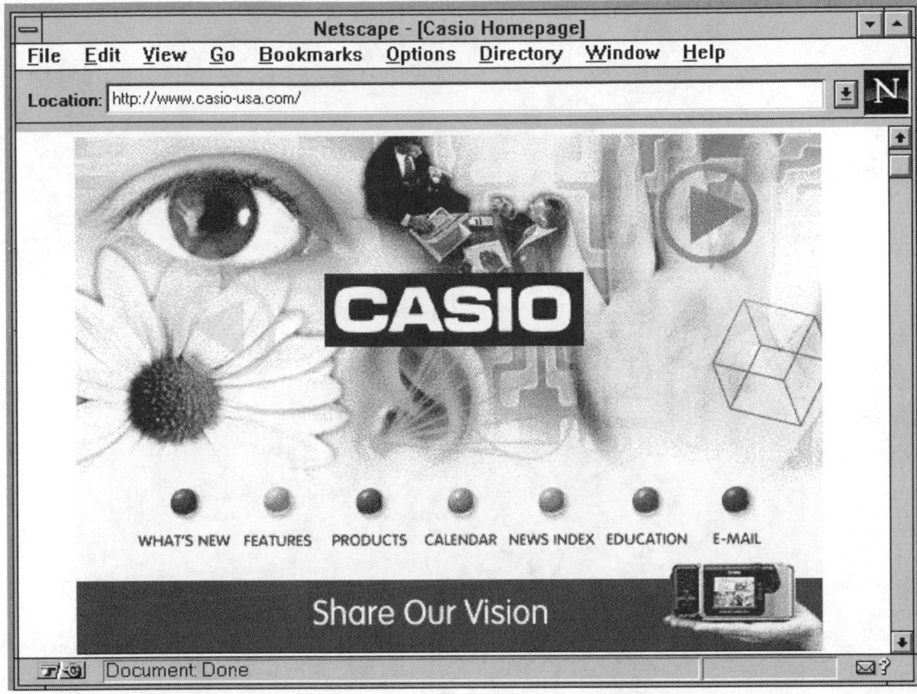


*The Casio home page.*

Casio product pages give you a photo of the product and then two or more pages discussing, explaining, and presenting features and specifications. This is far more information than you will find in any print ad or mail-order electronics catalogue. And you get to choose which product you read about.

This is a neat Web site offered by a huge company. It does its part in "giving back to the Net" with special features aimed at education. And it provides an excellent example of how one can build a corporate image (which is to say, make people feel good about your company) via the Web.

# 18

# Crafts & collectibles

IF you're selling a brand-name product, you can expect the manufacturer to do some promotion and advertising. And you can hope that most of your customers will have at least heard of the product. But what do you do if yours is a niche product or something you have created yourself? No big company is doing any advertising to build brand recognition, so you're pretty much on your own.

What you do, of course, is take small, inexpensive ads in the magazines, newsletters, and other publications that appeal to your niche. Maybe you can find a mailing list someplace targeted at your audience. But even bulk mail at the pre-sorted rate can be expensive.

If you're lucky, you'll get a one to two percent response rate. That's what Reader's Digest, Time-Life, and other professional direct-mail marketers hope for. Which means that to get 100 to 200 inquiries, you may have to send out 10,000 letters. Even if you can find a way to get the cost down to 50 cents a letter, that's still $5,000.

And of those 100 to 200 inquiries, how many will actually buy? Just to break even, you'll need to sell a $50 product to 100 people, or a $25 product to 200 people. It's a grim reality, we know. But the Net and the Web can help you break free—if you have the right product and market it properly online.

## Cards, Comics, & Collectibles

Web address: **http://www.teleport.com/~extreme/cards.htm**

Trading cards, memorabilia, comic books, and ephemera are ideal products to sell on the Net because each is unique. Every collectible baseball card, for example, is special—some have one or more "soft corners," others have "scuffing," and others have "slight warping." The better the condition, the better the price—for copies of the identical card. Same for comic books, autographed baseballs, and similar collectibles.

What's more, not only is each item essentially unique, it is located in a store or private collection someplace that may be thousands of miles from where a customer lives. Sure, there are trade shows, magazines, and "looking for" ads, but it all seems hit-or-miss. By putting collections on the Web, however, the chances of a buyer connecting with a seller are enhanced.

Extreme Marketing's "Cards, Comics, & Collectibles" page (Fig. 18-1) is not the most inspired site we have ever encountered. But it's on the right track. There is no built-in search function, so the trick is to get a page onto your screen and then use Netscape's "Find" function to look for items of interest. (Look for "Find" on the menu that drops down when you click on "Edit" in Netscape.)

The site also offers links to "Favorite Sports and Collectibles Related Sites," and information on donating cards to charity.

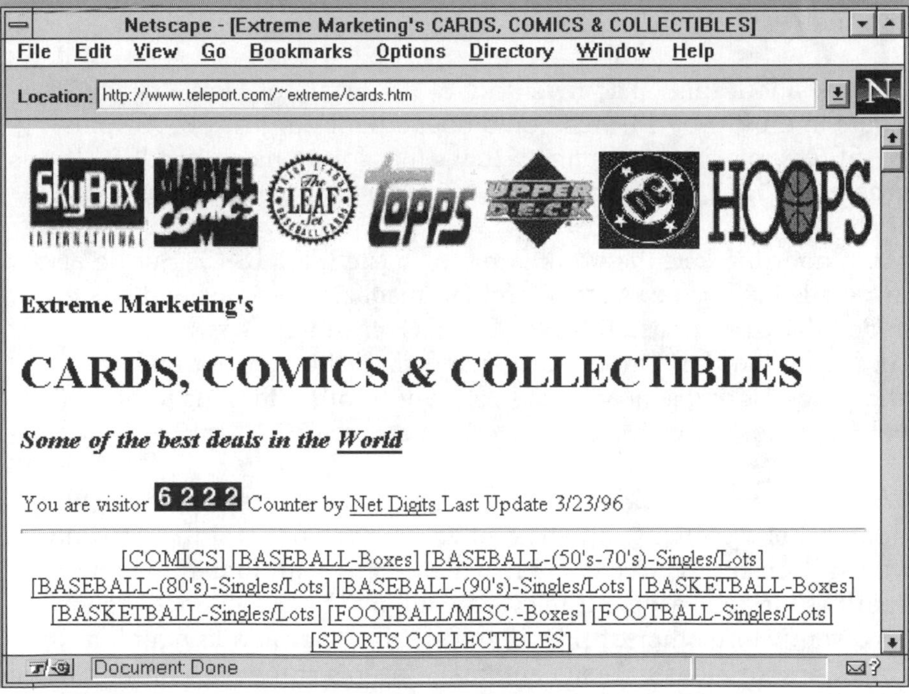


Figure 18-1

*Cards, Comics, & Collectibles on the Web.*

# ARJAY Enterprises & the Elvis Inventory

Web address: **http://www.aksi.net/rjay**

As the authors of numerous books about electronic information, we are well aware of what is available in the public records. Hunting and fishing licenses, powerboat registrations, voter registration rolls, Uniform Commercial Code filings, court records, and so on.

Our friend and professional public records searcher Lynn Peterson (**72262.2554@compuserve.com**) helped us write the public records chapter of *The Information Broker's Handbook* (McGraw-Hill). Lynn is master searcher, and we have been dazzled at what she can find.

So how about this: "The Inventory of the Estate of Elvis Presley." Yours in an 8.5-by-11-inch comb-bound book for just $6.95, plus $1.50 shipping and handling. How's that for a unique product! It was created by Richard Singer, and it is absolutely brilliant.

Mr. Singer markets the book at his Web site (Fig. 18-2). But he also takes ads in Elvis newsletters and fan magazines. Graceland has even added the book to its archives. The Elvis Inventory has been so successful that Mr. Singer has expanded on the concept and will shortly be issuing similar books relevant to other famous people. (We'd tell you who, but we've been sworn to secrecy!)

We only wish there were pictures. You can kind of see the "Sectional Sofa in Four Sections, upholstered in blue velour" and the "Twenty-one sofa cushions in yellow and white fabric, with Indian mirror sparkles" in the basement television room. The "Colt single-action revolver, with mother-of-pearl handle," the "German Lugger" (*sic*) and the "German Mousser" (*sic*) automatic pistols can be visualized, despite the mispellings.

But we sure would like to have seen photos of the "Selection of Dressing Robes and Silk Pajamas, some elaborately sequined, also with hats."

Figure 18-2

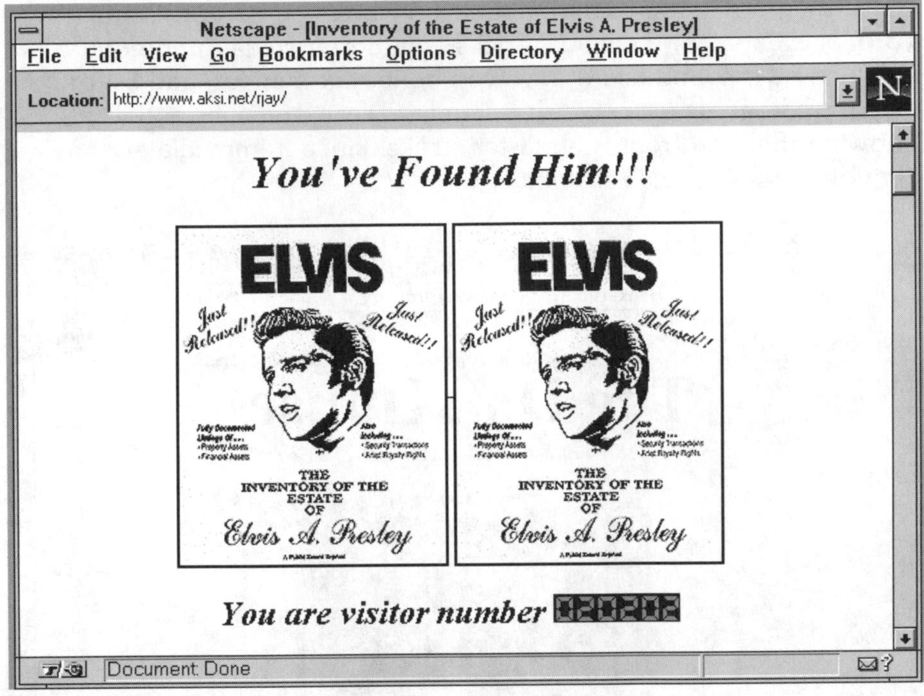


*The Elvis Inventory from ARJAY Enterprises.*

Richard Singer has a neat idea, nicely executed. (The page even includes a trivia question. Answer it correctly, and you get a copy of the book for free.) What he has going for him, of course, is that Elvis fans are passionate, on the Web, and more than happy to pay $6.95 for a public record reprint like this.

# The Doll House

Web address: **http://www.ultimate.org/DOLLS**

The Doll House is another excellent example of how a niche marketer can use the Internet to reach customers who would never have heard of the company any other way. After all, the Doll House is a retail store located in Edmond, Oklahoma, for Pete's sake! Yet it has over 5,000 collectible dolls in stock, and it does a great job of marketing them on the Web.

First, the graphic image that greets you when you go to this site (Fig. 18-3) is a photo of the actual bricks-and-mortar store in Edmond, followed by the land address, voice phone, fax number, and list of major credit cards accepted. It's simple, direct, and substantial. Showing the storefront is a master stroke, since it immediately connotes stability and reliability.

Figure 18-3

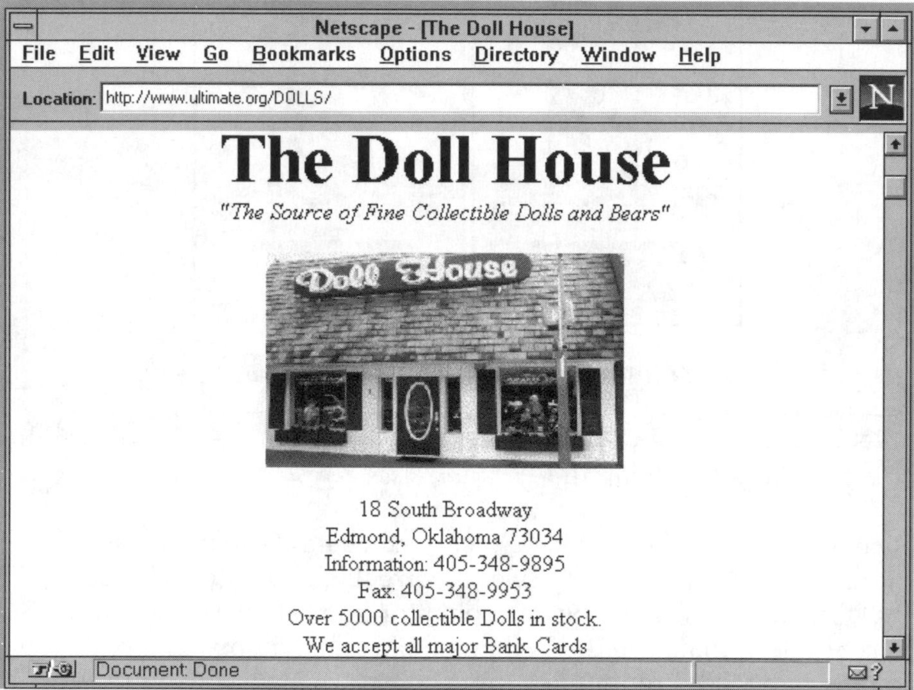


*The Doll House "storefront" on the World Wide Web.*

There are photos of dolls, many of which sell for $320 or more and are uncannily life-like. And there's an offer of a full-color brochure. We are not into collectible dolls, but the owners of this site appear to talk the talk and walk the walk. Definitely worth checking out.

## The Knitting Lodge

Web address: **http://www.knittinglodge.com/yarns**

Your co-authors are not into knitting, either. But with our fingers firmly on the pulse of popular trends, we know that knitting is making a comeback, big time! Not too long ago the *Wall Street Journal* carried a fourth-column cover story on knitting "camps" or "retreats," where both women and men go to do nothing but knit for a week or more under the supervision of a nationally known "super knitter."

Well, we do not know whether Joan-Marie Lodge is a super knitter or knot (get it!), but she has put up one heck of a neat Web site (Fig. 18-4). She calls it her Knitting Lodge, "a unique digital yarn boutique."

Figure 18-4

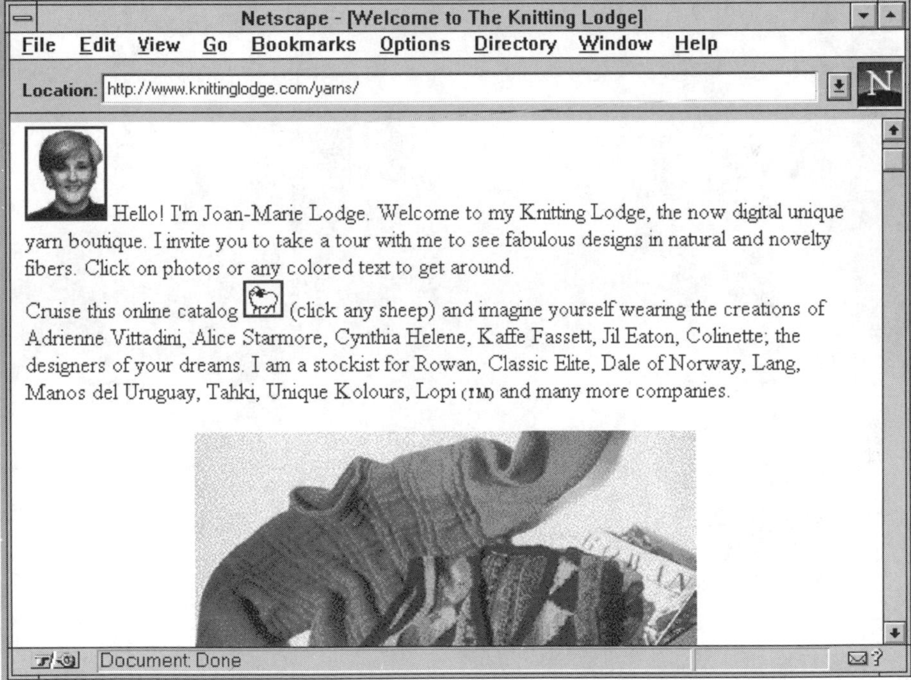


*The Knitting Lodge greeting screen.*

There's a nice, friendly, photo of Ms. Lodge, clickable sheep icons throughout, and driving directions should you plan to visit the shop in Cranston, Rhode Island. The toll-free 800 number appears on nearly every page. And the yarn, patterns, needles, and kits she offers are apparently top-of-the-line. Ms. Lodge speaks with authority, and with good humor.

So ask yourself, you're a knitter in, oh, Edmond, Oklahoma, and you would love to have materials from "Rowan, Classic Elite, Dale of Norway, Lang, Manos del Uruguay, Tahki, Unique Kolours, and Lopi"—but no local shop carries them. So you check the Web. Joan-Marie Lodge's Knitting Lodge comes up in your Yahoo! search, and there you are!

# 19

# Food, gifts, & novelties

# CHAPTER 19

FOOD, glorious food. And gifts and novelties, of course. This is a chapter with a high personal quotient on the part of your co-authors. We grew up in Ohio and Kentucky, where it's impossible to get good bread. Well, not "impossible," exactly. But not in the suburbs. There, they think really good bread is made by Pepperidge Farm.

We now live in a place with an abundance of good bread. But few of our readers are ever likely to have the pleasure of double-parking on a street in the Chambersburg section of Trenton, New Jersey, to pick up an unsliced loaf of Spolette from the Italian People's Bakery—within minutes of its coming out of the oven. Or of stopping by the gourmet store right up the road to pick up a half dozen freshly baked, authentic French croissants first thing in the morning.

There's no way to do that on the Internet, either. In fact, we're not even going to talk about bread in this chapter. But the point is the same. The Internet has brought gourmet, specialty foods to the heartland, and to the rest of the world. Not to mention gifts and novelties, which we will get to in a moment. But let's start with wine.

## Virtual Vineyards

Web address: **http://www.virtualvin.com**

Co-author Alfred has long been a wine snob. Not in terms of price, but in terms of origin. We may be able to get wonderful bread in the state of Pennsylvania, but with our system of state liquor stores, getting a really good selection of wine is a major problem. The French and Italian wines available from the state stores are cheaper, yet taste as good as—if not better than—those "imported" from California.

This is a simple fact. But it doesn't mean that California isn't producing great wine. As we discovered on a recent trip there to visit Alfred's brother, *the best stuff never makes it out of the state*! We're talking small wineries, with limited production, all of which gets snapped up by Californians.

Now however, thanks to the Internet, there is a site called Virtual Vineyards (Fig. 19-1). The company sells over $100,000 worth of wine a month. It offers in-depth information about the wines it sells and the wineries that produce them. There are special offers and monthly programs. And there is the "Ask the Cork Dork" question-and-answer feature.

Virtual Vineyards has been written up in many publications, for it is clearly one of the leading commerce locations on the Net. Don't miss it!

Figure 19-1

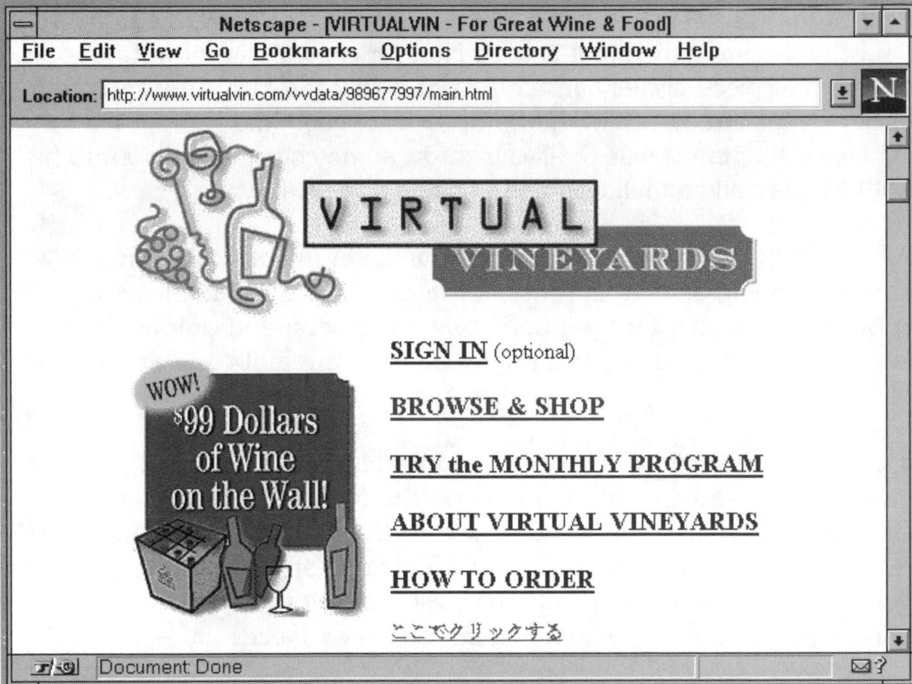


*Virtual Vineyards offers fine wines and foods on the Web.*

# Hot Hot Hot

Web address: **http://www.hot.presence.com**

Oh, boy! You never know, but probably one of the factors that brought us together (and that has kept us together for over 25 years) is that we have the same tastes in food. We both love pepper and spices and probably more salt than is good for us. Suffice it to say that when we eat at a Chinese restaurant, the only question for debate is which Szechuan dish each of us will have. And our favorite Garrison Keillor/Prairie Home Companion fake commercial is the one for "Ah-Hoo-Ah! Hot Sauce."

One of the greatest pieces of cooking advice we have ever heard is from Paul Prudhomme, the great chef of New Orleans. A fan of hot peppers and highly spiced dishes himself, he noted that the burn should be at the back of your throat, not at the tip of your tongue. And his method for achieving that effect was to always throw some chopped celery into his hot dishes to add a mellowing bit of sugar. (Try it, it works!)

All of which is by way of saying that, while in this age of namby-pamby cooking and vapid senses of taste, there are lots of people who adore hot peppers. Hot peppers, sweet peppers, and onions drenched in olive oil and grilled over an open flame is the ambrosia and nectar of the gods!

If you feel the same way, check into Hot Hot Hot (Fig. 19-2), one of many sites devoted to hot peppers on the Net. This Pasadena, California, specialty shop sold over $60,000 worth of hot sauces and related products over the Net in 1995. The shop itself offers over 400 fiery food products, including a large selection of cookbooks, salsa mustards, and an ever-expanding collection of sauces.

As you will see, Hot Hot Hot offers a "Frequent Fire Club" membership for $59 for three months, which entitles you to a "wild hot thing" each month for three months. Six-month and one-year memberships are also available. You'll find links to *Chile Pepper Magazine* and a "Gifts of Fire" feature to make it easy for you to send a really cool hot sauce to a friend.

Figure 19-2

*The Hot Hot Hot home page.*

Even if you personally cannot abide hot peppers, you should still visit this site. The reason is simple: Lovers of hot, spicy food are a minority. That's why most of the products on the shelves of American supermarkets are so bland. So spicy-food lovers represent the ultimate niche market. They know what they like. In fact, they are passionate about it. And they know that they can't get it from their local supermarkets.

Hot Hot Hot and other chile and hot-sauce sites can fill their needs. So of *course* they're going to buy. After all, at $25 or less, what have they got to lose? Disappoint them and they will never buy from you again. But satisfy them and you've got a customer for life.

The key point is not that hot peppers and sauces are food items. The key point is that they are *specialty* items that are not conveniently available to the large, widely dispersed numbers of people who want them. Read that sentence again, and burn it into your brain.

Leave food aside. Assume that you sell left-handed kitchen and woodshop tools (products close to our hearts because we are both left-handed). There may not be a large enough market in, say, Louisville, Kentucky, to open a shop dedicated to selling left-handed tools. Maybe New York and maybe Los Angeles. But definitely not just anywhere.

Yet there is this need, this desire, this demand. If only you can connect with it. That's what Hot Hot Hot does, and it is what you should think about doing on the Web. So go look at their site and see if you can't apply what they've done to your own product or service.

## Coffee Anyone???

Web address: **http://www.coffee-anyone.com**

If anyone in the 1980s had suggested that you put money into a chain of stores dedicated to selling on-demand cups of coffee, you would have said they were crazy. Coffee was supposed to be bad for you, and caffeine was utter poison. Herbal teas and bottled water were the order of the day.

Contrarians that we are, in the 1980s our concern was not cutting back on coffee. It was finding a better quality of coffee than the robusto-laced Maxwell House and other supermarket blends. Sorry, but Maxwell House, Folgers, and Chock-Full-of-Nuts coffees are to real coffee what Skippy, Jif, Peter Pan, and the other leading brands of peanut butter are to freshly ground peanuts. Ersatz, ersatz, ersatz! (You could look it up.)

As it happens, we were in Greenwich Village in the 1980s to see Wendy Wasserstein's *The Heidi Chronicles*. McNulty's Coffee store was nearby. We wandered in, and ended up establishing a relationship that has lasted for over a decade. Each month, McNulty's ships us six individually bagged pounds of whole coffee beans via UPS. A single phone call lets us change the bean selection. It is coffee drinker's heaven.

But what if you live in God's country, like upstate Idaho. Gad, what a beautiful place! But where do you get great coffee? Maybe you order it on the Net. Specifically, maybe you go to the Coffee Anyone??? site (Fig. 19-3).

Figure 19-3

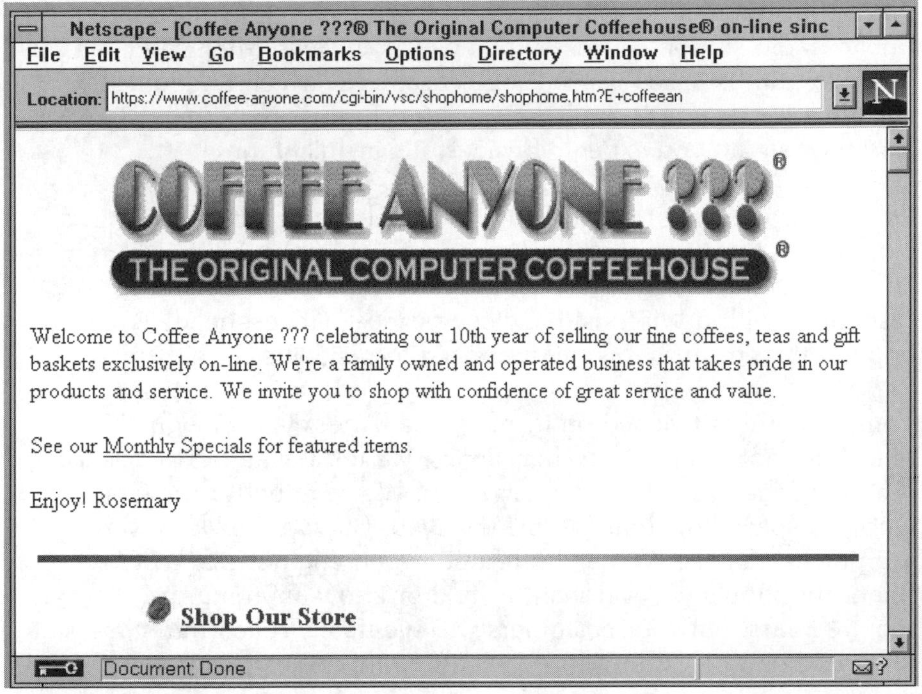

Netscape - [Coffee Anyone ???® The Original Computer Coffeehouse® on-line sinc
File Edit View Go Bookmarks Options Directory Window Help
Location: https://www.coffee-anyone.com/cgi-bin/vsc/shophome/shophome.htm?E+coffeean
COFFEE ANYONE ???®
THE ORIGINAL COMPUTER COFFEEHOUSE®
Welcome to Coffee Anyone ??? celebrating our 10th year of selling our fine coffees, teas and gift baskets exclusively on-line. We're a family owned and operated business that takes pride in our products and service. We invite you to shop with confidence of great service and value.
See our Monthly Specials for featured items.
Enjoy! Rosemary
Shop Our Store
Document: Done


*Coffee by mail from Coffee Anyone???*

The site was created by Wilson Internet Services, one of our favorites. And the company, known as "The Original Computer Coffeehouse," is run by Rosemary and Norm Belssner. These folks have done a splendid job. So, if yours is a specialty item of any sort, pay them a visit online and explore the site.

# Foamation World Famous Cheeseheads

Web address: **http://www.arcfile.com/cheesehead**

Finally, the two of us are so pleased to be able to tell you about Foamation Inc. and its line of "Cheesehead" products. This is a true story of both buyer and seller. And, just possibly, a story of how at least some products will be sold in the future.

From 1:00 to 3:00 pm on Saturday afternoons our local National Public Radio station carries "Whad'ya Know" with Michael Feldman. The program is based in Madison, Wisconsin, which undoubtedly accounts for its unabashedly leftward tilt. But it's NPR (or PRI), after all, so what can you expect? Besides, it's awfully funny!

On one program not too long ago, Mr. Feldman recounted a news story about the pilot of a small plane who saved his life by donning a "Cheesehead" foam hat just before crashing. The story had special resonance with a Wisconsin audience, since "Cheesehead" is apparently a term that is often applied to residents of that state.

Your co-authors twigged on it, of course. And, even though "Mr. Mike" did not offer any further details, we felt it was worth at least searching the Web. This is a key point. We have better things to do with our spare time than to surf the Web. But we are well aware of the power that the Web and Internet search engines place at our fingertips should we ever want to find or know anything. It will require years, but your customers will eventually reach this same state of awareness.

So, we did a search on "Cheesehead." A wonderfully unique term. (If it had been just "cheese" we were looking for, forget it!) Lo and behold, we discovered the Foamation site (Fig. 19-4), operated by the company that made the life-saving cheese-wedge-shaped foam headgear that saved that pilot's life.

The company is based in Milwaukee, and when we contacted Chris Becker there, he generously offered to send us samples of not only the "Original Cheesehead"—a cheese-wedge hat of the sort that is apparently popular with Green Bay Packer fans—but also a Cheesehead Cowboy hat, a Cheese necktie, and a pair of Cheese earrings. All made out of cheddar-colored foam.

This is a really neat site with a really neat attitude. It sells the ultimate in specialized novelty items, and does so successfully. Chris Becker is a peach of a guy (or should we say "cheese of a guy?"), and his site is full of good fun.

Figure 19-4

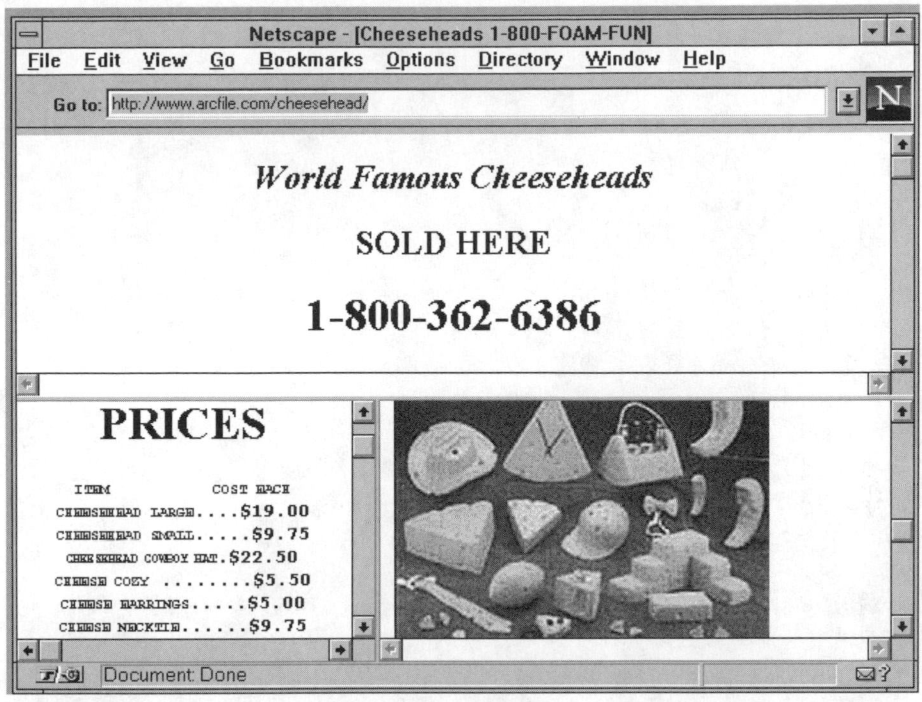


*Foamation promotes its "World Famous Cheesehead" and other products on the World Wide Web.*

If you have a similarly unique novelty item to sell, be sure to visit the Foamation site. And think about how you might make it easy for someone who hears about your product on the radio to jump on the Net and *find* you using one of the leading search engines.

# Multi-level marketing

# CHAPTER 20

MULTI-level marketing (MLM) has been characterized as the latest in a long line of get-rich-quick schemes. It has been said that MLM companies sell worthless products at prices that are grossly inflated in order to produce the margins necessary to provide a slice to every person in the marketing hierarchy, or *downline* as they call it in MLM organizations.

Probably there's a tad of truth to this in some multi-level marketing organizations—and there are hundreds of them. But if this were true of all MLM operations, such industry stalwarts as Amway, Mary Kay, Shaklee, Watkins, and others would have disappeared long ago. Just don't let your dream of owning your own business keep you from being as skeptical as you should be whenever anyone is asking you to invest money.

As you might expect, the parent companies of many MLM organizations have developed Web pages. But the quality varies. Amway has created a very informative site (**http://www.amway.com**) with lots of information about the company's products and business opportunities. Mary Kay, on the other hand, offers but a single page (**http://www.marykay.com**) consisting of a huge photograph and an 800 number to call for more information.

Interestingly, some of the best MLM Web sites you will encounter are the creations of individual MLM marketers interested in building their sales teams. That's what we'll focus on in this chapter.

## Multi-level marketing resources online

*If you're new to multi-level marketing and want to get an idea of what opportunities are available, you might try using one of the leading Internet search engines. However, you will probably be better off if you go to the Open market Commercial Sites Index instead. That way you will get only business-related hits. Point your Web browser at* **http://www.directory.net** *and look for entries containing the keyword "mlm" or "multilevel."*

*When we did this, the system came back with 143 MLM-related items. They ranged from "A1 Stop Smoking Guaranteed" to "Gold Merchants Guild" to "Wholesale Vacations Front Desk Pass." Click on any item, and you will be taken to its home page.*

*You should also check out the Network Marketing Emporium at* **http://www.cashflow.com**. *This site has a couple hundred links to MLM businesses. But it's not a mass directory. Listings cost $15 a month, and there can be only one listing for each MLM program. (If yours is already represented in the Network Marketing Emporium, you can request to be put on a waiting list.)*

*Membership includes up to six Web pages, e-mail forwarding from your Web page to any address you specify, listings with the leading search engines, and more. An auto-responder is available for an additional $10 a month. You can even opt to have the site set up your Web presence at a cost of $10 per page.*

*Clearly, this is site worth visiting if you're currently involved in multi-level marketing, looking for MLM opportunities, or just want to see how other multi-level marketers are using the Internet.*

# The NuSkin Feelgood Team

Web address: **http://www.feelgood.com**

The Feelgood Page (Fig.20-1) is one of the best MLM Web sites we've encountered. Created by Marion Stewart, a NuSkin representative, it offers much more than a pitch to become a representative yourself. It creates a team "clubhouse" atmosphere.

There are articles on health, nutrition, and personal care collected by team members. There's a bio of Marion Stewart and all kinds of information about NuSkin products. This is a terrific Web site that all current and prospective MLMers should visit.

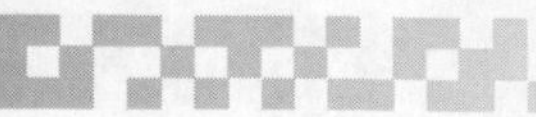

Figure 20-1

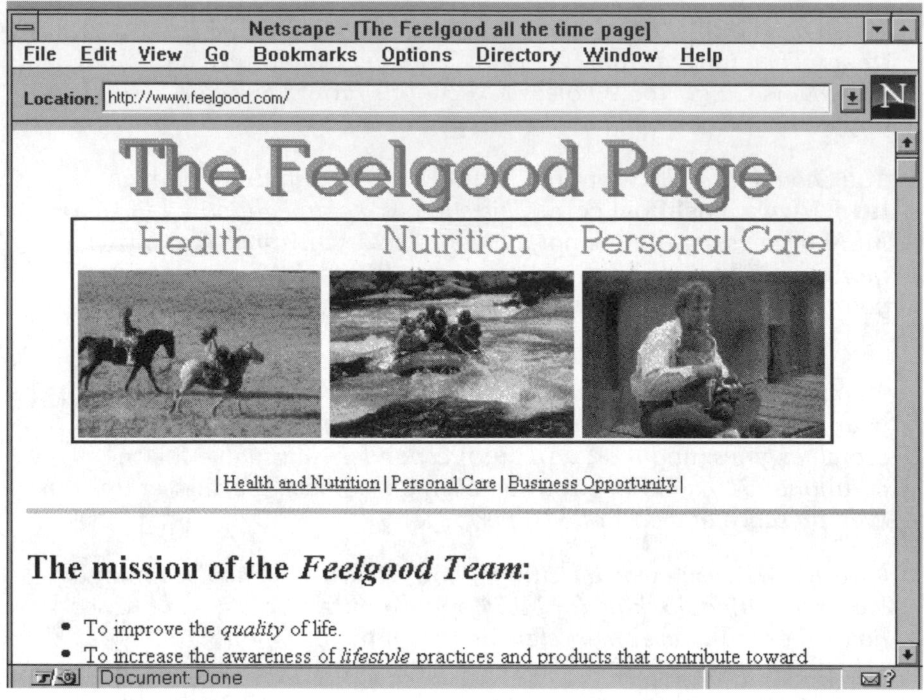


*The Feelgood Page was created by a NuSkin representative to build and support her marketing team.*

# Excel Telecommunications

Web address: **http://www.io.com/~exceljob**

Here's another example of an MLM rep creating a presence of his own on the Web. Based in Dallas, Texas, Excel Telecommunications was founded in 1988. It claims to be the fastest growing long-distance company in the U.S. In essence, you pay $50 to become a rep. You sell people on making Excel their long-distance carrier, and you get a percentage of whatever they spend each month.

This site, created by Excel independent representative Rexford Steele, does a thorough job of explaining the program, the products, and the "7-level" compensation plan.

Figure 20-2

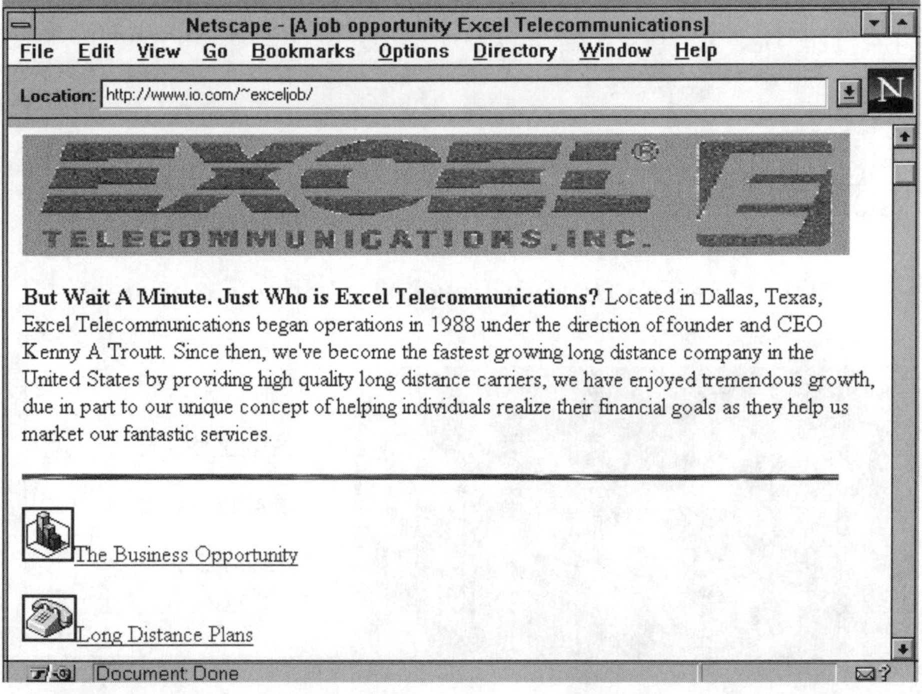


*Here's how one Excel representative uses the Web to build his downline.*

To see the site operated by the parent company, go to **http://www.exceltel.com**. This is an example of a parent company that has really done it right! In particular, check the "Representative's Guide to Advertising." This is an extensive feature designed to help reps like Mr. Steele create and place advertising, both in print and on online systems. There is advice here that *every* businessperson can use. Don't miss it.

# Watkins Products

Web address: **http://www.iwe.com/marshall**

JoAnne and Leonard Marshall have been Watkins reps for a dozen years, and they have created an attractive, cleanly designed page for themselves. Watkins makes food products like vanilla extract, spices,

Figure 20-3

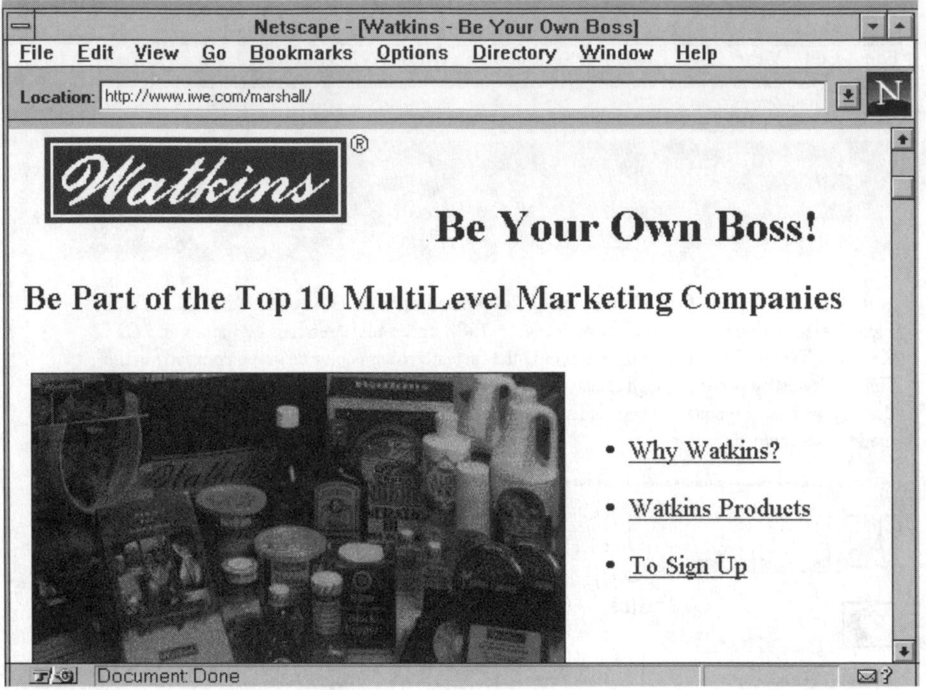


*This Web site is maintained by a husband-and-wife team who have been in the Watkins business for 12 years*

and chicken soup base; household cleaners; and health and beauty products.

The Marshalls maintain not only a voice and fax line, but also their own toll-free 800 number. And they encourage people to contact them by e-mail. Their Web site is not as ambitious as the other two in this chapter, but it does a good job of presenting the Watkins products and marketing concept. In our opinion, it's a good model to consider as you design your own site. Remember, you can always add more features later, after you've built a solid base to work from.

## Get the MLM FAQ!

*There seems to be a Frequently Asked Questions (FAQ) file for nearly every topic, and multi-level marketing is no exception. The MLM FAQ, however, is exceptionally good. So good that it's must reading for anyone currently involved in or contemplating joining an MLM program.*

*Written by Gary Fritz, a self-confessed MLM enthusiast, the FAQ nonetheless takes a very forthright and objective look at the field. Not only does the FAQ explain multi-level marketing, it also includes tips for succeeding, advice on the proper way to recruit on the Internet, a list of books on the subject, and a listing and description of a dozen or so leading MLMs.*

*To get a copy of the FAQ, point your browser at* **ftp://rtfm.mit.edu/pub/usenet/news.answers/mlm-faq**. *Alternatively, you can request a copy by e-mail. Send a message to* **mail-server@rtfm.mit.edu**, *and include the line "send usenet/news.answers/mlm-faq" in the body of the message.*

*The MLM FAQ is also posted every two weeks or so to the MLM newsgroup,* **alt.business.multi-level**. *To visit the newsgroup, point your browser at* **news:alt.business.multi-level**. *(Remember, there are no slashes in the "news:" URL.)*

# A

# FireCrystal Consulting

This appendix is designed to tell you about our company, FireCrystal Consulting, and how we can help you market your products or services on the Internet. If you have read and enjoyed this book, and if you are interested in having us help you establish a presence on the Net and the Web, skip the sales copy that follows and jump directly to the end of this appendix, where you will find information on how to contact us.

Otherwise, read on as we take our best shot at convincing you to pick up the phone or send us an e-mail query to arrange an appointment.

## Taken at the flood

There is a tide in the affairs of the Internet. No doubt about that. In fact, as you read this, the first Internet tide will have just about reached its peak. That's the tide of *Time* and *Business Week* magazine covers—plus untold stories in newspapers and other magazines—that has served to raise awareness of terms like "online" and "Internet" in the minds of the American public.

It's a tide we expected to hit the beaches around 1982, the year that the first edition of *The Complete Handbook of Personal Computer Communications: Everything You Need to Go Online with the World* came out. The industry's leading pundits and prognosticators thought so too, give or take a year.

And, of course, all of us were wrong!

At the time, not even the online industry appreciated the amount of hardware and software that would have to be moved into American homes or how steep the learning curve would be.

No one fully grasped the amount of spade work that had to be done. Families needed a good reason to buy a computer in the first place, and the price had to be right. Once purchased, they needed time to get familiar with the machine before taking the next step into the brave new world of modems and online communications.

## The gospel of the electronic universe

It took over a decade for the online tide to arrive. During which time we kept preaching the gospel of the "electronic universe" and its life-enhancing powers. Three editions of the *Complete Handbook*, plus one book devoted to CompuServe and another to GEnie, as well as *How to Look It Up Online*, *Internet 101*, *Online Resources for Business*, and more. It has taken some time, but the total number of Glossbrenner books sold now tops 350,000 copies.

So we are a "presence" in the online field. Some might even say a "fixture." Whatever. The fact is that we bring some very special credentials to the table. (This is the sales part—the part where we wheel in the heavy artillery to persuade you to hire us.)

## Who are your people?

Emily has close to two decades' experience in computing, marketing, and project management, including nine years with the IBM Corporation as a marketing representative and marketing manager for Fortune 500 accounts.

Alfred has written brochures, manuals, speeches, film scripts, booklets, press releases, and print ads for companies like AT&T New Media, Merrill Lynch, U.S. Trust, Dow Jones, Chase Manhattan, Sun Oil (Sunoco), Nissan, Monarch Life, Michelin, Berlitz, and others.

## Saving you time & money

Bottom line: We know corporate America. We know sales, marketing, and advertising. We know the Internet and the rest of the electronic universe—in depth.

If you want to offer your goods or services electronically, we at FireCrystal Consulting have the skills, the experience, and the credentials to save you time, money, and frustration. We can show you the best way to market your product on the Internet, the Big Three consumer systems, and bulletin board systems (BBSs).

We can also can keep you from making serious mistakes. Even as we write this, companies are being told that creating even a simple Web page will cost them $5,000 or more! But after reading this book, and especially after reading Chapter 10, "Setting up your Web site," you know better. A lot better.

## A free, five-minute consultation

We will be happy to spend five minutes on the phone with you to help you decide whether you should be on the Internet and the World Wide Web. Or whether it even makes sense for you to be doing any kind of electronic marketing. If you have read this book, you know we will tell you the truth.

If you feel it would be worthwhile to discuss things in detail, we will ask you to schedule a phone appointment—which you can charge to your Visa, MasterCard, or American Express, or pay with a check mailed to us in advance of the call.

## The next step

At the end of that initial consultation, you will have a very good idea of the best way to proceed. And, if you like, we can help you with any and all of the details—everything from creating and laying out the sales copy for your auto-responder message to planning the World

Wide Web pages that will present your products or services most effectively.

We will also show you which newsgroups and mailing lists to follow on the Internet, and which SIGs (Special Interest Groups) to check into on the Big Three consumer systems. We can help you avoid violating the online culture and getting flamed. We will advise you on ways you can "give back to the Net" by offering something free as a public service. If setting up your own on-site bulletin board system seems worthwhile, we can advise you on that as well.

## What makes you special?

No two products, services, or companies are exactly alike. Our goal at FireCrystal Consulting is to work with you to discover what makes your offerings special and to help you articulate those qualities on the Internet, on the World Wide Web, and in the electronic universe as a whole—in the most effective way possible.

As for what makes *us* special—aside from being truly wonderful people who are fun to work with—no one else can offer the same combination of writing and marketing skills and in-depth knowledge of the online world. If you like this book, you'll love what FireCrystal Consulting can do for you. Please give us a call!

FireCrystal Consulting
699 River Road
Yardley, PA 19067
Voice: 215-736-1213
Fax: 215-736-1031
**gloss@gloss.com**

# B

# The Internet Toolkit & Glossbrenner's Choice

Finally, the media has caught on. The key to empowerment is not in the hardware, it's in the *software*! Computers, by and large, are commodities. The artistry and the uniqueness are provided by software.

Thus, when you go online, the type and power of the computer you use are all but irrelevant. But the software you have available can make a great deal of difference, especially when you are offline.

It is that crucial software that we want to focus on here. How do you "unzip" a file? How do you "zip" a file into an archive that can be sent to someone else? How do you instantly delete all "trailing white space" from a text file? And what on earth do you do about those UU-CODED files you'll find on the Internet? For that matter, how can you quickly and easily encrypt a message so that only your correspondent can read it?

This appendix is designed to answer those questions. Certainly we can't anticipate absolutely every need. But with nearly 20 years of online experience, we have a pretty good idea of what most people are likely to require as they wade into cyberspace.

There isn't a file on any of the disks offered here that you can't get online from the Internet, America Online, CompuServe, Prodigy, or some bulletin board system. We know, because that's where we got most of these files ourselves.

We've located, tested, and selected the best programs and files for our own use. But it occurred to us that readers might appreciate the opportunity to benefit from our experience, not to mention the convenience of being able to get most of the tools they need from one place. So we've organized the files and programs *we* use on a regular basis and put them on disks.

The programs and text files contained on these disks are free. But the disks themselves, the postage, and the labor needed to make copies and put them in the mail are not. To cover those costs, we charge $5 per disk.

# The Internet Toolkit

We've organized our favorite Internet lists, guides, tools, and utilities into a collection of nine disks we call the Internet Toolkit. The majority of the contents of these disks are plain ASCII text files that can be read by users of both Windows/DOS machines and Apple Macintoshes, thanks to Apple's SuperDrive technology. (If your Mac was manufactured after August 1989, it is almost certainly equipped with one or more SuperDrives capable of reading 1.44 megabyte DOS-formatted disks.)

Here, then, is a quick summary of the disks in the Internet Toolkit and their contents.

## Internet Basics

This disk contains some of the best files we've come across to help new users get up and running on the Internet. Included are the famous Yanoff List of recommendations of great Internet sites to explore, a guide to the subject-specific lists of Internet resources available from the University of Michigan Clearinghouse, and a comprehensive list of Internet Service Providers (the POCIA List). The disk also includes *The Beginner's Guide to the Internet*, an excellent tutorial for DOS and Windows users.

##  Internet Compression & Conversion Tools

This is a collection of all the programs Windows/DOS users need to uncompress or unarchive the various files available on the Internet, along with a Glossbrenner-written quick-start guide showing how to use each one. Extraction programs range from those for ARC and ARJ files to ZIP, Z, and zoo. There's even a program to "unstuff" Macintosh-produced SIT files.

This disk also includes a program to deal with UU-CODED binary files—like the graphic images posted to some newsgroups. Capture the relevant newsgroup messages to disk, making sure that you get all of the parts of the image. Run the UU-CODE program against the captured file to convert the data into GIF, PCX, or other files. Then look at the images with Graphic Workshop or some similar program.

##  Internet FTP Essentials

On this disk you'll find an excellent FAQ on anonymous FTP, along with a list of FTP sites that's about as comprehensive as one can imagine. You will almost certainly be doing FTP via your Web browser, but your browser will deploy a thin candy shell over the FTP process. The files on this disk strip away the shell and help you make the most of what's really going on.

##  Internet Just the FAQs

Here are some of the best and most useful FAQ (Frequently Asked Questions) files on the Internet, covering topics such as finding e-mail addresses, compression, graphics, chat (IRC), Gopher, and Veronica. In writing this book, we've done our best to make this disk unnecessary. But we'd be the first to acknowledge that no book can cover everything. You'll find details on this disk that we did not have space to present in these pages.

##  Internet Mailing List Essentials

Internet mailing lists can be a valuable source of information as well as a powerful marketing tool. To help you identify the lists that might be applicable to your business or field of interest, we've assembled on this two-disk set two gigantic lists of Internet mailing lists—the SRI List of Lists and Publicly Accessible Mailing Lists (PAML). For each mailing list, you'll find a description of the list provided by the sponsor or creator, as well as information on how to subscribe.

##  Internet Making Money Disk

In the course of writing this book, we came across a number of excellent FAQs, lists, and guides of particular interest to online marketers. They cover topics like how to advertise on the Internet, multi-level marketing, promoting your Web site, international connectivity, the best business web sites, and so forth. We've assembled them all onto a single disk for those who want even more details about making money on the Internet than we could provide in the pages of this book.

##  Internet Newsgroup Essentials

Newsgroups are an important source of information. But they might also be the ideal spot to place a short, simple, message alerting people to your Web site and/or auto-responder. This disk includes the famous Lawrence List of newsgroups—thousands of them, in fact. Each with a witty, one-sentence description. Also included is the ROT-13 program Windows/DOS users need to read some of the raunchier jokes in some newsgroups.

##  Internet World Wide Web Essentials

This disk contains many text files concerning the World Wide Web, including the World Wide Web FAQ, the URL FAQ, *A Beginner's Guide to HTML*, and *A Beginner's Guide to URLs*.

It also includes three Windows/DOS programs. One is called DE-HTML and is designed to convert any saved HTML file into plain, single-spaced text. The second can convert .AU sound files into the .VOC format used by SoundBlaster-compatible soundcards. The third program, MOZSOCK.DLL, makes it possible to load any Winsock-compatible Windows program *without* automatically dialing the phone and going online. This is especially convenient when you want to use your browser to view saved HTML files without actually making an online connection.

##  Windows/DOS Tools & Utilities

We are big fans of shareware. But, you know, price really isn't the point. The point is artistry. Big companies rarely produce great software. That's because great software is always the product of a vision held either by one person or by a very small group of people. Great software is great art! And no committee or workgroup has ever created anything that could be mistaken for art.

In our opinion, the Windows/DOS shareware software on the following disks could not be mistaken for anything but art:

### Encryption Tools

Although the chances of it happening are slim, someone who really wants to read your electronic mail can probably find a way to do so. But should you ever want to encrypt a text or binary file so that *no one* can read it without the decoding "key," then this is the disk for you. Among other things, it includes Philip Zimmermann's famous "Pretty Good Privacy" program that's driving the FBI nuts!

###  Graphic Workshop for DOS

This program by Steven Rimmer is designed to help DOS users deal with nearly any kind of graphics file. No fuss, no muss. Get to DOS, key in gws, and you're ready to view, print, crop, scale, and convert to and from virtually every graphics file format going, including BMP,

EPS, GEM/IMG, GIF, JPG (JPEG), IFF/LBM, MAC, PCX, RLE, and TIFF, among others.

# Graphic Workshop for Windows 3.1 & 95

GWS for Windows does everything the DOS version does, and more. Including presenting you with a thumbnail screen showing you quick renditions of each graphic file on your disk. This saves time since it ensures that you will always load just the image you want. Use your Web browser to download a graphics file (remember to click on the *right* mouse button in Netscape) and save it to disk. Then look at, manipulate, or print it with this program.

# Idea Processing

PC-Outline is an incredible clone of the commercial idea-outlining program, Thinktank. Indeed, many former Thinktank users prefer this shareware product. PC-Outline lets you randomly enter information of almost any type (thoughts, plans, ideas, etc.) and then organize it into a hierarchical structure.

You can then go from viewing the lowest level of detail to a view that shows you only the highest, most important topics. You can also print the outline, copy it into another outline, or paste it directly into your word processor. Ideal for organizing projects, reports, books, and lists—or just organizing your thoughts!

# Instant File Management: QFILER, TSE, & Associates

QFILER (Quick Filer) by Kenn Flee gives you *complete* control over your files and disk directories. You can tag a group of dissimilar files for deletion or for copying to another disk or directory. You can easily move up and down your directory trees, altering the date and time stamps of files, changing their attributes, compressing, uncompressing, and peering into archives. You can also look at any file on the screen, copy it to your printer, and more. You will find QFILER much easier to use than the Windows 3.1 File Manager or similar DOS-based products.

Also on this disk is WHEREIS, a lightning-fast program for finding files on your hard disk. And TSE, the famous DOS text-editing program. TSE specializes in creating plain text of the sort you must use on the Internet and in most e-mail letters on other systems. Yet it gives you many of the convenience features of a full-blown word processor.

##  Text Search

This disk contains the programs BOOLE, LOOKFOR, SMARTDOC, and HUNTER. BOOLE is a Windows 3.1 program that makes it easy to search everything from a single file to your entire disk for words; phrases; and AND, OR, NOT occurrences. Thus if you searched for "Tom and not Bob," the program would not retrieve any file that contained both names. Only those files that contained "Tom" and did *not* contain "Bob" would be selected.

LOOKFOR is a fast DOS program that also lets you do AND, OR, wildcard, and proximity searches of text files. You can then print (to disk or printer) relevant file excerpts. SMARTDOC converts Windows 3.1 help files into plain text files and lets you print out entire Windows help files with fonts and formatting intact.

HUNTER is a "pattern- matching" utility. You can tell it to find things like phone numbers and dates without specifying *which* numbers or dates. You can also specify the kind of file (*.txt, *.wri, etc.) you want HUNTER to focus on, and you can target only those files of a certain size or age.

##  Text Treaters

This disk contains some 45 programs to manipulate, filter, and prepare a text file in virtually any way you can imagine. These

programs are particularly convenient when you're dealing with text you get from e-mail correspondents and Internet sites.

For example, a program called TEXT lets you remove all leading white space on each line of a file, remove all trailing blanks, or convert all white space into the number of spaces you specify. CHOP, will cut a file into the number of pieces you specify. CRLF makes sure that every line in a text file ends with a carriage return and a linefeed so it can be displayed and edited properly. There's also a package by Peter Norton to create an index for a report, document, book, or whatever.

# Order Form

You can use the order form on the next page (or a photocopy) to order the disks described here, as well as a selection of books by Alfred and Emily Glossbrenner. Or you may simply write your request on a piece of paper and send it to us.

We accept American Express, MasterCard, and Visa, and checks or money orders made payable to Glossbrenner's Choice (U.S. funds drawn on a U.S. bank, or international money orders). For additional information, write or call:

Glossbrenner's Choice
699 River Road
Yardley, PA 19067-1965
215-736-1213 (voice)
215-736-1031 (fax)
**books@mailback.com** (information about Glossbrenner books)
**gloss@gloss.com** (all other correspondence)

Glossbrenner's Choice Order Form
for Readers of *Making More Money on the Internet*

Name ______________________________________________

Address ____________________________________________

City ______________________ State _____ ZIP __________

Province/Country ____________________ Phone ___________

Payment [ ] Check or Money Order payable to **Glossbrenner's Choice**

[ ] Amex/MC/Visa ______________________ Exp ___ /___

Signature ___________________________________________

Mail, fax, phone, or e-mail your order to:

Glossbrenner's Choice
699 River Road
Yardley, PA 19067-1965

215-736-1213 (voice)
215-736-1031 (fax)
**gloss@gloss.com**

---

**The Internet Toolkit** (3.5-inch, DOS-formatted, 1.44MB)

____ Internet Basics
____ Internet Compression and Conversion Tools
____ Internet FTP Essentials
____ Internet Just the FAQs
____ Internet Mailing List Essentials (Disk 1 of 2)
____ Internet Mailing List Essentials (Disk 2 of 2)
____ Internet Making Money Companion Disk
____ Internet Newsgroup Essentials
____ Internet World Wide Web Essentials

**Windows/DOS Tools & Utilities** (3.5-inch, DOS-formatted, 1.44MB)

____ Encryption Tools
____ Graphic Workshop for DOS
____ Graphic Workshop for Windows 3.1
____ Graphic Workshop for Windows 95
____ Idea Processing
____ Instant File Management: QFILER, TSE, & Associates
____ Text Search
____ Text Treaters
____ Total number of disks × $5 per disk ____________

Shipping ($3 to U.S. addresses/$5 outside the U.S.) ____________

**Glossbrenner Books** (Prices include $3 for Book Rate shipping.)

____ *The Complete Modem Handbook*/MIS:Press ($38) ________
____ *Finding a Job on the Internet*/McGraw-Hill ($19) ________
____ *The Information Broker's Handbook*/McGraw-Hill ($38) ________
____ *Internet 101: A College Student's Guide*/McGraw-Hill ($23) ________
____ *The Little Online Book*/Peachpit Press ($21) ________
____ *The Little Web Book*/Peachpit Press ($18) ________
____ *Making More Money on the Internet*/McGraw-Hill ($23) ________
____ *Online Resources for Business*/John Wiley & Sons ($28) ________

TOTAL ________

Pennsylvania residents, please add 6% Sales Tax. ________

GRAND TOTAL ENCLOSED ________

# Index

3Com Corporation, 13

## A

addresses, 51, 143-144 (*see also* domain name system)
- finding E-mail, 148-149

Advanced Research Projects Agency (ARPA), 51
advertising
- announcement services (*see* announcement services)
- direct-mail, 152-154
- integrating online with other, 26-27
- Internet, 57-58, 226-228
- keeping it fresh, 27-28
- on BBS, 105-106
- online, 21
- on online service providers, 97-101
- specials/sales, 25-26

Alta Vista, 189, 203, 215
Amazon.com Books, 252-254, **253**
America Online, 5, 7, 13, 34, 46, 48, 59, 88, 92
- costs, 97-98
- E-mail, 149
- exploring, 116-118
- finding SIGs on, 101
- getting connected to, 108
- getting started, 115-116
- greeting screen, **93**
- marketing on, 97-101

announcement services, 234-247
- fee-based, 238-239
- free/automated, 235-238
- link-placement, 239-240
- locating, 242-243
- questions to ask, 243
- special interest pages, 243-246

Archie, 62
ARJAY Enterprises & the Elvis Inventory, 288-289, **289**
Arlen, Gary, 11
ARPANET, 53-54
ASCII, 39-40
AT&T, 124
auto-responders, 41, 158-168
- listing of, 162-163
- listing of vendors, 164-165
- picking a vendor, 163-165



**Boldface** numbers indicate illustrations

## B

bandwidth, 35-36
baud rate, 35
Bellovin, Steve, 216
Berners-Lee, Tim, 67-68
BigBook Yellow Pages, 210
binary number system, 39, 141-143
BinHex, 142
BizWeb Directory, 210
BMP files, 74
Bolt, Beranek, and Newman (BBN), 51
BookBound, 254-255, **255**
Brody, Herb, 11, 14
Buerg, Vernon, 219
buffer, 114
bulletin board system (BBS), 5, 7, 46, 91, 101-106
  corporate applications, 105
  features, 104-105
  graphics on, **103**
  marketing on, 105-106
  networks based on, 103-104
  setting up your own, 106
business
  commitment to using Internet, 31
  failures, 9-17
  rules for online selling, 25-31
  starting small and simple, 28-29
  successful, 20-31
bytes, 39

## C

cabling, modem, 112-113
cache, 82-83
Callihan, Steven, 193
Campus Wide Information Servers (CWIS), 159
Canter, Laurence, 153
Capitol Steps, 257-259, **258**
Cards, Comics, & Collectibles, 286-287, **287**
Casio, 282-283, **283**
Cassette House, 280-282, **281**
CBS, 16
character generator, 38
Chocolate Lovers' page, 245-246, **245**
Cochran, Johnnie, 7
Coffee Anyone???, 298-299, **299**
CommerceNet, 178
communications (*see also* modems)
  online, 34-41
  TTY, 114
Company Corporation, 262-264, **263**
compression, 75, 80
CompuServe, 5, 7, 13, 34, 46, 48, 51, 59, 88, 92-94
  costs, 97-98
  E-mail, 149-150
  finding SIGs on, 101
  getting started, 116
  greeting screen, **95**
  marketing on, 97-101
Computer Express, 270, **271**
consultants, 29-30, 177-178
  directory, 178-179
  FireCrystal, 311-314
  location of, 179-180
credit cards, security and, 195-197
Cuenet Systems, 164
Cybercon Inc., 164

## D

data encryption, 147-148, 319-320
databases, 89-90
DCX files, 74
DealerNet, 28, 37, **29**
debugging, 30-31
DejaNews, 61, 215
Dell Computer Corporation, 270-272, **272**
Delphi, 48, 91, 96
directory listings, 207-211
Doll House, 289-290, **290**
domain name system, 108, 118-119, 143-144
  choosing, 145-146
  registering, 145
DOS, 41-42, 75
dumb terminals, 114

## E

E-mail, 60, 72, 134-155, 214
  addresses, 143-144
  American Online, 149
  binary files, 141-143
  canned replies for, 138
  CompuServe, 149-150
  finding addresses, 148-149
  international, 144
  Internet, 136-141
  marketing/direct mail, 152-154
  MCI Mail, 150
  Prodigy, 150
  quirks with, 138-139
  security, 147-148
  sending to other networks, 148
  signatures, 150-152
  software features, 137-138
  tips and tricks, 139-141
Electronic News Network (ENN), 165
Ellis, Jim, 216
encryption, 147-148, 319-320
eWorld, 91
Excel Telecommunications, 305-307, **307**
Excite, 203

## F

fax-on-demand (FOD), 158
Federal Express, 264-265, **265**
FidoNet, 104
file formats, graphics, 74, 80
files, binary, 141-143
file transfer protocol (FTP), 62
FireCrystal Consulting, 311-314
FireCrystal Corporation, 166-167
flaming, 58
Foamation World Famous Cheeseheads, 299-301, **301**
frequency asked question (FAQ), 308-309
FrontPage, 176

## G

Gates, Bill, 71
Gateway, 10
GEnie, 91, 96
GIF files, 74
Global Network Navigator, 96
Gopher, 63, 72
Gore, Al, 47
Graphic Workshop for DOS, 320
Graphic Workshop for Windows, 320
graphics, 36-37, 73
  file formats, 74, 80
  HTML, 67-68
graphics interchange format (GIF), 74

## H

hard hyphen, 40
hardware, 190-192
Holly, James H., 10
Hot Hot Hot, 295-298, **297**
HoTMetaL Pro, 176
HTML Authoring Tools and Guides, 173
hypertext markup language (HTML), 67-68, 73, 84-85
  creating your own code, 172-173
  non-WYSIWYG editors, 175
  word processor HTML converters, 174
  WYSIWYG editors, 175-176

## I

IBM, 16
indexes, 205-206
InfoSeek, 97, 189, 203, 215
Internet, 13-14, 22-24, 34, 46-64
  access to from other service providers, 48-49
  advertising spaces for, 57-58
  anonymity of, 56
  case-sensitivity, 48
  concepts, 54-58
  connecting to, 115
  cultural issues, 56-57
  features, 58-64
  getting started on, 4-7
  history, 7-8, 46-50
  U.S. government and, 46-47
Internet Assistant, 176
Internet Basics, 316

Internet Compression & Conversion Tools, 317
Internet FTP Essentials, 317
Internet Just the FAQs, 317-318
Internet Mail, 210
Internet Mailing List Essentials, 318
Internet Making Money Disk, 318
Internet Newsgroup Essentials, 318
Internet Premium Plus service, 97-98
Internet protocol (IP), 146-147
Internet Relay Chat (IRC), 63
Internet service provider (ISP), 5, 81, 108, 118-126, 194-195
  choosing, 123-126
  features to look for, 124-125
  listing of, 127-129
  locating, 120-123
Internet Toolkit, 316
Internet World Wide Web Essentials, 319
InterNIC, 145

## J
Java, 74, 76, 80
Jennings, Tom, 104
Joint Photographic Experts Group (JPEG), 74
JPEG files, 74
Jughead, 63, 159

## K
Knitting Lodge, 290-292, **291**
Kodak Photo CD files, 74

## L
Lava Computer Manufacturing, 111
Lawrence, David C., 218, 223
LISTSERV, 160, 231
London Connection, 21-22, 42
Lycos, 203

## M
Magellan, 203
mail servers, 160-162
Mailback Auto-Responder Service, 165
mailing lists, 61, 229-232
Maine Cottage Furniture, 42, **43**, **44**
malls, 210-211
MCI, 124
MCI Mail, E-mail, 150
Mecklermedia Corporation, 121
media hype, xii
Metcalfe, Bob, 13
MicroNET, 7
Microsoft Corporation, 71, 76, 78
Microsoft Network (MSN), 91, 116
modems, 4
  communications software for, 113-114
  costs, 109
  external, 109-110
  internal, 110
  physically connecting, 112-113
  recommendations, 109
  speed, 35-36, 37-38, 109
Mosaic, 69
multi-level marketing (MLM), 304-309
multi-purpose Internet mail extensions (MIME), 142

## N
NAPLPS, 93
National Center for Supercomputing Applications (NCSA), 69
National Science Foundation (NSF), 54
Net Happenings, 229
NetCruiser, 70
NetPost, 240-241
Netscape, 70, 71, 72, 76, 79
  vs. Windows, 77-78
networks and networking, 50-51
  protocols, 52-53, 136
newsgroups, 55, 61, 72, 214, 215-217
  crucial points regarding, 217-218
  hierarchies, 220-221
  listings, 218-219
  searching offline, 219-220
NSFNet, 54
NuSkin Feelgood Team, 305, **306**

## O
O'Reilly & Associates, 14
online services (*see also* America Online; CompuServe; Prodigy)

communications-only systems, 90
connecting to Internet, 115
costs, 5
getting connected to, 108-129
information-only systems, 89-90
subscribers, 12-13
Open Market Commercial Sites Index, 210
Open Text Index, 203

## P

packet numbers, 51
packet switching, 51-52
PageMill, 176
PC cards, 111
PC-Outline, 320
PCT files, 74
PCX files, 74
PKZIP, 75
Post Office Protocol (POP), 136
PostMaster, greeting screen, **236**
Procomm Plus for DOS, 115
Prodigy, 5, 7, 12-13, 15-17, 48, 59, 88, 94
costs, 97-98
E-mail, 150
finding SIGs on, 101
getting started, 116
greeting screen, **95**
marketing on, 97-101
subscribers, 96
protocols, 52-53, 136
Providers of Commercial Internet Access (POCIA), 121

## Q

QFILER, 321
Quantum Computer Systems, 7
QuickTime, 75
QuoteCom, 266-267, **267**
QuoteCom Data Service, 161

## R

Raisch, Robert, 153-154
Rand Corporation, 50
Raskin, Robin, 30
ReplyNet, 165
RLE files, 74
Rutkowski, Anthony-Michael, 13

## S

saving, Web pages, 84-85
Scandinavian Computer Furniture, 272-274, **273**
search engines, 97, 189, 202-203
indexes and, 205-206
making the most out of, 203-204
weighting formula, 207
Sears, 16
security, transactions and, 195-197
serial ports, 112-113
Shoppers Advantage, 278-280, **279**
shopping, online, 8
Siegel, Martha, 153
SIMBA Information Inc., 11-12
Simple Mail Transport Protocol (SMTP), 136
SLIP/PPP connection, 119-120
soft hyphen, 40
software
communications, 113-114
order form, 323
Spafford, Gene, 218
special interest group (SIG), 98-101, 228
Spider, 176
SprintNet, 51, 124
SpryNet, 96
StuffIt, 75
Sun Microsystems Inc., 76

## T

Targa files, 74
telemarketing, 214
Telnet, 62-63, 72
terminal emulation, 113
Text Search, 321
Text Treaters, 321-322
The List, 121-123
The Source, 92

thumbnails, 42
Times Mirror Videotex Services, 10
Trintex, 16
Truscott, Tom, 216
TTY communications, 114
Tymnet, 51

## U

uniform resource locators (URLs), 72
universal asynchronous receiver/transmitter (UART), 110-111
UNIX, 75
USENIX, 216
UUENCODE, 142

## V

Veronica, 63, 159
videotex, 9
Videotex Industry Association, 11
Viewtron, 9-10
Virtual Vineyards, 294-295, **295**
Visual BASIC, 74, 76, 80

## W

Walnut Creek CDROM, 274-275, **275**
Ward, Eric, 240-241
Watkins Products, 307-308, **308**
Web Developer's Virtual Library, 173
Web page
- construction kit, 173-174
- consultants, 177-180
- creating your own, 172
- design tips, 186-190
- design/content, 184-186
- hiring a Webmaster for creating, 176-177
- making sure people find it, 206
- options for creating, 171-176
- testing your own, 189-190

Web sites
- costs, 193
- establishing, 24
- examples of the best, 181
- making visible, 204-205
- setting up hardware, 190-192
- setting up your own, 170-197
- visiting, 181-183
- Wilson Internet Services, 183-184

WebAuthor, 176
WebCrawler, 97, 203
WebPromote, 239
Wide Area Information Servers (WAIS), 64
Wilson Internet Services, 183-184
äWindham Hill, 256-257, **256**
Windows, 41-42, 75, 81
- vs. Netscape, 77-78

Windows/DOS Tools & Utilities, 319
WINSOCK.DLL, 81-82, 115
World Wide Web (WWW), 66-85
- browsers, 69-73, 81-83
- history, 67-68
- hypertext links, 83-84
- saving Web pages, 84-85

Worldata Services, 240
WPG files, 74

## X

X.25, 52
XyWrite, 105

## Y

Yahoo!, 97, 203, 208, **209**
- Web announcement services screen, **242**

## Z

ZyIndex, 64

# About the Authors

Alfred and Emily Glossbrenner are a dynamic husband-and-wife team who write and lecture widely on the online community. Alfred is the author of more than 40 online-related books, including *The Information Broker's Handbook*. He is regarded as one of the foremost authorities on online communications. Emily has nearly 20 years of experience in computers and marketing, including nine years with IBM. She and her husband have collaborated on several bestselling online guides, including *Finding a Job on the Internet* and *Internet 101*, now in its third edition.

FREEPORT MEMORIAL LIBRARY
[redacted]
3 1489 00397 9778

FREEPORT MEMORIAL LIBRARY

658.4038 Glossbrenner,
G Alfred.

Making more money on
the Internet.

DATE

DISCARDED BY
FREEPORT
MEMORIAL LIBRARY

Freeport Memorial Library
West Merrick Road
Freeport, N. Y. 11520

BAKER & TAYLOR